THE PUBLIC LAW OF WALES

Legislating for Wales

Thomas Glyn Watkin with Daniel Greenberg

UNIVERSITY OF WALES PRESS
2018

www.uwp.co.uk

British Library CIP Data
A catalogue record for this book is available from the British Library.

ISBN 978-1-78683-300-6
eISBN 978-1-78683-301-3

Typeset by Marie Doherty
Printed by CPI Antony Rowe, Melksham

THE PUBLIC LAW OF WALES

Legislating for Wales

Series Preface

For several centuries after the union of the two countries under the Tudors, the laws which applied in England and the laws which applied in Wales were almost exactly identical. Although administered differently in Wales by the courts of Great Session, the laws were not different. Only in the nineteenth century, barely half a century after the abolition of the Great Sessions in 1830, did laws begin to be made for Wales which did not apply in neighbouring England. The number of such laws however remained small when compared with those which were common to both countries. England and Wales was a single law district with a single law – the law of England and Wales, which was in reality English law.

Devolution has changed that situation significantly. The creation of the National Assembly for Wales and its subsequent acquisition of primary law-making powers has meant that there is now a growing number of differences between the laws which apply in Wales and those which apply in England. Although in the majority of cases, the laws of the two countries remain the same, there is an increasing divergence in the rules relating to those matters which have been devolved. In truth, there are now three bodies of law in England and Wales: one which applies only in Wales; a second which applies only in England, and a third which applies in both countries. Whenever the National Assembly legislates for Wales or the United Kingdom Parliament legislates only for England, the divergence increases. As that divergence increases, so does the importance that lawyers, law students and the public should be able to inform themselves of what the law is in Wales. People need to know the laws which govern their lives from the perspective of the society in which they live. In both countries, lawyers need to know what the law is on either side of the border.

The temptation has been to present the law which applies in Wales in terms of the law which applies in England, while merely noting the differences. As divergence increases, that approach becomes not merely unhelpful from a Welsh perspective, but unacceptable. The purpose of this series therefore is to present to the professions and to the public an account of the law as it applies in Wales in the areas where there is now divergence, and in so doing to both redress the deficit and provide the foundation for a legal literature to serve the distinct needs of Wales.

Thomas Glyn Watkin

Contents

Foreword

It is a pleasure and a privilege to welcome the fourth in this series of books which aims to present an account of the law of Wales in such a manner that not only treats Welsh law as a distinctive legal regime (distinct from a sub-species of English law), but which seeks also to meet the needs of all who live in Wales.

As the law of Wales will be very largely made by the legislature, it is essential that the legislative process is properly understood. There are some who share the view often attributed to Chancellor Otto von Bismarck that laws are like sausages; it is best not to see how they are made. Whether such a view is properly attributed to Bismarck is a subject of debate, but what is beyond debate is that the process of law-making must be properly understood. That is because a clear exposition of the process is essential in ensuring that it is a proper one. And a proper process is, in any age, but particularly in an age of populism, essential to the maintenance of democracy.

This work admirably sets out the entirety of the legislative process in Wales in a way that can be easily and readily understood not only by lawyers, but by all those interested in our democracy. It is comprehensive in its coverage as well as in its deep scholarship. For example, the chapter on competence and constraints of the National Assembly (chapter four) is an excellent summary of the difference between the UK Parliament and the subordinate parliaments in Scotland, Northern Ireland and Wales; as well as providing a detailed description of the limitations on the competence of the National Assembly.

Of particular interest are the innovative features that the National Assembly has adopted. Two examples are the drafting of legislation bilingually (considered in chapter eight) and the Committee stages of Welsh legislation (described in chapter seven).

I do not think it possible to over-emphasise the advantages of legislating in a proper bilingual manner as opposed to providing the translation of a text drafted monolingually and, when finalised, translated into a second language. In bilingual drafting, the right text for each language is considered as the draft progresses, and both texts can be changed to get the correct meaning. As the authors rightly stress, this has the added advantage of eliminating the risk of ambiguity. It is a notable achievement by the National Assembly to have adopted this progressive and modern approach, which gives true equality to the languages used in Wales.

The second example of innovation is the Subject Committee stage of considering Bills. This stage can be applied to Welsh legislation when there is a need for detailed expertise in the subject matter of the legislation. The ability of a committee to call evidence to assist it in scrutinising the broad policy proposals is of inestimable advantage, particularly for a small nation where it is not realistic to expect either the civil service or the legislators to have the necessary detailed expertise.

I very much hope that this book with its immensely clear description of the legislative process as it currently exists in Wales will assist those who seek to make that process more accessible and more democratic. The work covers the Law Commission proposals for the production of a codified form of law, which in a small nation is probably an indispensable necessity in providing proper access to the law. This work will also encourage more radical thinking with regard to making the legislative process more transparent and one in which many more people can readily participate.

I therefore warmly congratulate the authors on their achievement and enthusiastically commend the work to all interested in democracy in Wales.

The Rt Hon. the Lord Thomas of Cwmgiedd
July 2018

Preface

The law affects people's lives. It tells them what they may do and what they may not do. On occasion, it tells them how they must do things that they may lawfully do. It provides ways in which they can enforce and defend their rights. It frequently gives officials and public bodies powers which, when used, affect people's lives and well-being. Making laws is therefore a serious business. Those engaged in it need to bear in mind the effect their work has on the lives of others. Those others need to know and understand how the laws which affect them are made, so that they can engage with the work of the law-makers and, in a democracy, hold the law-makers to account for the quality of their work. 0-01

THE BOOK'S PURPOSE

The purpose of this book is to raise a critical awareness of what sound law-making involves, both among those who make the laws and among those who are affected by them. For the former, that awareness should ensure that they keep the effects of their work upon others firmly within view. For the latter, it should provide sufficient understanding to allow them to participate meaningfully in consultations and stakeholder engagements while laws are being prepared and passed, and to critically and confidently appraise the laws made. The book is not aimed solely, or indeed chiefly, at those who prepare and make legislation within the institutions of government, although it is hoped that they will find it of use. It is equally intended for the citizens whose lives are affected by legal change, whether individually or as members of voluntary organizations, charities, local communities or other entities with an interest in the quality of the laws which govern them and the society in which they live. 0-02

ITS APPROACH

For almost 500 years prior to the start of the twenty-first century, laws were made for Wales by the Parliament at Westminster. With devolution and the creation of the National Assembly, Wales has acquired another legislature. It does not replace the UK Parliament but shares in its law-making activity regarding certain subjects. Mindful of the length of time for which Westminster has made laws for Wales, of the fact that it still does so and of the undeniable reality that greater media attention is given to the UK Parliament than to the devolved institutions, this 0-03 book considers how legislation is made for Wales and not just in Wales. While the primary focus of attention will be law-making by the National Assembly and the Welsh Government, the rôle of Westminster and Whitehall will also be kept in view, and – recognizing that people are likely to be more familiar with the workings of the UK institutions – they will frequently be used to explain and strike comparisons with the newer, less familiar, Welsh institutions.

AN OVERVIEW OF ITS CONTENT

0-04 The book is divided into nine chapters.

Chapter one analyses the concept of legislation and its implications. It considers questions such as who can make laws and how, whether their law-making powers are limited, and whether their activities can be challenged. It examines the UK Parliament and the Welsh Assembly in terms of these questions, together with the relationship between those legislatures and the respective governments of the UK and Wales. It also considers the relationship between the UK and Welsh institutions as a consequence of devolution and the way in which this has developed.

Chapter two considers where ideas for legislation come from and how they are developed into policies. It addresses the need for thoroughness in the policy-making process in order to ensure that the effect on people's lives is fully appreciated. It links these issues with the function of legislative procedures in a modern democracy.

Chapter three considers when legislation is needed to deliver a policy objective, and the sort of legislative interventions which are available. It presents fundamental legal concepts, such as freedoms, rights and duties, which are the building blocks of legislative provisions. It considers the kinds of legislation which can be used and the choice of legislature. It assesses the pros and cons of the UK Parliament and the National Assembly for Wales as legislatures for Wales, and the importance of democratic principles in choosing whether to promote a proposal as a bill before a legislature as opposed to using the delegated powers of government ministers to legislate.

Having contrasted the unlimited legal sovereignty of the UK Parliament with the limited legislative competence of the Welsh Assembly, chapter four examines in detail the powers of the Assembly to make law. It compares the powers which the Assembly enjoyed until April 2018 (the conferred-powers model) with the powers it now has (the reserved-powers model). It also considers how laws made by the Assembly can be challenged for having exceeded the bounds of its legislative competence.

Chapter five moves away from the process by which legislation is prepared to consider by whom the work is done and their working practices both at Westminster and in Wales. It examines the working relationship between policy officials, government lawyers and the legislative counsel who draft the proposals to go to the legislature for consideration. It reflects on the importance of viewing the process as a project within which those working together need to respect each other's expertise without abdicating their critical judgement.

Chapter six then focuses on how the changes to the law which are to be proposed are expressed in the provisions of a bill to be sent to the legislature. It builds on the foundations of the legal concepts introduced in chapter three, which in turn reflect the policy choices addressed in chapter two. The structure of a bill and the function of its various provisions are discussed in terms of its accessibility and intelligibility by those who are to deliberate upon it and by those who will be governed by its terms if it passes into law.

Chapter seven examines the legislative procedures of the National Assembly when dealing with bills. It reflects on how the procedures deliver what representative democracy requires, and relates the work of the legislature in scrutinizing the bill to the preparatory work undertaken in its preparation. The opportunities for legal challenge to a bill's provisions and for intervention by the UK Government are also discussed.

Chapter eight considers how, after a bill has become law, its provisions come to be implemented. It examines in particular the use of subordinate law-making powers which may have been given to government ministers and how the courts will approach their task of applying and interpreting the law when called upon to do so when administering justice. How knowledge of this should affect the work of preparing legislation is also assessed.

Having considered the legislative procedures of the National Assembly in the preceding chapters, chapter nine deals with the same issues with regard to the UK Parliament and the institutions of the European Union. Both of these currently make laws which apply in Wales. It compares and contrasts the procedures of those bodies with Welsh practice.

At the time of writing, the United Kingdom remains a member state of the European Union, albeit that it has triggered the process of leaving and negotiations for the terms of its withdrawal are taking place. In an Afterword to the chapters, a brief glance at what the future may bring considers the uncertainties for devolution which attend withdrawal from the EU. Also ear-marked is the unresolved issue of what changes to the ways in which laws are administered in Wales may be desirable as a consequence of devolved law-making, as well as changes likely to be in the offing regarding the Assembly's name, the size of its membership and the methods by which it is elected.

The writing of this book had its origins in the authors' collaboration in creating, developing and teaching a course on the theory and practice of legislation for the Welsh Government. Although the work neither seeks to present, nor does present, any views other than the authors' own (which are not always shared!), they are indebted for the opportunity to work together which the Welsh Government's legislation course afforded, and in particular for the frequent discussions and exchanges of ideas with the staff organizing and teaching the course, as well as with the civil servants who have attended it. The last category are too numerous to list, but, among those who are, or have been, responsible for the course's delivery, the authors wish to thank Rachael Clancy, Charles Coombs, Richard Crowe, Lyndon Evans, Claire Fife, Louise Gibson, Elliott Gordon, Arwel Hughes, Carolyn Hughes, Victoria Minshall-Jones, Steve Lazell and William Whiteley. They also wish to acknowledge the interest and support of the staff of the Office of Welsh Legislative Counsel, and of Assembly Commission staff, including O. Gwyn Griffiths and Gareth Williams. They are, in particular, grateful for the detailed and helpful comments on an earlier draft of the work, given in a personal as opposed to a professional capacity, from Nicola Charles, John Spence and Paul Webb, as well as for the comments and suggestions of the University Press's anonymous peer reviewer. The support of the Press's staff, and in particular Sarah Lewis, the commissioning editor, has been outstanding throughout. All of this has benefited the authors' work enormously, even when they have not always agreed with or followed suggestions made. The authors alone are responsible for any errors, blemishes, infelicities of style or other shortcomings which remain.

Lastly, the authors wish to record that what began as an acquaintance and a professional partnership when their collaboration on the legislation course was initiated has since become a valued and lasting friendship. It is a friendship which bridges their different professional experience, geographical location and religious faith. Both wish to acknowledge and give thanks for the grace which inspires and sustains them and their work, together with the support of their respective families.

Thomas Glyn Watkin
Daniel Greenberg
January 2018

Acknowledgements

The Authors gratefully acknowledge the kind permission and courtesy of the following copyright owners in allowing their copyright material to be reproduced, quoted or referenced within this work:

under Open Government Licence v.3.0

extracts from statutes, statutory instruments, government documents and official transcripts within Crown Copyright, or published on-line by the National Archives;

court judgments published by the British and Irish Legal Information Institute (BAILII);

under fair dealing

The National Assembly for Wales Commission for references to the Standing Orders of the National Assembly for Wales;

The Incorporated Council of Law Reporting for England and Wales for extracts from the Law Reports;

William Collins Sons & Co. Ltd for the definitions from *Collins English Dictionary*;

Oxford University Press for the definitions from the *Oxford English Dictionary* and the quotation from the *Statute Law Review*;

Thomson Reuters (Professional) UK Ltd (Sweet and Maxwell) for the quotation from Daniel Greenberg, *Laying Down the Law*.

Table of Cases

Assembly Standing Orders

Table of Assembly Measures

Table of Assembly Acts

Table of Assembly Bills

Table of United Kingdom Acts

Table of Statutory Instruments

Chapter 1

Legislation and Legislatures

LEGISLATION: THE WORD AND ITS MEANING

The English word *legislation* is derived from two Latin words: *legis* from *lex* meaning 'an enacted law', and *latio* meaning 'a bringing forward' or 'a proposing'. The phrase *legis latio* was the technical expression used in ancient Rome to describe the proposing of a law or the bringing forward of a legislative proposal. 1-01

The meaning, or rather meanings, of the word *legislation* in modern English are not far removed from the word's etymological roots in Latin. Modern English dictionaries ascribe two meanings to the word. *Collins English Dictionary* gives these as: 1-02

> the act or process of making laws; enactment; and,
> the laws so made;

while the *Oxford English Dictionary*'s entry is similar:

> the action of making or giving laws; the enactment of laws; law giving;
> the enactment of a legislator or legislature; the whole body of enacted laws.

In both cases, the first of the meanings describes a process – the process of making laws, while the second meaning describes the end-product of that process – the law or laws so made.

IMPLICATIONS OF THESE MEANINGS

The meanings of the word *legislation* therefore imply certain things about legislation as a concept. It is implied that legislation in the sense of an enacted law is the end-product of legislation in the sense of a process of enacting, and – from the etymology of the word – that the process of enacting is the result of some person or some body having brought forward or proposed that an enacted law be made by that process. The word may be said to carry those implications. The implications are, as it were, the 'baggage' which the word carries. 1-03

These implications give rise to questions. If legislation in the sense of enacted law is the result of a process of enactment, who may enact such laws, and what is the process by which such enactment is achieved? If the process results from someone or somebody bringing forward or proposing that a law be made by the process, who may bring forward such a proposal? How is such a proposal to be brought forward? 1-04

How is it to be decided whether to enact the proposal in the form in which or with the content with which it is brought forward? Where and when can such proposals be brought forward, and where and when can they be enacted? Can any proposal be brought forward and enacted or are there topics which are not susceptible to such initiatives; in other words, what can be proposed and enacted? From where does the authority to bring forward such proposals come? From where does the authority to enact such proposals derive? Why are such proposals brought forward and why are they enacted? These are all questions which arise from a consideration of the meaning and root of the word, but they lead to an analysis of the concept of legislation itself.

Who can enact legislation?

1-05 A person who has the authority to make law is described as a legislator, while a body which has the authority to enact is termed a legislature. Such legislatures include Parliament and the National Assembly for Wales,[1] while when individuals, such as government ministers in Whitehall or Cardiff, exercise powers to make regulations in the form of what is called subordinate legislation, they act as legislators.

Where and when can legislation be enacted?

1-06 In the case of legislatures, such as Parliament or the National Assembly, they will conduct the activity of legislating in a place to which their members will have been summoned in order to perform that function. Likewise, there will be a time or times fixed for their meetings. In the case of legislators, on the other hand, their law-making may not be restricted to time and place in the same manner, although there will probably be other requirements regulating the manner in which they perform the task.

How is legislation enacted?

1-07 The manner in which a legislator or legislature performs the task of legislating raises the question of whether there is a process to be followed. In the case of a legislature there are likely to be procedures which allow for the proposals which are brought forward to be deliberated upon and scrutinized, with opportunity for the proposal to be altered or refined by being amended as part of that process. Even when a single legislator is making a law, he or she may be required or expected to follow a

[1] Under Government of Wales Act 2006 (hereafter GoWA 2006), s. 150A, inserted by Wales Act 2017, s. 16, the National Assembly has the power to change its name, together with that of the Assembly Commission and the name by which Assembly Acts are officially known. The power to change its name is governed by GoWA 2006, s. 111A, inserted by Wales Act 2017, s. 9, which requires such a decision to be made by an absolute majority of two-thirds of Assembly Members. See further, §7-67.

set procedure, for instance to ensure that he or she has consulted with those likely to be affected by the proposal and has considered the responses to such consultation.

When the appropriate procedures have been followed and completed, there 1-08
will be a formal mechanism for deciding that the proposal becomes law. In the case of legislatures, this may involve a vote of the members followed by a formal promulgation. In the case of a single legislator, it may involve the signing of a written document setting out the new law, followed by some form of publication.

What may be enacted?

The question of what a legislature may or may not enact or what a legislator may 1-09
or may not use legislative power to do concerns the legislative competence of that body or person. Some legislatures operate within limits which are themselves set by a higher law, often the written constitution of the country in question, while others may not be subject to such limitations. A single legislator who is untrammelled by any such limitations would be an absolute ruler or dictator. Where legislative power is entrusted to a single person it is therefore almost invariably itself subject to strict limitations with regard to the manner of its exercise.

Who may bring forward a proposal that a law be made?

If there is only one person who may bring forward such a proposal and that per- 1-10
son is the same person who can decide whether it should be made together with its final form and content, then one is indeed dealing with the dictatorship of an absolute ruler. If, on the other hand, any citizen is free to bring forward a legislative proposal and the entire citizen body is entitled to decide whether or not to enact the proposal following their consideration of it, then one is dealing with a very pure form of democracy. Most modern states opt for a position between these two extremes and allow representatives of the people to perform these tasks on behalf of the citizens as a whole, acting as the representatives of the citizens who will have chosen their representatives in regularly held elections.

Where does the authority to bring forward proposals or enact laws come from?

Where legislative proposals are brought forward, considered and decided upon by 1-11
representatives of the people, one can trace the authority to perform those tasks to the authority given by the people to their representatives in the process of election. That process, and the limits, if any, upon the powers of the representatives once elected, may be set out in the written constitution of the state. Where there is no written constitution and no limits to the law-making powers of the representatives once elected, the question of whence the authority to legislate derives becomes more difficult. Almost always, there is an element of 'which came first, the chicken or the egg?' to such inquiries – but that does not mean that the question is in any way trivial, nor that attempts to answer it lack usefulness.

Why is a proposal being brought forward and why should it be enacted?

1-12 If the person or persons bringing forward a proposal for scrutiny by others has to persuade them as part of the process of consideration and scrutiny of the merits of the proposal, then those bringing forward the proposal need to be able to produce convincing, cogent reasons for asking that their proposal be enacted. There needs therefore to be – usually for practical reasons rather than strict legal necessity[2] – a clear, well-thought-out policy behind the proposal. Although only the legislature may have the power to decide upon the proposal, in a free society the policy behind it may well be debated more widely by the people, and organs such as the press and the media.

THE PHASES OF LEGISLATION AS AN ACTIVITY

1-13 There are therefore certain features that will be common to the making of an enacted law in any circumstances.[3] These common factors are sometimes described by legal theorists as the phases of the legislative process. They are three in number.

1-14 First, there is the introductory phase. This is the phase in which the proposal is brought forward. Those who are able to bring forward such proposals are said to have the legislative initiative.

1-15 Secondly, when a proposal has been brought forward by those with the legislative initiative, the proposal will be subjected to consideration and scrutiny, during the course of which it may undergo changes in the form of amendment. This is termed the deliberative phase.

1-16 Finally, when the process of deliberation has ended, the question remains of whether the proposal as it has emerged from the deliberative phase should become a law, that is whether it should be enacted. This is the decision-making phase, the third and final phase of the legislative process as a whole.

1-17 These three phases can be identified whenever and wherever laws are made, regardless of whether one is dealing with an ancient or a modern society, regardless of whether one is contemplating a dictatorship or a democracy. In a dictatorship, it is likely that only one person may bring forward legislative proposals and that

[2] 'Usually' because it has been stated in the Supreme Court that where a devolved legislature is considering whether, on a fair balance, the benefits of achieving the proposed legislation's aim outweigh the disbenefits resulting from the restriction of a right protected by the Human Rights Act 1998, the courts will be prepared to weigh the benefits of the measure proposed against the disbenefits to other interests, and the weight it will attach to the legislature's choice will depend upon the extent to which the legislature has been put in a position to evaluate the various interests. Admissible background material, such as White Papers, explanatory documentation and ministerial statements during debate, will be used by the court in evaluating the relevant considerations and forming its own judgment. See *Recovery of Medical Costs for Asbestos Diseases (Wales) Bill: Reference by the Counsel General for Wales* [2015] UKSC 3, at ¶¶52, 56, *per* Lord Mance, discussed further §§3-11–3-20; 8-36–8-44.

[3] *Enacted law* is used to mean any law made by a legislature or a legislator.

same person will consider their content and decide as to whether they will become law, while in a democracy the tasks are likely to be shared by the people or their representatives. Sometimes the legislative initiative will be confined to those who are members of the legislature, as is the case with the United Kingdom Parliament. Sometimes persons who are not members of the legislature but are members of the government will be allowed to bring forward proposals. In that event, they may be allowed to speak to those proposals in the legislature but probably not be allowed to participate in the decision-making phase. The legislative initiative may also be enjoyed by certain public bodies, for instance regional assemblies or parliaments can bring forward proposals in the national parliament in some countries where some but not all legislative power has been devolved. Indeed, in some countries the people themselves may be permitted to bring forward proposals which their representatives must then deliberate upon. In Italy, for example, the legislative initiative can be exercised by any 50,000 electors. They can submit a proposal in the form of a Bill to the Italian Parliament, which must then consider it, although, of course, there is no guarantee that it will be passed and become law. Such a broad approach to the exercise of the legislative initiative is a form of direct democracy.[4]

The deliberative phase will almost certainly involve the legislature as a whole or 1-18
committees from within it considering the merits of the legislative proposal viewed as a whole and scrutinizing the content of the proposal in detail to consider how it is intended that the proposal should be carried into effect. In carrying out these tasks, persons and bodies from outside the legislature may be given the opportunity to comment on the proposal and submit evidence regarding it in writing or by giving oral testimony. During this phase, there will generally be opportunity for changes to be made to the proposal as a consequence of the deliberations. The questions therefore again arise as to who may propose such changes, by whom and how will the merits of the proposed changes be considered, and who can decide whether or not they should be made. The process of amending legislative proposals during deliberation therefore exhibits once more the three phases identified earlier with regard to the legislative process as a whole: who may propose; who may deliberate; who may decide. The process of dealing with an amendment is a microcosm of the process of dealing with a proposal as a whole; it is the legislative process in miniature.

Finally comes the decision-making phase. This will almost certainly involve 1-19
the members of the legislature as this ultimately is the key function they are elected to perform, but it may also involve others. Within the legislature, there may be more than one chamber that has to consider and decide upon the proposal. Where there is only one chamber, the legislature is said to be unicameral. The National Assembly for Wales, the Scottish Parliament and the Northern Ireland Assembly, together with the German *Bundestag* are examples of unicameral legislatures. The United Kingdom Parliament and the United States Congress, on the other hand, have two chambers, an arrangement described as bicameral, the two chambers

[4] See the Italian Constitution, *Costituzione Italiana*, art. 71.

being the House of Commons and the House of Lords in the UK Parliament and the Senate and the House of Representatives in the case of the US Congress. Participation in the decision-making phase may not, however, be restricted to the members of the legislature. On some issues, the people may be included in the process by means of a referendum on the proposed or enacted law. Thus, in Italy once more, direct democracy can be discerned in the right of any 500,000 electors to call for a referendum on a law which has been passed by the two chambers of the Italian Parliament, in which case, if a majority of those who vote in the referendum are opposed to the law, it is as a consequence abrogated. Some laws are not susceptible to such an abrogative referendum, for instance laws concerning the state's treaty obligations and taxation. However, popular referenda have been held on laws concerning such issues as divorce, abortion, hunting with guns, environmental issues and nuclear power.[5]

1-20 The completion of the decision-making phase may involve the formal promulgation of the enacted law by the head of state. This may or may not be part of the decision-making process. There may, however, be an opportunity prior to such promulgation for the proposal as passed to be challenged before the courts on the grounds that the legislature has exceeded its powers in agreeing to the proposal. Such a possibility is common in countries which have a written constitution and in which the legislature has to exercise its powers within the limits of that fundamental law. Such an opportunity also exists where the legislative powers of a devolved legislature are subject to legal limits. This is the case with the National Assembly for Wales. The opportunity to challenge proposals which have been agreed prior to final promulgation should not be confused with the continuing right of citizens to challenge enacted laws on the grounds that a legislature has exceeded its powers. The former is part of the law-making process; the latter is not.

1-21 It is not only devolved legislatures and the legislatures of countries with written constitutions that have limited legislative powers. The same is true of legislators to whom legislative power is delegated by national or regional legislatures. It is not uncommon for government ministers or other public bodies to be given such delegated powers to make laws, which laws are then described as delegated or subordinate or secondary legislation, terms which are more or less synonymous. Even where it is one person, such as a government minister, who has the power to make such laws, the three phases of law-making can still be identified. A proposal to make subordinate legislation will come from the minister or be presented to him to adopt by his officials. He will deliberate by taking advice from his officials and possibly by engaging the public through going out to consultation. On the basis of such deliberation, he will decide to make the law, usually by signing a document, called a statutory instrument, containing the subordinate legislation he is making. His signature may in itself be sufficient to make the law, but he may be required to submit it to the legislature and give them opportunity to annul it, or he may even be required to submit the document to the legislature for approval. There are

[5] Ibid., art. 75.

various ways in which the decision-making phase may be organized but, whichever way is chosen, its presence can be identified. The three phases are always present.

TERMINOLOGY

A legislative proposal before the United Kingdom Parliament or before the National Assembly for Wales is referred to as a Bill. It remains a bill until it is finally passed into law by receiving Royal Assent, at which point it ceases to be a bill and becomes an Act, either an Act of Parliament or an Act of the Assembly, according to which legislature passed it into law. 1-22

Acts of Parliament are also frequently referred to as statutes. This term is not often encountered in relation to Assembly Acts, probably because the legislation which gave the Assembly the power to enact laws states that such laws are to be known as 'Acts of the Assembly'.[6] Assembly Acts are quite properly regarded, however, as part of statute law, that is law which is enacted or made. 1-23

In the same way as it was instructive to consider the etymological root as well as the meaning of the word *legislation*, so too it is useful to reflect on the implications of the 'baggage' carried by the words *Act* and *Statute*. The word *act* has an everyday meaning in English; an act is something which one performs. Thus one speaks of one's acts and omissions, the things which one does or does not do. Technical, specialized meanings of the word *Act* flow from this central, everyday meaning. Thus, an act in a play in the theatre is something which is performed. With regard to legislation, it is pertinent therefore to ask why are Acts so-called? What is it that they do? 1-24

Acts in the sense of Acts of Parliament or Assembly Acts are so-called because they invariably do something, and what they always do is change the law. That is what an Act does, and it is because it does something that it is called an act. A similar technical use of a word in a legal context derived from its everyday meaning in ordinary language is the word *deed*. A deed in everyday language is again something that is done; one speaks of doing one's good deed for the day. A deed in a legal context, however, is a written document, but such legal documents are called deeds because they do something. Thus, one can change one's name by deed, or transfer property by executing a deed. Such documents are not the evidence of what one has done; they are the means of doing it. Without the deed, the change or transfer would not be accomplished. A deed does something, although unlike an Act it transfers legal rights which exist under the law rather than changes the law itself. The technical legal meaning in each case is derived from and reflects the word's everyday meaning in the language. 1-25

Describing an enacted law as a statute exhibits a different perspective. The English word *statute* comes, like the word *legislation*, from a Latin root, in this case *statutum est* meaning 'it has been decided'. A statute therefore is something which 1-26

[6] GoWA 2006, s. 107(1).

has been decided. What it has decided is that the law should be changed, that the act of changing the law should be done. The words, *Act* and *statute*, reflect two facets of legislation: the activity of changing the law, and the end product of that activity, a recorded decision of the change made. The need for the decision to be recorded and thereby known is important for its accessibility to those affected by the change which it records.[7]

THE LEGISLATIVE INITIATIVE

1-27 The legislative initiative is concerned with the question – who may bring forward a proposal that the law be changed? It was shown above that this question is answered differently in different societies. It will now be considered in the context of two legislatures which regularly legislate for Wales, namely the United Kingdom Parliament and the National Assembly.

The United Kingdom Parliament

1-28 The legislative initiative within the UK Parliament lies entirely with the members. Only Members of Parliament may introduce legislative proposals in the House of Commons, and only peers may introduce bills in the House of Lords. No one else may do so.

The National Assembly for Wales

1-29 The position in the National Assembly is slightly – but perhaps significantly – different. Bills may be introduced into the Assembly by Assembly Members, but may also be introduced by the Counsel General, the chief legal adviser to the Welsh Government.[8] The Counsel General may be an Assembly Member, but need not be one.[9] Originally, when the Assembly was established in 1999, the Counsel General was a civil servant and not a political appointee. However, in 2007, the position was changed and the appointment became a political one. Between 2007 and 2011, and again since 2016, the post was held by Assembly Members, but between 2011 and 2016, it was held by Theodore Huckle QC who was not an Assembly Member. Undoubtedly the rationale for allowing the office to be held by a person who is not elected to the Assembly is to guard against there not being a suitably qualified

[7] This poses a problem for those engaged in the drafting of legislative proposals. Should they draft for those legislating, so that it is clear to them what changes are proposed and, if approved, so as to provide a clear record of those changes, or should they aim to provide a clear statement of the law in the wake of those changes? It is perhaps too readily assumed that one text can perform both functions and perform both well.

[8] GoWA 2006, s. 110(1).

[9] GoWA 2006, s. 49.

person among the members. Nevertheless, by allowing a non-member to hold the post and to have the right to introduce legislative proposals into the Assembly, the Welsh arrangements have within them something foreign to the tradition of the UK Parliament, something which indeed has a distinctly European flavour to it. The Counsel General is also permitted to speak and answer questions within the Assembly, but is not allowed to participate in its decision-making if he is not a member.[10]

THE AUTHORITY TO ENACT: DELIBERATION AND DECISION-MAKING

The United Kingdom Parliament

If one asks the question 'who or what is the legislature of the United Kingdom?', 1-30
the answer can be found by examining the enactment clause which introduces most Acts of the UK Parliament. This reads:

> Be it enacted by the Queen's most Excellent Majesty, by and with the advice and consent of the Lords Spiritual and Temporal, and Commons, in this present Parliament assembled, and by the authority of the same

Most readers of an Act of the UK Parliament will pass over this clause as a traditional, ritual formula, adding nothing to the substance of the enactment. Yet it is highly significant as it sets out clearly where the authority to legislate lies in the United Kingdom. The wording expresses the exercise of law-making authority – 'Be it enacted …' – and makes it clear who possesses that authority: by whom is it enacted? – 'by the Queen's most Excellent Majesty', but not acting alone, for it is also enacted 'by … the Lords Spiritual and Temporal, and Commons', that is by the House of Lords consisting of the Lords Spiritual (the archbishops and bishops who represent the established Church of England) and the Lords Temporal (all the other peers) and the House of Commons, the MPs elected by the people to represent their interests. The Lords and Commons are also said to have advised and consented to the law's being enacted, recording the fact that they have deliberated upon the enactment when it was still a proposal and have consented to it, that is it has been passed by each House as a part of the final decision-making phase. It is recounted that this has all been done in the 'present Parliament assembled'[11] and asserts boldly that it is done 'by the authority of the same', that is by the authority

[10] The right to speak and participate in Assembly proceedings was originally also granted to another non-member, the Secretary of State for Wales, but the Secretary of State's right has been removed by the Wales Act 2017, s. 15, repealing GoWA 2006, s. 32(1). The Secretary of State was never able to exercise the legislative initiative.

[11] See below, §8-27 and corresponding n. 23, for the significance of this phrase for the interpretation of statutes.

of the Queen acting with the advice and consent of Parliament and by Parliament's own authority. Thus it is that the legislature of the United Kingdom is 'the Queen in Parliament'.

1-31 It is significant that the authority of Parliament to legislate is asserted rather than demonstrated as deriving from a legal or constitutional source. This leads to the questions, what is the source of that authority and what is its nature?

The authority to legislate: legal and political sovereignty

1-32 The classic exposition of the authority of Parliament to legislate is that developed by the constitutional lawyer, Albert Venn Dicey. Dicey described the legal sovereignty of Parliament as follows. 'Parliament has', he wrote, '... the right to make or unmake any law whatever; and ... no person or body is recognized as having a right to override or set aside the legislation of Parliament.'[12]

1-33 What Dicey described in these words is the position of Parliament in the legal arrangements of the United Kingdom. Parliament can enact any change whatsoever to the laws of the United Kingdom; there are no limits upon the competence of Parliament to make laws. Further, what Parliament enacts cannot be overridden or set aside by any other body, and the bodies which Dicey particularly had in mind were the courts. One cannot argue before a court in the United Kingdom that a parliamentary enactment is not a valid law, or at least not unless another parliamentary enactment has deprived the first of its validity.

1-34 This is very different from the position of legislatures in other countries, particularly those in which the legislature operates within the context of a written constitution. Thus, for instance, the power of the US Congress to enact legislation is not limitless, but must be exercised in accordance with the US constitution and Bill of rights. If the Congress oversteps its legal power to make law, the law so made can be challenged by the citizen and set aside by the US Supreme Court. Congress does not have the right to make or unmake any law whatever; and there is a body, the Supreme Court, which does indeed have the right to override or set aside Congress's enactments. The same is true in many European countries with written constitutions where the legislatures may make law only within the limits set by that higher, fundamental law from which all powers in the state are derived, and where a constitutional court can police the law-making of the legislature and set aside its enactments if they overstep the mark.

1-35 The authority of the UK Parliament to make law is therefore not subject to any legal limits, but that is not to say that it is completely uncontrolled. Dicey recognized that, even if there were no legal limitations upon Parliament's power to legislate, there were political checks. These political checks Dicey ascribed to what he termed the political sovereignty of those who periodically elected the members of the House of Commons. '[T]he will of the electors', he wrote, 'shall by regular and constitutional means always in the end assert itself as the predominant

[12] A. V. Dicey, *An Introduction to the Study of the Law and the Constitution* (London, 1885), pp. 39–40.

influence in the country. But this is a political, not a legal fact. The electors can in the long run always enforce their will. But the courts will take no notice of the will of the electors.'[13]

The political check upon the unlimited legal power of Parliament to legislate lies in the power of the electorate to vote out representatives with whose legislative work it disagrees and elect different ones, and in so doing vote out an unpopular government. General elections were the 'regular and constitutional means' by which 'the will of the electors' could 'always in the end assert itself'. Between elections, however, there was little or nothing which this political sovereign could do. However unpopular the legislature became and however obvious it might be that a forthcoming election would bring a change, until the election was lost, the legislature remained the legal sovereign and the courts would enforce the laws it made regardless of their unpopularity. 1-36

This again is very different from the position in countries where sovereignty is regarded as vested in the people rather than in the parliament. In Italy, as has been said, if 500,000 electors are unhappy with a law passed by their Parliament, they are entitled to call for a referendum on that one law or indeed on certain provisions within it. Without the need for a general election or a change of government, they are able by this means to reclaim their sovereignty on a single issue and, if the referendum delivers a popular vote against the enactment, they can override and set aside the law made by the legislature, not because it has overstepped the limits of their Parliament's law-making powers, but because they are unhappy with the manner in which that power has been exercised within its legal limits. 1-37

Legislation and the House of Lords

Dicey's words concerning political sovereignty emphasize the powers of the electorate, the fact that the will of the electors can assert itself by constitutional means. They appear, however, to overlook the fact that while the members of the House of Commons are elected, the peers in the House of Lords are not. The question therefore arises as to how the political will of the electors can be asserted against the unelected upper Chamber. 1-38

The answer to this question can be found in the provisions of the Parliament Acts, the first of which was passed in 1911. The background to its passing has connections with Wales in that it was the rejection by the House of Lords of the so-called People's Budget of the Liberal Chancellor of the Exchequer, later to be Prime Minister, David Lloyd George, which provoked the constitutional crisis that gave rise to the 1911 Act. Under its terms, if a bill which had been passed twice by the House of Commons had been rejected twice in the House of Lords, if the House of Commons were to pass the bill a third time, then on that third occasion it could be presented for Royal Assent despite the Lords' rejection. In effect, the Commons – as representatives of the will of the electors – could assert their will. 1-39

[13] Dicey, *Introduction*, pp. 73–4.

1-40 The first Act to progress to Royal Assent in this manner, in effect bypassing the House of Lords, also has a close connection with Wales. It was the Welsh Church Act 1914, which disestablished the Church of England within Wales. The enactment clause of that statute rehearses the constitutional change which lay behind and authorized its passing. It reads:

> Be it enacted by the King's most excellent majesty, by and with the advice and consent of the Commons, in this present Parliament assembled, in accordance with the provisions of the Parliament Act, 1911, and by the authority of the same, as follows:

Like the version quoted earlier, the clause expresses the law-making authority – 'Be it enacted' – and records by whom it is exercised – 'the King', but this time it is not by the Lords and Commons, but solely by the Commons and only with their, not the Lords', advice and consent. The deviation from the norm is also explained – 'in accordance with the provisions of the Parliament Act 1911' – before finally the authority of the King and the Commons to legislate in this manner is asserted. A second Parliament Act in 1949 reduced the number of occasions upon which the Lords' rejection is needed before a bill can 'leap-frog' to Royal Assent.

1-41 The provisions of the Parliament Acts pose questions regarding both the rôle of the House of Lords in the three phases of the legislative process and the source of the authority to legislate. While the Parliament Acts do not affect the legislative initiative of the peers (introductory phase) nor their right to scrutinize bills (deliberative phase), under the Parliament Acts they can in truth be excluded from the decision-making phase. The amended enactment clause used on such occasions recognizes this exclusion and also the legal consequence that the authority to legislate in this manner is itself derived from pre-existing legislation.

The National Assembly for Wales

1-42 Against this background of the deliberation and decision-making phases of the legislative process within the UK Parliament and that body's authority to legislate, certain questions can be examined about the law-making of the Welsh Assembly. Again, one can begin by analysing the Assembly's enactment clause, which reads:

> Having been passed by the National Assembly for Wales and having received the assent of Her Majesty, it is enacted as follows.

The first difference to strike the reader may be the absence of the words 'Be it enacted'. The clause does not express law-making authority. It merely states that 'it' – the text which follows 'is enacted'. Nor is the reader told by whom what follows is enacted; there is nothing equivalent to what follows the word 'by' in the equivalent clause of UK parliamentary enactments. Instead, a process is recorded as having taken place: the proposal has been passed by the Assembly and has received the Queen's assent. That process has taken place and 'it is enacted'. Why that process authorizes that consequence is not recounted.

The answer to the question of where the authority to make law in that fashion derives is to be found, as with legislation made in accordance with the Parliament Acts, in pre-existing legislation. In the case of the Welsh Assembly, the relevant statute is the Government of Wales Act 2006. Part 4 of that Act gives the Assembly the power to make laws, to be called Acts of the Assembly, which can make any provision that can be made by an Act of the UK Parliament.[14] However, the Assembly does not enjoy the same degree of legal sovereignty as the UK Parliament. It cannot, in Dicey's words, 'make or unmake any law whatever'. Instead, its right to make law, its legislative competence, is limited by the powers given to it by the 2006 Act. The powers and their limitations are contained in Part 4 of, and Schedules 7A and 7B to, the Act.[15] Unlike the UK Parliament, the powers of the Assembly to make laws are subject to legal limits and not just political control by its electorate. 1-43

Having identified legal limits to the law-making powers of a legislature, the question then arises: what occurs if those limits are transgressed? Who can question or challenge the power of such a legislature? Where and when can they do so? Who can decide whether the legislature has exceeded its powers, and what are the consequences of such a decision? These questions do not arise regarding the UK Parliament's law-making because of its legal sovereignty: it can make or unmake any law whatever and no person or body can override or set aside its legislation. As the Assembly cannot make or unmake any law whatever but must legislate within its limited competence, the question arises as to who may be able to override or set aside its proposals or enactments. For the Welsh Assembly, as for other legislatures operating within limits, the answer is the courts. 1-44

If a bill which has been passed by the Assembly is thought by the government of the United Kingdom to be in whole or in part outside the Assembly's competence, then the senior law officer of the UK government, the Attorney General, may refer it to the Supreme Court of the United Kingdom for the issue of competence to be determined. As the highest court in the land, the decision of the Supreme Court will resolve the issue in a manner which will be binding whenever a question arises about the challenged provisions in the future.[16] The chief law officer of the Welsh Government may also refer a bill or certain of its provisions to the Supreme Court. It may be thought odd that the Welsh Counsel General should 1-45

[14] See GoWA 2006, s. 108A(1), inserted by Wales Act 2017, s. 3. The original s. 108(1), which was replaced by s. 108A(1) specifically stated that Assembly Acts could make any provision that could be made by an Act of Parliament. Were the Assembly to exercise its power to change its name, the designation 'Acts of the Assembly' could also be changed: see GoWA 2006, s. 150A, inserted by Wales Act 2017, s. 16.

[15] The competence was originally granted by Part 4 of, and Schedule 7 to, the 2006 Act, but the Wales Act 2017 has since amended Part 4 and replaced Schedule 7 with Schedules 7A and 7B.

[16] See below, §8-31, for a fuller discussion of the doctrine of binding precedent.

wish to refer a Welsh Assembly bill to the Court, but it must be remembered that not every bill passed will be a government bill, and – very importantly even in the case of government bills – there are good reasons for wishing to see any doubts about competence cleared up before a bill becomes law.

1-46 Both the Attorney General and the Counsel General have only a limited amount of time to decide whether to refer an Assembly bill to the Supreme Court. The bill does not progress to Royal Assent until the issues raised in such a reference have been resolved. The period of time allowed for them to make a reference is four weeks from the date on which the bill is passed by the Assembly. They must make their reference within that window of opportunity or else hold their peace. The same is not, however, the case with others.

1-47 Even after a bill has received Royal Assent and become an Assembly Act, it is open to anyone involved in litigation before a court in the United Kingdom to raise a question as to whether any provision in an Assembly Act relevant to the determination of that litigation was within the competence of the Assembly. Provided the challenge is not frivolous or vexatious – for example, raised to waste time or otherwise cause delay – the court before which the issue is raised will be required to determine it in the manner set out in Schedule 9 to the 2006 Act. That schedule makes provision for the determination of Welsh devolution issues before courts in England and Wales, Scotland and Northern Ireland. Devolution issues include questions regarding the competence of the Assembly to have legislated. If the courts find that the Assembly has exceeded its competence in passing the law in question, their determination can override and set aside the law made by the Assembly. In this regard, therefore, Assembly Acts are more akin to the legislation made by legislatures operating in countries with a written constitution where similar challenges leading to similar consequences are a possibility.

THE EXECUTIVE BRANCH OF GOVERNMENT

1-48 Constitutional theorists distinguish the power of a legislature to make law from the powers of the executive to govern under the law. Both of these powers are then distinguished from those of the courts or the judiciary to administer justice in accordance with the law. The separation of these three powers – the legislative, the executive and the judicial – is seen as being crucial to the existence of a free society and the avoidance of dictatorship.

1-49 In some countries, the doctrine of the separation of powers is almost religiously observed. In the United States, for example, it is absolutely forbidden for a member of the administration, the Presidential government, to be a member of the Congress. In the United Kingdom, on the other hand, government ministers are without exception members of one or other of the two Houses of Parliament, as this is what allows them to be questioned and held accountable politically for the manner in which they exercise their executive functions. Their legal accountability is another matter, to which the discussion will return.

THE GOVERNMENT OF THE UNITED KINGDOM

The formation of the government of the United Kingdom is a process which is followed by convention, not by rule. In other words, in the absence of a written constitution, the manner in which a government is formed is not dictated by law, and the process is not one which is justiciable in the courts. It is a matter of convention, albeit that theorists refer to such conventions as being constitutional conventions. 1-50

By convention, following a general election, the Sovereign asks the leader of the party which has won the greatest number of seats in the House of Commons to form a government. If the party in question has an overall majority in the Commons, then it is clear that in government they will command the confidence of the House. If, however, that party does not have an overall majority, the leader will have to consider whether to attempt to govern as a minority government or seek an accommodation with one or more of the other parties so as to construct a working majority. Such an accommodation may or may not necessitate the formation of a formal coalition, that is a party grouping which then, as a group, has an overall majority of seats and therefore is assured of having the confidence of the House. The leader of the party or party group which accepts the Sovereign's invitation to form a government becomes the Prime Minister. 1-51

Instantly, therefore, it is clear that the doctrinal distinction between the legislative and executive powers of government is blurred within the United Kingdom. It is blurred because the result of a general election determines not only the composition of the legislature but also the identity of the government, and if the government has a working majority then in effect it controls the legislative branch of government. Again, it is worth comparing this situation with the constitutional arrangements in the United States where the separation of powers doctrine has been more thoroughly assimilated. There, elections to the Congress in no way determine who will be President; the election of a president as head of the executive is an entirely separate matter. The President and his Secretaries of State have to govern under and within the laws made by the Congress, and may have difficulty in promoting legislative change. This can appear bizarre to a British observer who is accustomed to governments being able to promote changes to the law with relative ease when possessed of a majority in the House of Commons. 1-52

Once appointed, the Prime Minister then chooses the other government ministers. Technically, they are nominated by the Prime Minister and appointed by the Crown, but by convention – yet again – the Sovereign accepts the Prime Minister's advice. The holders of the principal posts in the government, the Secretaries of State, together form the cabinet. These ministers are sometimes referred to as Ministers of the Crown. The reason for this is not simply that they are technically appointed by the Crown; they also possess executive functions which were at one time exercised by the Sovereign in person but which are now – by convention – exercised in the Sovereign's name by his or her ministers. These functions are not given to the ministers in statutes passed by Parliament; they are inherent to their 1-53 offices as ministers of the Crown. These functions are sometimes called prerogative powers.[17] Ministers also enjoy common law powers, derived for them as for citizens from the ordinary law of the land, enabling them, for instance, to sue and be sued in the courts in their ministerial capacity.

1-54 However, by far the greater part of ministerial duties and powers derive from functions entrusted to ministers by Parliament, having been conferred on them by statute. These are functions which are given them by law, and therefore they are legally accountable for their lawful exercise,[18] as well as being politically accountable for what they do before Parliament. It is this second requirement that ministers be politically accountable for their actions to the representatives of the people that makes it a necessity that ministers be members of one or other House of Parliament. If the Prime Minister wishes to appoint a person from outside Parliament to the cabinet, that person must either be elected to the House of Commons, by persuading a member from the governing party to retire and create a vacancy to be filled in a by-election, or more usually by giving the person a peerage and a seat in the House of Lords. When government ministers are members of the Lords rather than the Commons, they are not directly accountable to the representatives of the electors in the lower house, and it is therefore necessary for there to be a junior minister in the department in question who can be held to account for the department's actions in the Commons. When the minister is an MP in the Commons, it is customary for there to be a government peer to act as spokesman for the department in question in the Lords.

1-55 As well as the Prime Minister and the other ministers of the Crown, the government also comprises its law officers. The chief law officer of the United Kingdom government is the Attorney General, and the Attorney's deputy is the Solicitor General. Both are appointed from among those government MPs and peers who are legally qualified. With over 600 members of the House of Commons[19] and an even greater number of members of the House of Lords, finding suitably qualified individuals does not pose a problem. The law officers are not members of the cabinet, but the Attorney General regularly attends cabinet meetings.

The subordinate law-making powers of ministers

1-56 One of the functions which statutes frequently confer on ministers is the power to make subordinate legislation. In effect, such powers delegate to the executive arm of government a function of the legislature. Such legislation is therefore often referred to as delegated legislation. It is delegated in that the power to make it is

[17] The Ministers of the Crown Act 1975, s. 8(1) defines *Minister of the Crown* as 'the holder of an office in Her Majesty's Government in the United Kingdom'.

[18] Whereas private individuals are said to be free to do as they wish as of right until the law provides otherwise (see below, §§3-07–3-08), public officials or bodies, such as Ministers, on the other hand, are said to have no right to do anything other than that which the law empowers them to do.

[19] At the time of writing, the number is 650, with over 800 peers in the House of Lords.

given by Parliament to its chosen delegate, and subordinate in the sense that it is made under the requirements for its making which have been set by Parliament. The statute which gives the minister the power – often called 'the parent Act' – comes first; the exercise of that power after. Thus, statutes made by the legislature are termed 'primary legislation', and 'subordinate legislation', made by those with delegated authority to do so, is termed 'secondary legislation'. The terms 'subordinate', 'delegated' and 'secondary' legislation are used virtually interchangeably. Such delegated powers to make subordinate legislation are not only given to ministers, but are frequently, for example, given to local authorities or other public bodies.

Subordinate law-making by UK ministers

A government minister making subordinate legislation is a member of the executive 1-57 exercising a function which properly belongs to the legislature. In other words, the exercise of this function, albeit under statutory authority, contravenes the principle of the separation of powers.

That being the case, the issue arises as to how the legislature safeguards its rôle 1-58 as the proper law-making body. To allow the minister a free hand to exercise the power delegated without any check would be to abdicate the rôle entrusted to the legislature by the electorate. As well as therefore defining carefully the nature and extent of the power delegated, the legislature can also ensure that the power is exercised only in accordance with its express or implied approval.

This is done by requiring that the minister, when exercising the power to make 1-59 subordinate legislation, submit the legislative proposal in writing to the legislature in the form of a statutory instrument either for the legislature to approve the proposal or at least to have the opportunity of disapproving. If express approval must be sought, the statutory instrument containing the subordinate legislation is said to be subject to affirmative procedure; if the instrument received implied approval by the legislature not disapproving of it, it is said to be subject to negative procedure. It is for the legislature to determine, when granting the subordinate law-making power to the minister, which of these procedures should apply. The parent Act will state which procedure is to apply. Although there is no set form of words for the imposition of either procedure, the affirmative procedure is often created by words such as the following stating that the statutory instrument:

> must be laid before, and approved by a resolution of, each House of Parliament.

This requires that the instrument be expressly approved by both the Commons and the Lords before becoming law. The negative procedure on the other hand, again there being no set formula, is often imposed by stating that the statutory instrument containing the subordinate legislation:

> is subject to annulment in pursuance of a resolution of either House of Parliament.

Here, the subordinate legislation is set to take effect unless either the Commons or the Lords take steps to annul it. This recognizes that the subordinate legislation is valid by reason of the minister's signing the statutory instrument. The rôle of Parliament is to require annulment it if it disapproves, else the content remains valid. Only one House need require annulment, as its disapproval effectively indicates that the instrument is not approved by Parliament as a whole.

1-60 What Parliament either expressly or impliedly approves by way of these two procedures is what the minister has done when exercising the powers given by the legislature. The minister is nevertheless able to do only those things which the legislature has empowered him to do; he or she must act within the limits of the powers granted. If the minister, or any other body to which functions have been delegated, including the function of making subordinate legislation, has exceeded the power granted, the exercise of that power can be challenged. Challenge may come from any person or body with a legitimate interest in its exercise, and such challenges are made before the courts. The usual form for such a challenge is by means of the procedure known as judicial review.[20] Exceeding the limits of the powers granted, acting *ultra vires* or beyond the powers, renders the exercise of the function unlawful and therefore invalid. The courts will quash the exercise of the function for such illegality, as they will also do if the power has been exercised in a manner which is wholly unreasonable, procedurally improper or in a manner which is incompatible with Human Rights legislation. It must be emphasized that, in policing the exercise of executive powers, the courts are not agreeing or disagreeing with what a minister or administrator has done; they are rather ensuring that what is done is a proper exercise of the power granted. With regard to the merits of his actions, the minister is politically accountable before Parliament. Before the courts, he is answerable for the lawfulness of those acts.

THE HISTORY OF WELSH DEVOLUTION

1-61 Devolution of governmental powers to Wales has been a gradual process; in Ron Davies' famous words, it has been a process not an event.[21] That process began with the granting of executive functions relating to Wales to one of the ministers of the United Kingdom government, the Secretary of State for Wales. It continued with the transfer of many of those functions to the National Assembly, and later the transformation of that body into a legislature for the Welsh nation.

[20] See below, §§3-66–3-71; 8-22–8-23. For a comprehensive examination of judicial review as it relates to Wales, see David Gardner, *Administrative Law and the Administrative Court in Wales* (Cardiff, 2016).

[21] R. Davies, *Devolution: A Process Not an Event*, The Gregynog Papers, Vol. 2, No. 2 (Cardiff: Institute of Welsh Affairs, 1999).

The Secretary of State for Wales

The office of Secretary of State for Wales was created by the incoming Labour government led by Harold Wilson in 1964. There had been a lengthy campaign for the creation of such a cabinet ministry for much of the previous century.[22] Thereafter, when it was thought appropriate to allow legislation to be implemented differently in Wales, executive functions and subordinate law-making powers in relation to Wales could be given to the Welsh Secretary when granting equivalent powers to one of his cabinet colleagues for England. Pre-existing powers of this nature in certain areas were, in the early years of the office, also sometimes transferred to the Welsh Secretary. Thus, for example, large tranches of such functions relating to local government, housing and public health were transferred in 1965, and powers relating to agriculture in 1969. Further such transfers were made in 1978.[23] 1-62

More frequently, however, particular functions were given to the Secretary of State for Wales in individual statutes which granted the equivalent functions to other government ministers in relation to England. It was never the case that the Secretary of State for Wales was granted the entirety of the functions relating to a particular policy area such as education or health as a matter of principle. Even when substantial numbers of functions were transferred under Transfer of Functions Orders, the functions were individuated by reference to their original creation by statute. The Secretary of State therefore acquired his powers by a process of piecemeal accumulation, and the question of whether he could exercise a particular power had to be determined by reference to the individual grant and not according to any general principle that functions relating to a broad area of law should be exercised by him in relation to Wales. 1-63

From 1964 onwards, therefore, certain executive functions were exercised for Wales by its Secretary of State. This meant that legislation made for England and Wales by the UK Parliament could be implemented and administered differently in Wales from the manner of its implementation and administration in England. The Secretary of State for Wales, when given the powers, could make subordinate legislation for Wales different from that made by one of his cabinet colleagues for England. Once made, that subordinate legislation could carry into effect and govern the manner in which the policy behind the enactment was achieved in Wales. The policy itself, however, was still that of the UK government, and the primary legislation giving it effect that made by the UK Parliament. With regard to the 1-64

[22] See T. G. Watkin, 'Dadleuon Dichellgar a Datganoli' / 'Devious Debates and Devolution', in T. G. Watkin (ed.), *The Welsh Legal Triads and Other Essays* (Bangor, Welsh Legal History Society, vol. 11, 2015), pp. 96–132.

[23] The functions were transferred by Orders in Council, a form of subordinate legislation made by statutory instrument: see the Secretary of State for Wales and Minister of Land and Natural Resources Order 1965, the Transfer of Functions (Wales) Order 1969 and the Transfer of Functions (Wales) (No. 1) Order 1978. Such orders have become generally known as Transfer of Functions Orders or TFOs.

exercise of his powers, it was to the UK Parliament that the Secretary of State was politically accountable, even though that body represented a much broader swathe of the electorate than those affected by the Secretary of State's exercise of his functions. The Secretary of State was not directly accountable to the people of Wales. The subordinate legislation made by him, for example, was laid before the two Houses of Parliament at Westminster for approval or possible annulment by the affirmative and negative procedures respectively. This 'democratic deficit', as some called it, was the subject of some criticism, particularly during the 1980s and early 1990s when the UK government was of a different political persuasion to the majority of MPs elected from Wales.[24]

The National Assembly for Wales 1999–2007

1-65 With the return of a Labour government under Tony Blair in 1997, steps were taken to remedy this perceived democratic deficit. A referendum of the Welsh electorate was held on the question of whether Wales should be given a National Assembly. By the narrowest of margins,[25] the people of Wales voted in favour of having their own Assembly, and the consequence was the creation of the National Assembly for Wales by the Government of Wales Act 1998. That Act created the Assembly as a body corporate with both legislative and executive functions.

1-66 The Assembly's legislative functions were limited to the making of subordinate legislation. It was thus a very different body to the Scottish Parliament, created in the same year, which could pass primary legislation in the form of Acts. The powers of the Assembly to make subordinate legislation were given by transferring to it, either in the 1998 Act itself or in subsequent Transfer of Functions Orders, the vast majority of the subordinate law-making powers previously exercised by the Secretary of State. Although the areas to which these powers related were listed as eighteen fields in Schedule 2 to the Act, the Assembly did not acquire the totality of functions belonging to those fields. What the Assembly acquired were individually identified functions which the Secretary of State for Wales had gradually accumulated since 1964. In other words, the Assembly inherited the bulk of those functions, the balance remaining with the Secretary of State and some falling to be exercised jointly by the Assembly with the Secretary of State or concurrently by either one or the other. The difference made by the creation of the Assembly lay not in the law-making powers that would be exercised but in the manner of their exercise and the nature of the political accountability of those exercising them, for the Assembly Members, unlike the Secretary of State, were accountable to

[24] While the Conservative Party was in government from 1979 until 1997, the Party won eleven of Wales's thirty-six seats in the 1979 general election, fourteen of the thirty-eight seats in 1983, eight of the thirty-eight in 1987, and six of the thirty-eight in 1993. At the general election which returned Labour to power in 1997, the Conservatives failed to win any one of the forty seats in Wales.

[25] On a turnout of 50.1%, 50.3% voted *Yes* and 49.7% voted *No* – 559,419 as against 552,698, a majority of just 6,721.

the electors of Wales at the four-yearly Assembly elections. Thereafter, additional functions were conferred in the same manner.

Again, unlike the Scottish devolution settlement, the Welsh settlement did not create an executive arm of government separate from the legislature. Instead, as stated above, the Assembly was a body corporate with executive as well as legislative functions. Its executive functions were to be carried out in its name by a First Secretary and other Secretaries, acting for and in the name of the Assembly. This was markedly different to the separation of the legislative and executive power at Westminster and at Holyrood, where in both cases a government with a separate identity to that of the legislature was accountable to the legislature for its actions. This combination of legislative and executive functions in one body in Wales was soon thought by many to be unsatisfactory, as were the limited law-making powers which it had been given.[26] 1-67

The National Assembly for Wales 2007–2011

These causes of dissatisfaction were dealt with by the passing of a second Government of Wales Act in 2006. This Act ended the existence of the Assembly as a body corporate combining – or confusing – legislative and executive powers. Instead, for the future, the Assembly was to be a legislature, with an executive, called the Welsh Assembly Government, separate from it and accountable to it in the manner of the UK government and Parliament and the Scottish executive and Parliament. 1-68

A change was also made to the legislative powers of the Assembly. The 2006 Act contained two models of legislative devolution for Wales. The first, contained in Part 3 of, and Schedule 5 to, the Act, gave the Assembly the potential to acquire primary law-making powers. If acquired, these powers would give the Assembly the competence to make laws for Wales, in the form of Assembly Measures, the provisions of which would have equivalent effect in Wales as those of an Act of Parliament. Such powers were to be granted by the insertion into Part 1 of Schedule 5 to the Act of 'matters'. These matters were to be inserted into one of twenty fields listed in that Part of the Schedule, each of which reflected an area of the law in which first the Secretary of State and later the Assembly had been given executive functions and subordinate law-making powers. Once a matter had been inserted into the Schedule, the Assembly would have competence to legislate 'in relation to' that matter for Wales, subject to certain restrictions and the requirement 1-69

[26] Even before the Assembly had served its first four-year term, the Richard Commission was established to review the satisfactoriness of the Welsh devolution settlement and recommended substantial changes: Commission on the Powers and Electoral Arrangements of the National Assembly for Wales, Report 2004. The UK government brought forward its proposals in a White Paper, *Better Governance for Wales / Trefn Llywodraeth Well i Gymru* (2005), which was the background to the proposals that formed the basis of the Government of Wales Act 2006. Some, but by no means all, of the Richard Commission's recommendations were followed.

to comply with European Union laws and the Convention rights set out in the Human Rights Act 1998. Matters could be inserted into the Schedule in one of two ways: either they could be inserted by provision in an Act of the UK Parliament, or the Assembly could promote a Legislative Competence Order, popularly known as an LCO (generally pronounced 'elco'), which, if approved by both the Assembly and both Houses of Parliament at Westminster, would be made as a form of subordinate legislation termed an Order in Council, made by Her Majesty in the Privy Council. This in effect ordered that the matter be inserted into the Schedule to the 2006 Act. Matters could only be inserted by LCO if they related to one or more of the fields listed in Part 1 of the Schedule. Technically, this restriction did not apply to the Act of Parliament route as, Parliament being sovereign, it could not restrict itself in this way as a matter of law, although in practice it would be likely to stick to the principle. In effect, the Assembly was intended to gradually acquire primary law-making powers through the gradual accumulation of such powers, mirroring the manner in which subordinate law-making powers had been granted over the previous four decades. Subordinate law-making powers were set to be periodically converted into primary law-making powers.

1-70 Obtaining legislative competence by these means, particularly the LCO route, proved to be a time-consuming and frustrating process during the lifetime of the Third Assembly (2007–11). As a consequence, the Assembly unanimously supported moving to the second model of legislative devolution set out in the 2006 Act.

The National Assembly for Wales 2011–2018

1-71 This second model of legislative devolution was contained in Part 4 of, and Schedule 7 to, the Government of Wales Act 2006. For this model to come into force, the Act provided that there had to be approval for such a development by the Welsh electorate in a referendum. That referendum was held in early March 2011 and the electors approved moving to the system of the Assembly Act provisions contained in Part 4 and Schedule 7.

1-72 This was the scheme of legislative devolution which operated in Wales until 1 April 2018. Under Part 4 of the 2006 Act as originally enacted, the Assembly was empowered to enact primary legislation for Wales, the provisions of which, like those of the earlier Assembly Measures which they replaced, had equivalent effect in relation to Wales as the provisions of an Act of the UK Parliament. Although once more subject to some general restrictions and having to be compliant with European Union law and the Convention rights contained in the 1998 Human Rights Act, Assembly Acts could make provision in relation to any one or more of the subjects set out under the twenty headings in Part 1 of Schedule 7. There were well over a hundred subjects to be found under those twenty headings. The headings were basically the same as the fields in Schedule 5 of the previous settlement, but whereas the fields necessitated the gradual, piecemeal insertion of matters, the headings of Schedule 7 were already populated with subjects when the 2006 Act was passed. The subjects once more reflected the areas of law regarding which first the Secretary of State and later the Assembly had acquired executive functions and subordinate law-making powers, but the Assembly's competence to enact primary legislation was in relation to the subjects and not the executive functions on which they had been based.[27] Areas covered by the subjects within which executive functions had never been devolved were excluded from the subjects by means of the exceptions listed under the twenty headings in Schedule 7.[28]

This granting of legislative competence by means of listing the subjects in relation to which a legislature can make law has become known as the conferred-powers model of legislative devolution. It differs from the model employed in granting legislative powers to the Scottish Parliament and the Legislative Assembly in Northern Ireland, where the devolved legislature is given power to legislate with regard to any subject at all provided the provisions of such legislation do not relate to a number of matters reserved to the UK Parliament. This approach is referred to as the reserved-powers model. There was much debate as to which model would better serve Wales. Once more, during the lifetime of the Assembly that was utilizing the Assembly Act provisions for the first time, a commission was established to review the satisfactoriness of the Welsh devolution settlement. This was the Silk Commission. It reported in 2014 and recommended that Wales should move to a reserved powers model of devolved law-making.[29] The UK government once again brought forward its own proposals the following year in which it agreed to implement some, but again by no means all, of the Silk Commission's recommendations.[30] After much discussion, these formed the basis of the reserved powers model enacted for Wales in the Wales Act 2017. 1-73

The National Assembly for Wales 2018–

The latest Welsh devolution settlement therefore is that which has been created by the Wales Act 2017. Despite the fundamental change to the settlement which it inaugurates, the 2017 Act has made the change by means of amending Part 4 of the 2006 Act and substituting two new Schedules, numbered 7A and 7B, replacing the original Schedule 7. 1-74

[27] See *Agricultural Sector (Wales) Bill: Reference by the Attorney General of England and Wales* [2014] UKSC 43, at ¶42.

[28] A twenty-first heading, *16A Taxation*, was added to Schedule 7 by the Wales Act 2014.

[29] *Empowerment and Responsibility: Legislative Powers to Strengthen Wales / Grymuso a Chyfrifoldeb: Pwerau deddfwriaethol i gryfhau Cymru* (Commission on Devolution in Wales, 2014). This was the second report of the Silk Commission, having already recommended tax-raising powers in its first report: *Empowerment and Responsibility: Financial Powers to Strengthen Wales / Grymuso a Chyfrifoldeb: Pwerau Ariannol i Gryfhau Cymru* (Commission on Devolution in Wales, 2012). It was the first report that led to the granting of some tax-raising powers in the Wales Act 2014, which inserted heading, *16A Taxation* into Schedule 7.

[30] *Powers for a Purpose: Towards a Lasting Devolution Settlement for Wales / Pwerau at Bwrpas: Tuag at Setliad Datganoli sy'n para i Gymru* (Cm. 9020, 2015).

1-75 The Welsh reserved-powers settlement, like its predecessors, limits the Assembly's legislative competence to enacting provisions that apply in relation to Wales, and continues to require that Assembly Act provisions be compatible with both EU law and the Convention rights incorporated into UK domestic law by the Human Rights Act 1998.[31] Within those limitations, and others set out in the General Restrictions upon the Assembly's legislative competence in the new Schedule 7B, the Assembly now has competence to legislate provided it does not do so in relation to the reserved matters in the new Schedule 7A. These, however, are considerable in number, and there has been much debate over whether the move to a reserved-powers model has enhanced the Assembly's powers or contracted them, and even greater doubt as to whether the new settlement has delivered the promised clear devolution settlement that would stand the test of time.

1-76 The Assembly is composed of sixty members, forty of whom are elected to represent geographical constituencies coterminous with those used to elect MPs to the House of Commons. These are elected by means of the 'first past the post' method of election, whereby the candidate with the largest number of votes is elected. The remaining twenty members are elected to represent five electoral regions, each region returning four AMs. These regional members are elected by a method of proportional representation which is meant to ensure that the views of those electors who supported unsuccessful candidates in the forty 'first past the post' seats do not go entirely unrepresented. The system was designed to ensure that the Assembly's membership reflected the diverse views of its electorate and to prevent one party dominating on a virtually permanent basis. In that no party has yet secured a comfortable working majority in the five Assembly elections which have taken place since 1999, the scheme would appear to have delivered its objective.[32]

1-77 Assembly elections originally took place at four-year intervals, but the introduction of fixed, five-year parliaments at Westminster in the wake of the 2010 UK general election led to the life of the Fourth Assembly, elected in 2011, being extended to five years to avoid the next election being held in the same year – and

[31] The passage of the Wales Bill, which became the Wales Act 2017, coincided with the referendum on the UK's continued membership of the European Union, so-called *Brexit*. While it is clear that the UK's withdrawal from the European Union will inevitably have significant implications for the devolution settlement in Wales, as in Scotland and Northern Ireland, it is not at all clear at the time of writing what those implications will be. The legal position is therefore described in this volume as it currently stands and will stand until withdrawal actually occurs, namely that devolved legislation has to be compatible with EU law to be valid. The same applies to compatibility with the Convention rights, despite indications that changes to human rights law may be proposed at UK level.

[32] The Wales Act 2017 has given the Assembly competence to legislate so as to amend the laws relating to its membership and the method of their election. Such changes would require the support of an absolute majority of two-thirds of its members: see GoWA 2006, s. 111A, inserted by Wales Act 2017, s. 9. Consideration has been given to doing this: see *A Parliament that Works for Wales: The Report of the Expert Panel on Assembly Electoral Reform* (November 2017).

month – as the following UK general election. After 2016, Assembly general elections will continue to be held at five-year intervals.[33]

Following an Assembly general election, the AMs who have been elected assemble at the Senedd in Cardiff Bay, where it is their duty at their first meeting to elect a Presiding Officer and a Deputy Presiding Officer from among their ranks.[34] These must not come from the same political group. The Presiding Officer fulfils functions roughly equivalent to those of the Speakers in the two parliamentary Chambers at Westminster, albeit that at Westminster the functions of that office in the House of Lords differ from the rôle of the Speaker in the Commons.[35] 1-78

That done, the next task of the Assembly is to nominate a First Minister to head the Welsh Government.[36]

THE WELSH GOVERNMENT AND THE WELSH MINISTERS

Having elected a Presiding Officer and a Deputy Presiding Officer, the Assembly then has one month within which to nominate from among its members a person to be First Minister of the Welsh Government. If no one is nominated within a month, there has to be another Assembly general election.[37] If one of the political parties has an overall majority within the Assembly, that being thirty-one seats or more, then that party can successfully nominate its leader to be First Minister. If no party has an overall majority, then to successfully make a nomination either the support of another party must be obtained or else one or more of the other parties must be prevailed upon to abstain in the voting so as to allow a successful nomination to be made. The nomination is made to Her Majesty the Queen and it is by the Sovereign that the First Minister is appointed. 1-79

When appointed, the First Minister can then choose the other Welsh Ministers. These must be chosen from among the Assembly Members; persons from outside the Assembly are not eligible. Again, technically, these are appointed by the First Minister nominating them to the Queen who formally appoints them. Although appointed by the Crown, they do not exercise prerogative powers, and therefore never act *in lieu* of the Sovereign but only in consequence of having been given 1-80

[33] GoWA 2006, s. 3(1), as amended by Wales Act 2014, s. 1(1). The holding of a UK general election in 2017 has, however, broken the pattern that might otherwise have been anticipated.

[34] GoWA 2006, s. 25.

[35] The Speaker in the Commons is a much older office, dating back to the fourteenth century, while the office of Speaker in the House of Lords was created by section 18 of the Constitutional Reform Act 2005, the Lord Chancellor having previously performed the rôle.

[36] GoWA 2006, s. 47.

[37] GoWA 2006, s. 5(3).

powers by either Parliament or the Welsh Assembly.[38] The First Minister may appoint up to twelve Welsh Ministers or Deputy Welsh Ministers, but no more than that. This safeguards against there being too few government members left in the Assembly to perform duties that government ministers are not permitted to fulfil.[39]

1-81 As well as the First Minister, the Welsh Ministers and the Deputy Welsh Ministers, the Welsh Government[40] also has a Counsel General, who is the chief legal adviser to the Welsh Government. The Counsel General is also appointed by the Queen on the nomination of the First Minister, but the First Minister is required to obtain the consent of the Assembly to that nomination before forwarding it to the Sovereign. The same process has to be followed if the First Minister wishes to remove a Counsel General from office. The Counsel General may or may not be an Assembly Member, but even if not an AM, the Counsel General is permitted to speak and participate in Assembly proceedings, and to introduce legislative proposals, but never to vote.[41] That the Counsel General, as a member of the executive, can participate in the work of the legislature despite not being a member of that body, introduces into the government of Wales an element which is very common in other countries but not present in the UK Parliament – the possibility of members of the government being appointed from outside the legislature. This is possible in many European countries, and in the United States there is a total ban on members of the executive being members of either legislative Chamber. While it is only the Counsel General who is so favoured in Wales, the development is significant, and it raises the question whether it might be desirable to allow further members of the government to be appointed from outside the

[38] For this reason, it is submitted that the Welsh Ministers are not Ministers of the Crown as are their counterparts in the United Kingdom because all of the Welsh Ministers' powers are derived from statute. For the contrary view see Rhodri Morgan, *Rhodri: A Political Life in Wales and Westminster* (Cardiff, 2017), p. 272, and evidence given by Mark Drakeford AM to the UK Parliament's Exiting the European Union Committee: *http://data.parliament.uk/writtenevidence/committeeevidence.svc/evidencedocument/exiting-the-european-union-committee/the-uks-negotiating-objectives-for-its-withdrawal-from-the-eu/oral/48622.pdf* at Q1305, p. 16.

The devolution settlement in the Scotland Act 1998 provides for the Scottish executive to have all of the statutory and prerogative powers that pertain to the Scottish Parliament's legislative competence unless such executive powers are not specifically reserved: Scotland Act 1998, s. 53. Nevertheless, the Scottish ministers are not Ministers of the Crown according to the unamended definition in the Ministers of the Crown Act 1975; see above, n. 17.

The Wales Act 2017 has, however, given the Welsh Ministers executive ministerial functions, allowing them, for instance, to bring and defend actions at common law within their devolved competence: GoWA 2006, s. 58A, inserted by Wales Act 2017, s. 19.

[39] The Assembly now has competence to legislate so as to change the permissible number of Welsh Ministers and Deputy Welsh Ministers. Once more, such changes would require the support of an absolute majority of two-thirds of its members: see GoWA 2006, s. 111A, inserted by Wales Act 2017, s. 9.

[40] This is now the official statutory title of what had previously – misleadingly – been officially called the Welsh Assembly Government: Wales Act 2014, s. 4(1).

[41] GoWA 2006, s. 49.

Assembly on the same terms. Such a move would alleviate, to some extent, the problem of depleting the number of government members available to carry out duties on Assembly committees. The Counsel General, it should be noted, is not one of the Welsh Ministers.[42]

The Welsh Ministers exercise functions which have been given to them by statute. When the National Assembly as a body corporate with both legislative and executive functions ceased to exist in 2007, and the new-style Assembly became the Welsh legislature and the Welsh Assembly Government (as it was then called) Wales's executive, the Welsh Ministers inherited the executive functions and subordinate law-making powers which had previously belonged to the old-style Assembly. In other words, that mass of accumulated functions and subordinate law-making powers which had been acquired bit by bit by the Secretary of State for Wales between 1964 and 1999, and thereafter been acquired by the Assembly, now passed to the Welsh Ministers. They continue to acquire such functions and powers when granted them by Assembly Acts, and also by Acts of the UK Parliament. With regard to their subordinate law-making powers, the Welsh Ministers proceed in roughly the same manner as their Westminster counterparts, making such legislation in the form of statutory instruments which are either to be laid before the Assembly for its approval – the Welsh version of affirmative procedure – or laid before the Assembly so that there is opportunity for the Assembly to annul an instrument with which it is unhappy – the Welsh version of negative procedure. Whereas at Westminster the power to make subordinate legislation in this manner is generally given to 'the Secretary of State' – a phrase interpreted to mean any one of the government ministers, in Wales such powers are generally given to 'the Welsh Ministers' collectively, although a power can be given expressly to the First Minister or the Counsel General. Statutory instruments are made by being signed by the individual minister concerned who is identified at Westminster as 'one of Her Majesty's Principal Secretaries of State' and in Wales as 'One of the Welsh Ministers'. 1-82

As is the case with UK government ministers, the Welsh Ministers when exercising functions given to them by statute, including the function of making subordinate legislation, must act within the limits set by the statute in question, and their exercise of such functions can be challenged before the courts by those with a legitimate interest in their proper exercise by means of judicial review. This is another example of how limited law-making power results in laws which are capable of being challenged. 1-83

[42] The Secretary of State for Wales was originally entitled to participate in Assembly proceedings, but was prohibited from voting in the Assembly: GoWA 2006, s. 32(1), repealed by Wales Act 2017, s. 15.

THE CIVIL SERVICE AND THE ASSEMBLY COMMISSION

1-84 The creation of the office of the Secretary of State for Wales in 1964 led to the establishment of a UK government department to serve the Welsh Secretary and the other ministers and under secretaries serving Wales. Thus was created what was called the Welsh Office. Like other departments of state, the Welsh Office was served by a body of civil servants working as part of the Home Civil Service.

1-85 With the opening of the National Assembly in 1999, the office of the Secretary of State was reduced greatly in size as a very substantial part of its work then passed to the Assembly. The vast majority of the civil servants in the Welsh Office were transferred to serve the Assembly, while remaining a part of the Home Civil Service. When the legislative and executive functions of the Assembly were reallocated in 2007 to the new-style Assembly and the Welsh Assembly Government respectively, while a body of civil servants, constituted as a single government department, remained to serve the Government, others were transferred out of the civil service to work for the new-style Assembly as employees of the Assembly Commission, a body specifically created by the 2006 Act to hold the legal rights and obligations pertaining to the Assembly.[43] The Assembly staff were to be the counterparts of the Parliamentary Service at Westminster.

THE CHALLENGE OF LEGISLATING FOR WALES

1-86 From 1964 until 2007, first for the Secretary of State and after 1999 for the National Assembly, civil servants in Wales were involved in preparing legislation. However, the laws then made were almost always in the form of subordinate legislation. Very occasionally, the Welsh Office would promote a bill in the UK Parliament, important examples being the Welsh Language Acts of 1967 and 1993. Generally, however, Welsh Office civil servants and their successors working for the old-style National Assembly between 1999 and 2007 were concerned with implementing the legislative policies made at Westminster by framing suitable subordinate legislation for Wales under powers given by the parent Act of Parliament.

1-87 With the Assembly acquiring primary law-making powers first in the form of Measures in 2007 and then in the form of Assembly Acts in 2011, the Welsh Government and its civil servants had themselves to begin to frame policy initiatives to be carried into effect by means of primary legislation on a regular basis, rather than think mainly in terms of how best to implement policies made elsewhere. Likewise the Assembly in 2007, with eight years' experience of scrutinizing subordinate legislation, had to begin the task of scrutinizing proposals leading to primary legislation. Whereas departments of state in Whitehall were accustomed to bringing forward legislative proposals in the form of bills as well as thereafter implementing those bills by subordinate legislation, the same had not been true

[43] GoWA 2006, s. 27.

to anything like the same extent for the Welsh Office. The change was therefore destined to be challenging.

Difficulties manifested themselves in various ways following the advent of primary law-making powers in 2007. On the part of the Assembly, accustomed as it had been since 1999 to seeing virtually every item of subordinate legislation made in its name, there was an understandable reluctance to cede subordinate law-making to the Welsh Ministers without retaining the opportunity to debate such proposals and approve them by an affirmative procedure. There was resistance to the use of the negative procedure with only the opportunity to annul. On the part of the Assembly Government, there was at times a discernible tendency to view primary legislation as the vehicle by which ministers obtained subordinate law-making powers, thus in effect recreating the context in which legislation had been made before 2007. This may indeed have been exacerbated by the fact that, where the early Assembly had very broad subordinate law-making powers, the executive would have striven to achieve policy goals by using the only means at their disposal – subordinate legislation. Having developed techniques for achieving this, policy officials might be loathe to abandon them in favour of the untried method of primary law-making rather than sticking to the tried and tested path. Achieving policy goals by means of subordinate legislation may fairly be said to have been the familiar 'comfort zone' of Welsh Government. Between 2007 and 2011, the difficulties and delays which arose when trying to obtain legislative competence for the Assembly from Westminster under Part 3 of and Schedule 5 to the 2006 Act meant that the effort of obtaining that competence often left little time to develop legislative proposals for enactment once the relevant competence was obtained. The upshot was that the subsequent Assembly Measure was often framed so as to allow more time for the development of those proposals by giving Welsh Ministers powers to make subordinate legislation to carry the policy into effect – a return to the 'comfort zone' of Welsh Government by passing 'framework' legislation. 1-88

With the enhanced legislative competence that the Assembly acquired in 2011 under Part 4 of and Schedule 7 to the 2006 Act, the difficulties and delays of the previous processes became a thing of the past and both the Assembly and the Welsh Government had the opportunity to develop effective working practices to embrace the new situation of being able to legislate for Wales on a broad range of topics. This is arguably even more true with the advent of a reserved-powers model of legislative competence. The succeeding chapters of this book will seek to establish what good legislative practice requires and involves in the contemporary Welsh context so that the challenge of legislating for Wales can be successfully embraced. 1-89

Chapter 2

From Ideas to Policy

LEGISLATION, GOVERNMENT AND THE RULE OF LAW

It is the function of a legislature to make laws by a process of proposal, scrutiny and enactment. It is not the function of a government to make law. Rather, it is the principal function of a government to govern within the limits of the law as it stands. A government is itself subject to the law. It governs under the law. This is partly what is meant by the phrase, 'the rule of law'. 2-01

This basic proposition may seem somewhat foreign to British eyes. It is illustrated more clearly in the governmental arrangements of the United States. There, enacted laws are made by the Congress, and it is not open to any member of the government, from the President downwards, to be a member of Congress. There is a clear separation of the legislative and executive powers. The administration is expected to govern in accordance with the law as it stands, and has no ready means of changing that law in order to advance its policies. It frequently has to struggle to get legislative proposals accepted and enacted by the Senate and the House of Representatives. 2-02

This is very different from what the position has usually been in the United Kingdom. The government of the United Kingdom is by convention formed by the party with the greatest number of seats in the House of Commons. If that party, as again has usually been the case, actually has the majority of seats in the Commons, it will be able to ensure that its legislative proposals will be passed by the lower house, and the convention by which the unelected House of Lords does not frustrate the will of the democratically elected House of Commons means that a majority government can in effect ensure that its legislative proposals are enacted and become law. Unlike the position in the United States, therefore, governments in the United Kingdom are accustomed to being able to change the law as they wish in order to promote their policies. Indeed, in many respects, legislation has come to be seen in the United Kingdom as the means by which the government implements its policies.[1] As will be seen, this is not always beneficial, as it can confuse the means for advancing a policy goal with that goal's implementation and its achievement. 2-03

[1] This is what led to Lord Hailsham's famous consideration that a UK government with a majority in the House of Commons was an elected dictatorship: see Lord Hailsham, 'Elective Dictatorship', The Richard Dimbleby Lecture, *The Listener*, 21 October 1976, p. 496, and his *The Dilemma of Democracy* (London and Glasgow, 1978), p. 126: see the reference to the latter in *AXA General Insurance Limited* v *The Lord Advocate (Scotland)* [2011] UKSC 46, at ¶¶50–1, *per* Lord Hope.

THE NEED FOR LEGISLATION

2-04 Legislation is not therefore *the* means by which a policy is achieved. It is *one* of the means which can be used to achieve a policy outcome. It is sometimes the case that enacting a law in itself produces the outcome which is required. Examples of such legislation would include statutes abolishing the death penalty or allowing homosexual couples to marry. Once the Act comes into force, the policy goal it was intended to achieve has in fact become the case. More usually, however, the provisions of an Act have to be implemented, and only as they are implemented and after their implementation does it become clear whether the statute has achieved what it was intended to deliver. Thus, for instance, statutes that have as their aim a reduction of crime or the advancement of education or an improvement in public health do not deliver their intended objectives simply by being enacted.

2-05 Legislation is not therefore a magical process by which policy goals are achieved by being placed on the statute book. Nor is it a process aimed at securing the approval of the legislature for a policy. In the case of a government, approval for its policies will in many cases have been obtained directly from the people through the endorsement of its manifesto at a general election. That endorsement of its programme of government delivers the mandate of the people for its implementation, and no further endorsement by the legislature is needed if the government can implement its policies without having to change the law. However, if the government requires the law to be changed in order to achieve its programme, then the further approval of the representatives of the people will be needed, not to approve the policy but to approve the means by which the government has chosen to carry it into effect.

2-06 This distinction has been neatly encapsulated by one of the later twentieth-century's most distinguished judges, Lord Diplock, when he said:

> What Parliament enacts are not policies but means for giving effect to policies.[2]

Legislation is needed when the chosen means for giving effect to a policy necessitates a change in the law.

2-07 Changing the law means that the rules by which the lives of citizens are regulated are being changed. This may mean that additional duties are going to be imposed on them, duties which may entail sanctions, such as punishment, for their breach. It can also mean that citizens are to have additional entitlements given to them or powers enabling them to achieve certain goals for themselves. It may also mean conferring powers on public officials or public bodies, which in turn will allow them to affect the way in which citizens live their lives.

2-08 Simple politeness would require that before a person was given an entitlement or a power, and even more so before extra duties were imposed upon them, they should be notified that this was intended, given an opportunity to consider the

[2] *DPP* v *Bhagwan* [1972] AC 60 at 82.

suggestion, ask questions concerning it and themselves suggest adjustments to it, and finally agree or disagree to its being implemented. Such individual involvement in the approval of changes to the rules regulating the lives of citizens has not been practicable in communities with large populations. Instead, the citizens elect representatives to perform those functions on their behalf. The function of the legislative process is to afford the representatives of the people the chance to consider changes to the rules on behalf of the people affected by them. Notification becomes the introductory phase; the chance to consider, question and make alternative suggestions becomes the process of scrutiny and amendment during the deliberative phase; and the chance to agree or disagree becomes the consent given or withheld in the decision-making phase. What simple politeness might seem to require is embodied in the formal mechanisms of the legislative process, the representatives ultimately being accountable for the manner in which they discharge their responsibilities when the time comes for them to seek re-election, the 'regular and constitutional means' by which the political sovereignty of the people is asserted.

That this is more than just simple politeness but a fundamental principle of democratic government is again encapsulated in the words of a later twentieth-century judge. In a lecture following his retirement, Lord Oliver of Aylmerton said: 2-09

> the citizen ... is entitled in a democratic society to have the rules by which his life is to be regulated properly debated and scrutinized by his elected representatives.[3]

It is this principle of democracy which is carried into effect by the legislative process. It can be lost sight of when a government is capable of forcing its proposals through the legislature by dint of having a majority. In such circumstances, the process can appear to be no more than an elaborate ritual, a rigmarole which has to be performed to get a legislative proposal onto the statute book. Perhaps it is then, more than ever, that the underlying democratic purpose of the process needs to be recalled, together with its very real connection with the rule of law.

IDEAS FOR LEGISLATION

The ideas forming the basis for policy initiatives which may require legislation for their achievement can come from a variety of sources. Some will have involved the electorate in their adoption; others will not. Whether there is a popular mandate for a change will be relevant to how the proposal is developed and how the legislature is to respond to it. 2-10

[3] Lord Oliver of Aylmerton, 'A Judicial View of Modern Legislation' [1993] *Statute Law Review* 1, at 3.

Manifesto commitments

2-11 Political parties obtain a mandate from the people for their policy ideas by placing those ideas before the electorate in a manifesto prior to a general election. Voting for a candidate is taken to indicate support for the ideas set out in the manifesto of the political party to which that candidate belongs. A successful candidate obtains a mandate to deliver the ideas set out in his party's manifesto, and the party which has the greatest number of successful candidates will form a government with a mandate to pursue those ideas during its term of office.[4]

2-12 The incoming coalition government formed by the Conservatives and Liberal Democrats in 2010 made an important change to the electoral arrangements of the United Kingdom. Up until then, Prime Ministers had had the power to call a general election at a time of their choosing, provided that the lifetime of a Parliament did not exceed five years.[5] The power to dissolve Parliament and call an election was a prerogative power of the Crown, exercised on the advice of the Prime Minister as the chief Minister of the Crown, the convention being that the monarch follows the advice of his or her ministers. The Fixed-Term Parliaments Act 2011 changed this, by requiring that for the future general elections were as a rule to be held at regular intervals of five years, voting to take place on the first Thursday in May in each fifth year. This should have meant that it would now be possible to predict with some certainty the dates of UK general elections. However, the Fixed Term Parliaments Act 2011 permits a general election to be called before the expiry of the five-year term if there has been a successful motion of no confidence in the government or if the House of Commons agrees to an early election with at least two-thirds of the members voting in favour.[6] This second scenario materialized in 2017, thus in effect thwarting the policy in the infancy of its operation.

2-13 Fixed-term parliaments should make it possible for political parties to plan and prepare their manifestos in a more orderly fashion. In particular, they should be in a better position to ensure that the policy ideas for which they seek a mandate, which if successful would become commitments to the electorate, are affordable and realistically achievable. This raises the question of how political parties not currently in government are to work out whether their ideas are affordable and capable of achievement. It is understood that government departments in Whitehall have requested the opportunity to assist political parties in their manifesto preparations

[4] The legal concept of mandate derives from the Roman law of consensual contracts, whereby one person commissioned another to perform tasks on his behalf. The school of mediaeval jurists known as the Commentators used the concept to explain the legal basis of representative government which was emerging in the communes of Italy, from where it has acquired its modern meaning of the commission given to a political party or individual to carry out policies which gained support through an electoral victory.

[5] The maximum five-year term had been instituted by the Parliament Act 1911, replacing the seven-year maximum under the Septennial Act 1715.

[6] Fixed Term Parliaments Act 2011, s. 2.

in the six months leading up to a general election so as to ensure such an outcome. They should now be able to perform this service because one should be able to calculate when that six-month period will be.

In terms of the working of democracy, this is a highly significant development in that it should ensure that electors are given realistic choices between affordable, achievable alternatives, and be confident that this is the case. Manifesto commitments will not contain the possibility of electoral disappointment when their lack of practicality is discovered by a party coming into government. Utilizing the resources of the civil service to achieve that goal by its providing the necessary evidence and analysis appears not only reasonable but proper in the interests of good government, for political parties not in government and still less ordinary voters are otherwise massively disadvantaged in attempting to make such calculations for themselves. It could end political debate at election time as to whether other parties' commitments are affordable – an issue which the electorate is not truly in a position to judge, and therefore is an argument rooted in raising fears. Electors could make confident choices between realistic alternatives. 2-14

In passing, it is worth noting that the National Assembly for Wales has, since its creation, operated on a fixed-term basis.[7] Thus, it was always possible for such support to be provided to the competing parties. Welsh institutions have been in a position not merely to anticipate but to run ahead of developments at United Kingdom level, provided they are not wedded to slavishly following Whitehall and Westminster practices regardless of their suitability.[8] 2-15

From the point of view of legislative development, one of the worst features of uninformed manifesto commitments is the tendency of political parties to state that, if elected, they will legislate to achieve a particular goal. Often, such statements are made in ignorance of the fact that the goal may not require legislation for its achievement. Sometimes this results in unnecessary legislation having to be passed simply to fulfil the manifesto commitment, wasting legislative time and resources. Such commitments also contribute to the fallacy that legislation itself delivers the policy. Lord Diplock's reminder that legislation does not enact policy but the means for giving it effect deserves to be recalled here, and it is to be hoped that informed support in the framing of manifestos can bring an end to such unnecessary commitments and assist in correcting the misconception that, simply by legislating, policy goals can be delivered. 2-16

[7] The Assembly's fixed term was originally four years, but this has now been increased to five years as a consequence of the change to fixed-term five-year Parliaments at Westminster, in order to avoid the two election dates ever falling at the same time: compare GoWA 1998, s. 3 and GoWA 2006, s. 3 (four-year term) with Wales Act 2014, s. 1 (five-year term).

[8] It is understood that the opportunity has been taken and that Welsh politics has already for some time benefited from informed input into party manifestos.

Government departments

2-17 Not all policy initiatives requiring legislation for their implementation originate in the manifestos of political parties. Indeed, research carried out with regard to legislation during the 1970s discovered that during that decade manifesto commitments counted for only a minority of such developments. The vast majority arose from the activity of government departments themselves.[9]

2-18 This should not be surprising. Civil servants working in government departments are well positioned to observe how existing policies are working and to make suggestions both as to how to improve the working of those policies or even to draw attention to the need for them to be fundamentally reconsidered or replaced. They also have access to important bodies of evidence and the tools to analyse it effectively.

2-19 Clearly, where a political party is in government, civil service input of this sort regarding the working of existing policies may well result in the incorporation of proposals for change in that party's manifesto. Therefore the line between ideas which arise from manifesto commitments and those which are generated by the working of government departments is not a clear one. If government departments are permitted to provide support to political parties generally in the preparation of their manifestos, the line will become even more blurred. However, the blurring of the line may result in clarifying what is realistically achievable.

Assembly Members, Assembly Committees and the Assembly Commission

2-20 It is not only the government that may promote policy ideas that require legislation for their achievement. As all Assembly Members are entitled to introduce legislative proposals, backbench members from both the government and opposition parties – that is all AMs who do not hold government office – can come up with ideas for legislating. Under the Standing Orders of the National Assembly, ballots are held on a regular basis under the terms of which AMs who are successful in the ballot have an opportunity to bring forward legislative proposals in the form of bills.[10] This allows them the opportunity to fulfil commitments made to the electorate at the time of their election, even where their party did not make it into government.

2-21 Similar ballots are held of backbench MPs in the House of Commons to allow them to bring forward bills, and at Westminster members of the House of Lords are also able to bring forward legislative proposals. Given that the time allocated for government bills at Westminster is limited and competition for a place in the government's legislative programme keen, it is not uncommon for proposals which have not won a place in the programme to be handed down to backbench MPs on the government side to promote as private members' bills. Such a tactic is capable of

[9] See Michael Zander, *The Law-Making Process* (6th edn, Cambridge, 2004), p. 2, quoting R. Rose, *Do Parties Make a Difference?* (2nd edn, London, 1984), pp. 72–3.

[10] SO 26.84–94.

being employed in the National Assembly should the time for Welsh Government business prove insufficient to accommodate all of the items it would wish to advance. Such handout bills will have been developed by government departments in the same manner as the government's own bills, and drafted by its drafting counsel.[11]

Where the initiative has not come from the government but from the backbench member himself or herself, there is nothing to stop the bill being passed if it finds the support of a majority of the members. Where the government does not have a majority capable of defeating the bill, it behoves it to take such proposals seriously, and to devote civil service time and resources to ensuring that the consequences of the bill being passed are fully scoped. This may result in the government undertaking to support the bill in return for the backbench member accepting certain changes so as to bring the bill into line with government policies or to make it administratively and legally workable. It is not unusual for backbench bills to receive such support in the National Assembly.[12] No doubt this is a consequence of the fact that majority government by one party has not yet occurred in the Assembly's history. Nevertheless, it has made for a more inclusive style of politics, with backbench proposals regularly being considered on their merits rather than being voted down for purely party political reasons. 2-22

Assembly Committees, with responsibility for scrutinizing the development and implementation of policies in relation to the various areas of government, can also be a source of ideas for legislative change. The Assembly Standing Orders recognize them as a potential source of such ideas, even though strictly their proposals have to be introduced by an Assembly Member serving the committee.[13] As with private members' bills, such committee bills cannot safely be ignored by a government lacking a working majority. 2-23

Standing orders also recognize that the Assembly Commission can develop legislative ideas, although again any proposals will formally be introduced by an Assembly Member who is also a member of the Assembly Commission.[14] Its proposals must relate to its functions as the body corporate serving the legal and administrative needs of the Assembly. In that capacity, it has promoted legislation. Indeed, the first Assembly Act to receive Royal Assent under the enhanced powers given by Part 4 of, and Schedule 7 to, the Government of Wales Act 2006 was an Assembly Commission bill – the National Assembly for Wales (Official Languages) Act 2012, which made Welsh and English the official languages for all Assembly business. 2-24

[11] See further below, §9-09.

[12] Examples include the Healthy Eating in Schools (Wales) Measure 2009, the Playing Fields (Community Involvement in Disposal Decisions) (Wales) Measure 2010, and the Mobile Homes (Wales) Act 2013. The Recovery of Medical Costs for Asbestos Diseases (Wales) Bill, also such a bill, failed to become an Act because its provisions were found to be outside the Assembly's legislative competence: see *Recovery of Medical Costs for Asbestos Diseases (Wales) Bill: Reference by the Counsel General for Wales* [2015] UKSC 3 (the *Asbestos Diseases* case).

[13] SO 26.80–83.

[14] SO 26.84.

Civic society

2-25 It is not only from within the institutions of government and the legislature that ideas for legislative change may come. There is nothing to prevent such ideas being developed and promoted from outside the Assembly and the Welsh Government. Interest groups and pressure groups, being part of wider civic society, may campaign for the promotion of particular policies and seek to have the law changed to ensure their achievement. In some countries, it is even open for a minimum number of electors to present a bill to the legislature and require that it undergo scrutiny and debate, albeit that they cannot require that it be passed.[15] Although the voters of Wales do not enjoy the right to introduce legislative proposals into the Assembly for deliberation, any more than do the electorate of the House of Commons at Westminster, there is nothing to prevent their seeking to influence an Assembly Member or an Assembly Committee to do so on their behalf. One such proposal which found favour with an Assembly Committee resulted in the passing of the Active Travel (Wales) Act 2013.[16]

Events

2-26 There are occasions when the need for legislation is not the consequence of a period of consideration and reflection as to how best to achieve a policy goal but rather the result of an immediate and pressing need for urgent action requiring a change in the law. At the United Kingdom level, examples of events requiring legislative action are acts of terrorism resulting in the passing of legislation to safeguard the public from such acts. In Wales, since the creation of the Assembly, urgent legislative action has been required to deal with emergencies such as an outbreak of avian 'flu' among birds, which could have spread to the human population, or, on two occasions, of foot and mouth disease among cattle. In these cases, it was secondary legislation made by ministers by means of statutory instrument that was needed, and there may even be a duty to legislate in such circumstances. However, the Standing Orders allow for the passage of Government Emergency Bills by an accelerated procedure where the need arises.[17]

The Law Commission of England and Wales

2-27 The Law Commission was established by statute in 1965 with the purpose of reforming the law. As Scots law is distinct from the law of England and Wales and

[15] Italy is one such example, where 50,000 electors to the Chamber of Deputies can present a bill for debate, thus exercising a popular legislative initiative.

[16] This had originally been advocated by an interest group promoting sustainable transport policies, called SusTrans.

[17] SO 26.95–104. One such emergency bill was passed by the Fourth Assembly – the Agricultural Sector (Wales) Act 2014, which is discussed further below, §§4-12–4-14 and nn. 11 and 12.

Scotland has its own law courts, a separate Law Commission was established for Scotland in the same year. Northern Ireland acquired its own Law Commission in 2007.[18]

As the Law Commission for England and Wales, the Law Commission can propose reforms to the law and submit draft bills for introduction into Parliament by the United Kingdom government. It can now also submit proposals to the Welsh Government, complete with draft bills for introduction to the Assembly. At Westminster, a special accelerated procedure has been devised for Law Commission bills that deal with technical reforms to the law rather than the implementation of a political policy. There is currently no such procedure in place in Wales, but Law Commission proposals for reform of the law have found favour with the Welsh Government and have been enacted by the National Assembly.[19] The Law Commission deserves therefore to be recognized as a source of ideas for Welsh legislation. 2-28

PROPERLY THOUGHT THROUGH POLICY

Ideas are one thing; a policy is another. The difference between the two lies in the amount of thought and work that has gone into its development. A frequently-heard criticism of a policy goal is that it was worked out 'on the back of an envelope' or 'fag packet'. Essentially this suggests a failure to take the time and trouble to undertake a proper development of the policy. It has been said that 'well-intentioned legislation, properly thought through and competently executed, is a powerful force for good'. Conversely, it has been recognized that 'ill-intentioned legislation, poorly thought through or incompetently executed, can cause untold unfairness and misery'.[20] Unfortunately, it is also the case – and perhaps the greater problem – that well-intentioned legislation, if poorly thought through or incompetently executed, can also result in those consequences. 2-29

The unfairness and misery will be felt by those whose lives fall to be regulated by the legislative rules that are made. It is to avoid such consequences that those who are responsible for thinking through the ideas, developing the policies and executing the intentions need to do so properly and competently. Methods of working need to be developed and maintained to ensure that the work is properly and competently done.[21] 2-30

[18] The relevant legislation is the Law Commissions Act 1965, and the Justice (Northern Ireland) Act 2002 (as amended), s. 52(2) and (3). The Northern Ireland Law Commission ceased operating in 2016 owing to budgetary constraints.

[19] For instance, the Renting Homes (Wales) Act 2016.

[20] Daniel Greenberg, *Laying Down the Law* (London, 2011), p. 272.

[21] When rights protected by the Human Rights Act 1998 are involved, this becomes even more important given the majority view expressed concerning the quality of legislative decision making in the devolved legislatures in the *Asbestos Diseases* case: see below, §§3-11–3-20; 8-36–8-44.

POLICY: THE WORD, ITS MEANING AND THE IMPLICATIONS

2-31 The English word, *policy*, is derived from the Latin word, *politia*, which can mean 'the state' or 'the administration'.[22] It is not unconnected with the verb, *polire*, which means 'to polish' or 'to finish'. It conveys the sense, therefore, of something being fashioned into a finished state, a finished state which is the result of careful crafting and polishing, resulting in an elegant end-product.

2-32 The meaning of the modern English word is given in dictionaries as 'a plan of action adopted or pursued by an individual, government, party, business, etc.'[23] Connecting this with the word's etymology would suggest that such a plan of action will have been carefully crafted and be adopted in a polished state, finished in a somewhat greater sense than simply having been completed.

2-33 A policy, therefore, according to the dictionary definition requires that there be a plan of action, which requires that those who are promoting it know what they intend to do and how they intend to do it. For the plan of action to be adopted similarly requires that one knows why one intends to do it and why one intends to do it in the particular way envisaged by the plan of action and not in other ways. The pursuance of the plan of action likewise entails that how the plan is to be implemented has also been scoped.

2-34 The focus of this plan of action will be what it is that the policy aims to achieve. This may be the overcoming of a problem of some sort that is perceived to exist, or effecting some improvement that is deemed to be of benefit. Either way, there will be a goal to be targeted and what that goal is needs to be clearly defined, as will the means by which it will be possible to determine, after the plan of action has been pursued, whether the goal has in fact been achieved. Both the problem that is being addressed and the goal that it is sought to achieve need to be clear at the outset. The idea requires clarification.

THE ACTION AND ITS CONSEQUENCES

2-35 Once the nature of the problem that it is sought to resolve or the improvement that it is sought to deliver have been clarified, questions arise as to the manner in which this is to be accomplished. Addressing this broad question will entail focusing on some detailed issues. The following questions will need to be asked and answered:

Who must be affected to achieve the goal?

2-36 The lives of which individual citizens, families, communities or work-forces will have to be affected by the plan? Which public bodies, local authorities, private

[22] It was used in Latin as the title of Plato's work known in English as *The Republic*.

[23] *Collins English Dictionary*.

companies or businesses will of necessity find their activities and responsibilities affected? The persons practising which trades or professions, or working in which industries will have to feel the effects?

How must they be affected to achieve the goal?

In what way will the people identified above find that their lives, activities, responsibilities or working practices are being affected? Will they be required to do things which they are not currently required to do, or find that they are no longer permitted to do things which they are currently allowed to do? Will they be given new rights or entitlements, or be given the means to enable them to achieve for themselves things which they are either currently not able to achieve or else not achieve easily or effectively? 2-37

Where must they be affected in that way to achieve the goal?

Is it intended that the persons identified be affected in the manner identified everywhere or only in certain places? For instance, is the plan to affect only rural communities or urban communities, or only coastal, lowland or upland areas? 2-38

When must they be affected in that way to achieve the goal?

Is it envisaged that the persons identified are to be affected in the manner identified in the places identified all at once or will the changes be implemented gradually? Will there be any discretion as to when the changes should be implemented, and, if so, who will exercise that discretion and how? 2-39

And perhaps most importantly of all:

Why must they be affected in that way in those places at those times to achieve the goal?

In many respects, this is the key question, for it calls upon those advocating the changes which the policy anticipates to justify their adoption and the pursuit of this plan of action. Justification will be required by those who scrutinize what is proposed both as a formal part of the legislative process and as the institutions of civic society – the press, radio, television – interrogate the policy and its proponents. Unconvincing or unsatisfactory answers to this question can damage the credibility of the policy and of those who are advocating it. 2-40

What are to be the consequences of their being so affected?

This question concerns the desired outcomes of the policy. The idea will have been to solve a problem or produce a benefit of some sort for the people of Wales. 2-41

The solution or the benefit is intended to result from pursuing the plan of action that it is intended to adopt. The consequences desired may be changes to the legal entitlements, responsibilities or powers of the individuals or institutions concerned. They may be social, aimed at supporting or changing patterns of living, by providing schools, medical care or housing in proximity to local communities or effective transport links between population centres and places of work. Economic outcomes, such as the attraction of new industries or the creation of a work-force with new skills may be sought, and financial outcomes may involve increasing the spending power of those in work and their families. Finally, but far from unimportantly, there are likely to be political consequences if the desired outcomes are achieved, as it may result in an increase in the credibility and popularity of, and therefore support for, the government or the party which has achieved the goal.

EFFICACY AND IMPACT

2-42 A distinction is sometimes drawn between the intended effects or efficacy of a policy and the policy's impact.[24] Whereas *efficacy* is used to demarcate the results which were intended or may be taken to have been intended by its proponents, by *impact* is meant the consequences which are actually brought about in practice. These may or may not correspond, and there is always a risk that some unintended consequences which were not foreseen prove to be very unfortunate for those affected by them. In the worst cases, this is where what should have been a powerful force for good turns out to be a cause of unfairness or misery for the people unintentionally affected.

2-43 A robust process of policy development needs therefore to ensure that no consequences are unforeseen. If there are to be unfortunate consequences for some, they need to have been foreseen, considered and decided to be a price worth exacting to promote the objects which the policy is meant to achieve.[25]

2-44 To prevent such unforeseen consequences arising, a second set of questions, similar to and complementing the first, need to be asked and answered, addressing all possible outcomes rather than just those that are desired.

Who might be affected in achieving the goal?

2-45 Although the idea may be to affect one particular class of person, it may be important to define that class to ensure that others do not fall into it inadvertently. For instance, legislation meant to prevent those claiming housing benefit from claiming for properties which are more spacious than they need (the so-called 'bedroom tax'), if targeted on the basis of the number of residents in a property and the

[24] See D. R. Miers and A. C. Page, *Legislation* (2nd edn, London, 1990), pp. 204–6.

[25] These words are based on those of Lord Diplock in *DPP* v *Bhagwan* [1972] AC 60 at 82, which are discussed later, §3-06.

number of bedrooms it has, may inadvertently include families where a family member is not resident because serving in the armed forces or working away from home but hoping to return. A person living alone and claiming benefit for a three-bedroom property may seem to fall squarely within the class to be affected, but if that person is able by living there to offer support to their son or daughter's young family living nearby or an elderly parent in the same community, the effect on those others of forcing the claimant to move to a one-bedroom property at some distance needs to be considered. These possibilities need to be identified and a decision taken as to whether such persons need to be included in the affected class or not, and, if not, whether they need to be specifically excluded and how.

How might they be affected?

Continuing with the previous example, the idea would be to get people living in properties of a size greater than their residential requirements to move to smaller properties and thereby reduce the benefits payable. However, if the persons concerned are in employment but earning a low income, unless smaller properties are available in the same locality, they may be forced to give up a job because unable to travel to it or to afford to travel to it. The reduction in housing benefit may therefore be cancelled out or surpassed by a payment in unemployment benefit. Likewise, if the person forced to move is, as a consequence, unable to provide support to the young family, one of the parents may have to work shorter hours or even give up work to provide that support, or the elderly relative may have to rely on social services for support or move into residential care at a cost to the taxpayer exceeding the amount of benefit saved. 2-46

Where might they be affected?

A policy, for instance, of building a major road to lessen journey times between north and south Wales would be intended to benefit travellers and carriers of freight by road, but would impact on the owners of property, including farms, near the new route. Attracting traffic to the new road would relieve traffic on other roads and avoid congestion in the small towns that were bypassed. However, businesses such as petrol stations along the now quieter routes would be adversely affected and might even have to close. This effect could be felt over a wide area. 2-47

When might they be affected?

The introduction of a new school curriculum to benefit pupils might be timed to commence at the start of a new school year. However, if staff had to attend preparation events during the previous school year, pupils completing their studies at that time might suffer disruption to their learning as a consequence. 2-48

And perhaps, once again, most important of all:

Why might they have to be affected in that way to achieve the goal?

2-49 When unfortunate consequences flowing from achievement of the policy goal have been foreseen, those promoting that policy face a difficult choice. Do they seek to avoid those consequences for those adversely affected by providing that the persons concerned are to be protected from the consequences or compensated for their loss, or do they abandon the policy initiative altogether because of those consequences, or do they press ahead in the belief that the adverse consequences for some are a price worth paying for the benefit of others. The choice is for those who must decide upon the policy and how it is to be implemented. What is important is that such unfortunate consequences are foreseen, and that those promoting the policy are able to provide justification for their infliction upon those who will suffer as a result.[26]

What will be the consequences if they are so affected?

2-50 The consequences, as the examples have shown, can again be of various sorts: social in the case of the families no longer able to rely on one another for support; economic and financial for the businesses who lose out as a consequence of the new road. Sometimes intended beneficial consequences may be at odds with undesirable and undesired ones, as when the work, jobs and prosperity which a new industry may provide in a locality threatens damage to the environment. As always, there may be political consequences at the ballot box for a party that presses ahead with unpopular measures in the teeth of opposition, or for that matter a party which opposes change which is desired by a significant section of the electorate. The worst political consequences may however await the party that or the individual who becomes aware of the adverse consequences only after the policy has been adopted or its implementation commenced – in other words, whose policy development has been less than thorough, compromising the quality of the policy itself and the credibility of its advocates.

2-51 The scoping of one particular sort of consequence is, with the introduction of the reserved-powers model of devolution, now the subject of a statutory requirement. The Wales Act 2017, section 11 has inserted a new section 110A into the Government of Wales 2006. This section requires that the Standing Orders of the Assembly require the person introducing a bill to make a written statement on or before the bill's introduction setting out the potential impact, if any, of the bill's provisions on the justice system in England and Wales. This is termed a 'justice impact assessment'.

[26] Again, this has become of increased importance where issues of human rights are involved as a consequence of the majority judgment in the *Asbestos Diseases* case discussed further below, §§3-11–3-20; 8-36–8-44.

ANSWERING THE QUESTIONS: EVIDENCE AND ANALYSIS

In order to determine who must or might be affected, how must they or might they be affected, etc., it is necessary to assemble the evidence needed to answer those questions and to analyse it rigorously so that the answers arrived at are reliable. The temptation merely to assemble the evidence that supports the idea needs to be firmly resisted. Almost certainly, a policy based on incomplete evidence will be exposed as such when it undergoes formal scrutiny by elected representatives, but also – and perhaps more damagingly – in the media. Every effort therefore needs to be made to ensure that all, not some, of the relevant evidence is gathered. Government ministers will have the support of their civil servants to do this, and backbench Assembly Members the support of the Assembly's own research service. Ideas that come from outside these areas will nevertheless have the benefit of these resources if they are adopted by the government, a backbencher or an Assembly Committee. 2-52

Officials charged with assembling the relevant evidence are likely to find themselves pressured to complete the work within a shorter timescale than thoroughness demands or with resources which do not match the task. As public servants, they should make clear the consequences of cutting corners.[27] The price of doing so with undue haste is likely to be paid when the failure to foresee unfortunate consequences is exposed by opposition parties and the media. The price may be political embarrassment or even failure. 2-53

Not all of the evidence may need to be freshly gathered. Use can and should be made of existing sources of information, such as the findings of research carried out by universities. If it becomes clear that there are gaps in the evidence needed, the option of conducting further research or of inviting appropriate external bodies to conduct such research on one's behalf should be borne in mind. Contributions from and consultation with interested parties, stakeholders and the public generally may be appropriate, both to obtain evidence and to test the ground with regard to ways of delivering the change required. Confidentiality may sometimes preclude such outreach, and resources may limit the extent of such engagement. Effective consultation should always be aimed at harnessing the expertise of those consulted 2-54

[27] The Civil Service Code deals with the issue in its requirement of Objectivity, where it states:

Objectivity

You must:

- provide information and advice, including advice to ministers, on the basis of the evidence, and accurately present the options and facts
- take decisions on the merits of the case
- take due account of expert and professional advice.

You must not:

- ignore inconvenient facts or relevant considerations when providing advice or making decisions
- frustrate the implementation of policies once decisions are taken by declining to take, or abstaining from, action which flows from those decisions.

and allow them to challenge what is being proposed; it should not be an exercise in enlisting support for the policy, or simply carried out to be able to say that it has been done. Among those who are most usefully and properly consulted are the persons or bodies who have been identified as those who are to be or who might be affected by the policy, those whose activities significantly affect the issues under consideration, those with information, knowledge and expertise regarding the matters in question, and those who control or influence important factors relating to the issue. These may well include other agencies of government, not all of which may be sympathetic to the policy under consideration. Therefore, careful thought and planning need to go into considering who to consult and how to go about consulting them to obtain the best results from the consultation. This entails seeking to understand the perspective of the consultees and approaching them appropriately.[28]

2-55 The accumulation of evidence in itself is not enough. The evidence needs to be subjected to rigorous testing and analysis. Care needs to be taken that evidence is accurate and objective, even though it is going to be used to build a case for a particular policy. Its quality needs to be assured, as does the credibility of its sources. It needs to be relevant, and those compiling it need to be wary of sources that may present evidence with their own agenda in mind, even if it coincides with the policy being promoted. A robust policy cannot be constructed on the basis of patchy or one-sided evidence.

When the evidence has been fully gathered and subjected to rigorous, critical analysis, it must be asked whether, on that evidence, there is a case for change.

THE CASE FOR CHANGE

2-56 The evidence as analysed should provide an answer to the question of whether there is a problem to be solved or whether there is room to improve some aspect of life for the people of Wales. In assessing whether a solution is feasible or an improvement possible, that is whether there is a case for change, certain factors will need to be borne in mind.

2-57 First, it must be asked whether the change can be effected in a manner which is consonant with existing policies favoured by the proposers. Policies need to be consistent in their response to problems which are similar in nature. In the case of a government proposal, consistency in this regard goes to the credibility of its programme of government as a whole. It will need to be assessed whether the change fits in with policies relating to equality, diversity and inclusion, sustainable development, social justice, the alleviation of poverty, the promotion of public health, employment and economic growth. The change should not conflict with

[28] On consultation and the benefits of working with stakeholders, see further below, §§5-35–5-42.

or undermine policies regarding the environment, rural communities, the rights of children and young people, privacy and the promotion of the Welsh language.[29]

It is particularly in such areas as these that 'unfortunate, unforeseen consequences' need to be avoided at all costs. The potential impact of the change on the people of Wales with regard to these issues needs to be carefully considered by analysis of the evidence, for questions regarding them will have to be addressed in justifying the policy to the Assembly and its Committees as well as to the press and the media. It is unlikely in the extreme that these issues will be overlooked by those seeking to challenge the change, whether constructively or otherwise. 2-58

The change will need to be thoroughly and accurately costed, so that any increased burden on the revenue is identified and shown to be capable of being supported by the budget. Questions with regard to this issue are again certain to arise. 2-59

The means at the disposal of the promoters of the policy by which their proposed change is to be brought about also need to be analysed. The impact on the lives of the people of Wales needs to be clear and justifiable. This includes the manner in which it is intended to manage the implementation of the change, which may also have cost implications. 2-60

Finally, the question of how those proposing the change intend to evaluate in due course whether it has actually delivered the solution to the problem it was intended to solve or the improvement it intended to make. It is not unusual for policies to be severely criticised for failing to provide for an efficient method of assessing whether or not they have been successful. It is a frequent criticism of successive United Kingdom governments that they legislate regarding a particular subject, such as education or criminal justice, before previous legislation on the topic has even had a chance to be evaluated.[30] 2-61

While it is important to assess objectively whether there is, on the evidence, a case for change, the decision as to whether there is a case for change may in the end be a political one. Analysis of the evidence may suggest that existing policies are working effectively to deal with any problem which has been identified, but if a manifesto commitment has been made and the electorate has voted for the party with that commitment in its programme, the political justification for change cannot be gainsaid. However, the manner in which it is to be accomplished may yet be determined on the evidence. 2-62

[29] Indeed, unless it is proposed to repeal the earlier legislation, there would be a duty on the government to ensure compliance with, for instance, the Well-being of Future Generations (Wales) Act 2015, Part 1 of the Environment (Wales) Act 2016 and the Rights of Children and Young Persons (Wales) Measure 2011.

[30] See the concerns expressed by the House of Commons Public Accounts Committee regarding the Department for Communities and Local Government's delay in evaluating the success or otherwise of its 'Help to Buy' scheme: House of Commons Public Accounts Committee, *Help to Buy equity loans*, 2nd report of Session 2014–15 (HC 281, 18 June 2014). See also, G. Palmer, 'Law Making in New Zealand: Is There a Better Way?', (the Harkness Henry Lecture) (2014) 22 *Waikato Law Review*, 1–40 (Victoria University of Wellington Legal Research Paper Series, Palmer Paper No. 82/2015).

GENERATING OPTIONS

2-63 The next stage in developing the policy will be to examine the possible methods by which the change required can be accomplished. It is important that the full range of options is scoped, for the proposal will be subjected to scrutiny in the Assembly and by civic society, and even those who agree that there is a case for change may still disagree with the method of effecting it which has been chosen and be minded to advance their own suggestions of how to proceed. If the full range of options has been assessed and subjected to challenge and criticism, the reasons for rejecting other suggested avenues will be ready to hand. Governments are again fiercely criticised if they fail to look at more than one option of how to proceed, limiting themselves to their own, one idea.[31] The same bank of evidence and analysis will be used to generate these options as was used to make the case for change, and each option should be evaluated objectively, in terms of the criteria used to assess the case for change, namely consonance with other policies, impact, cost, the mechanisms for effecting the change by means of that option and how well it can be managed and evaluated if that particular option is preferred. It will be necessary in certain circumstances to share with the Assembly and its committees the alternative options which have been scoped.[32]

THE PREFERRED OPTION

2-64 Each of the options which have been identified will be alternative plans of action, and identifying the preferred option will be the decision of which is to be adopted and pursued. How the action is to be pursued will be part of the plan of action itself.

2-65 The same five factors which were used in assessing whether there was a case for change and in identifying the various options will again be pertinent in making this choice. Thus, it will be relevant as to which of the options best fits with the government's perspective and its whole programme of policies. This will inevitably be heavily influenced by the political colour and beliefs of the party or parties in government, and it may well be that the choice of the preferred option will be dictated by what has been promised in a manifesto or incorporated in a coalition agreement. Some options may be ruled out for similar reasons.

[31] See again the House of Commons Public Accounts Committee's criticisms of the Department for Communities and Local Government for failing to assess any alternative options before going ahead with its 'Help to Buy' scheme: ibid.

[32] This is required to be in the Explanatory Memorandum by the Standing Orders (SO 26.6), and may be referred to by the courts in determining, where an issue of protected human rights is involved, whether the Assembly was or had been put in a position where it could properly evaluate the various interests involved: see *Recovery of Medical Costs for Asbestos Diseases (Wales) Bill: Reference by the Counsel General for Wales* [2015] UKSC 3, at ¶56, *per* Lord Mance.

The impact which the choice will have on the people of Wales will also be a determining factor, taking into account not only the outcomes which the proponents of the policy wish to occur, but also the avoidance of those consequences which they do not want to see happen. When making the choice, it may be necessary to face up to the fact that achieving the policy goal may result in undesired consequences for some, and the difficult decision taken that the price to them is worth paying to achieve the benefit to others. Such unpalatable elements should be recognized and admitted.[33] 2-66

Undoubtedly, the cost of the various options will be a factor in choosing between them, and it is therefore important that the costs which have been identified are accurate and reliable. 2-67

The mechanisms which are to be employed will also be a factor in making the choice. When considering whether to legislate for Wales, the question of whether the Welsh Ministers have executive powers to achieve the policy goal without needing to have primary legislation enacted will be a persuasive factor if the government does not have a majority in the Assembly, and the legislative competence of the Assembly will be key if the Welsh Government does not want to have to engage with Whitehall and Westminster to deliver the policy. The urgency of delivering the desired outcomes may also be a factor in preferring a mechanism that can be rapidly employed and over which the government has control. 2-68

Finally, the ease or otherwise with which the administrative bodies charged with implementing the policy will be able to do so can influence the choice of approach, as may the question of how straightforward it will be to evaluate whether the policy has delivered the desired results.[34] This may be key to making those responsible for the policy's adoption and implementation accountable to those affected and the public generally for the success or failure of their choice. 2-69

Choosing the preferred option marks the adoption of the policy, and the option chosen is the plan of action incorporating the method chosen for pursuing it. Once adopted, the questions posed earlier when developing the idea into a policy should have been answered. It will now therefore be clear: 2-70

who is to be affected and who is not to be affected;
how they are to be affected and how they are not to be affected;
where they are to be affected and where they are not to be affected;
when they are to be affected and when they are not to be affected;

[33] Failure to do so could again be a factor in the determining whether a fair balance had been achieved in weighing the public benefit of the goal to be achieved against the detriment to individuals involved where the courts had to consider a qualified protected right under the Human Rights Act 1998, as in the *Asbestos Diseases* case.

[34] The five factors identified as relevant to making the case for change, identifying the possible options and choosing the preferred option are sometimes referred to as 'the delivering results principles', or more recently 'the policy development principles'. Regardless of what they may from time to time be called, their relevance is unaffected.

and once more perhaps most importantly:

> why they are to be affected and why they are not to be affected.

One of the principles of the rule of law identified by Lord Bingham was that the laws of the land should apply equally to all, save to the extent that objective differences justify differentiation.[35] Objective differences therefore need to be identified to justify why some but not others are to be affected. In addition, the consequences of all of these outcomes will have been assessed – social, economic, financial and political, together with any legal consequences flowing from the policy choice which has been made.

2-71 One legal question which will have been or which will need to be addressed is whether what is intended will require a change in the law for its implementation. Any such change in the law will be effected by legislation. Legislation is needed only if it is necessary to change the law to give effect to the policy. If it is, the means for giving effect to the policy will need to be the subject of a legislative proposal. If it is not necessary to change the law, the government can implement the policy administratively, and much criticism is levelled at governments which resort to legislation when it is not necessary. The following chapters deal with the situation where some sort of change to the law is needed, because the policy can only be delivered by changing the law, that is by legislating for Wales.

[35] Tom Bingham, *The Rule of Law* (London, 2010), p. 55.

Chapter 3

From Policy to Proposal

Legislation is needed to change the law. When those who have developed the plan of action have adopted their preferred option for pursuing it, they will need to know whether it is necessary to change the law to achieve their goal in the manner in which they have decided to achieve it. At this point, it is essential that they have access to competent legal advice to ascertain whether what they propose requires a change in the law. It may have been necessary previously to seek legal advice in order to discover the possible legal consequences of the various options they identified and considered in developing their policy; however, now it is essential. If it is found that it is necessary to change the law in order to give effect to the policy, from this point at the very latest, lawyers need to be part of the team which will pursue the plan of action adopted.[1] 3-01

THE CHANGES TO THE LAW THAT CAN BE MADE

Legislation can be used to change the law in a variety of ways. It can be used to place people under duties, requiring them to perform some conduct, or prohibiting them from doing so. Where such duties already exist, legislation can change the nature of the duty in some way, or even remove the duty altogether, leaving individuals free to do as they wish with regard to the conduct in question. In consequence of imposing or removing duties, legislation is capable of restricting or enhancing the freedom of those it affects. Thus, legislation may impose a duty on persons not to smoke in certain public places, or it may alter the duty placed on motorists not to drive at speeds in excess of 30 miles per hour in built-up areas to one of not driving at a speed in excess of 20 miles per hour. Equally, it can take away the obligation to obtain a licence to keep a dog which is more than six months old. 3-02

As well as placing people under duties, legislation may be used to give people rights to certain things or certain services. It may provide them with entitlements, which they may claim from others, who will be under duties to meet those expectations. Likewise, existing entitlements may be taken away from all or some of the people who currently enjoy them, or the nature of that to which they are entitled may be changed. Thus, legislation may give people a right to certain benefits if they are unemployed or over a certain age. The nature of those benefits can be changed, so that for instance a benefit currently paid in cash may for the future be paid in kind. Legislation may also deprive people of benefits to which they are currently entitled, by for instance changing the age at which a state pension becomes payable or introducing a means test to determine whether any benefit is payable. 3-03

[1] On the formation and composition of the bill team, see below, §§5-02–5-34.

3-04 Legislation can also empower people to achieve things for themselves by giving legal significance to their actions and supporting their choices with the mechanisms of the legal system. This can allow citizens to achieve things for themselves with a certainty and confidence that would otherwise not be guaranteed. A simple example is that of the will. A person who wants to ensure that his property will pass to particular individuals on his death may tell his wife and children, his friends and wider family what his wishes are. He may choose to tell them by word of mouth at various times, by letters and e-mails, or in the course of telephone conversations. However, some of these persons may die before him, others forget what he has said or have only a vague recollection, and their recollections may differ or even conflict. The law therefore provides a simple mechanism to allow such a person to achieve his wishes. It simply asks that he write his wishes down, sign his name, and have two persons who are not to benefit add their signatures as witnesses of his having signed. If he has done this, then, on his death, the whole apparatus of the legal system becomes available to carry his wishes into effect. The law has empowered him to achieve for himself what, without its help, he would have been unable to achieve with any certainty.

3-05 Among those who may be given powers to achieve things, or even placed under duties to do so, are public officials and public bodies, including the institutions of government. Ministers and local authorities may be given powers to enable them to build roads, schools and hospitals, or to organize the manner in which education or health care is provided. Duties may be placed upon them to perform certain functions in order to safeguard public health and welfare, and to ensure public safety and security. There is a danger that, when it comes to considering how to change the law in order to achieve a policy goal, those who are closely involved in the work of government and public administration tend to think solely or primarily in terms of the duties and powers of public bodies; they see legislation as changing the law in order to give powers to ministers or public authorities. This is indeed one way of changing the law, but it should not dominate at the expense of other means of giving effect to a policy or force those other means from view. This has been a particular risk in Wales as a consequence of the fact that from 1964 until 2007, only by such means was it possible for the particular institutions of Welsh government, from the Secretary of State or the National Assembly downwards, to give effect to their policies.[2]

FREEDOM AND LEGISLATION

3-06 Changing the law to place duties upon citizens or to give them rights or powers, or to confer powers or place duties upon ministers and other public bodies, is one means of giving effect to a policy. Legislation, as was stated by Lord Diplock in

[2] See above, §§1-86–1-89.

the 1970s,[3] is the process of enacting such means of giving effect. Lord Diplock recognized that in many instances the duties imposed involved a curtailment of freedom for those who were subject to them.

> Those means [of giving effect to policies] often involve imposing upon private citizens fresh obligations or restrictions on their liberties to which they were not previously subject.[4]

He went on to characterize this as:

> the price, by way of deprivation of freedom to do or not to do as they wish, which Parliament is prepared to exact from individual citizens to promote those objects to which the Act is directed.[5]

What Lord Diplock said of Parliament is equally applicable to any legislature, including the National Assembly for Wales.[6] Legislation as an end product affects the freedom of citizens, possibly as 'a powerful force for good', but perhaps as a source of misery and unfairness. Legislation as an activity has as its object proposing such changes and deciding whether to make them and produce those effects, and in so doing seeking to ensure that good effects are the result and bad effects avoided. The thoroughness and rigour of the process of policy development had the same aim. That aim again deserves to be prominent in the process of converting the policy goals into the legislative proposals which will be the means of giving them effect by changing the law.

FREEDOM OR LIBERTY AS THE DEFAULT POSITION

It is often said that freedom or liberty is the default position with regard to the law 3-07
of the United Kingdom and indeed of other free societies. What this means is that an individual is free to do or not to do something as he or she wishes unless and until the law requires them either to do or not to do that thing. Unless the law requires a person to perform or to abstain from performing a particular conduct, he or she is free with regard to that conduct. It is a matter of personal choice for

[3] *DPP* v *Bhagwan* [1972] AC 60 at 82.

[4] Ibid.

[5] Ibid.

[6] Indeed, where the price which a devolved legislature such as the National Assembly is prepared to exact involves interference with a freedom protected by the Convention rights which have been incorporated into the domestic law of the United Kingdom by the Human Rights Act 1998, the courts will be prepared to examine whether the legislature has evaluated the various considerations involved satisfactorily: see *Recovery of Medical Costs for Asbestos Diseases (Wales) Bill: Reference by the Counsel General for Wales* [2015] UKSC 3, at ¶¶52, 56, 67, *per* Lord Mance.

the individual whether to engage in that behaviour or not. No one can compel the individual to do the thing in question nor to refrain from doing it.

3-08 This is sometimes described by saying that the individual has a right to do the thing in question. The word *right* in English has, however, more than one meaning.[7] In this context, its meaning is the freedom to do or not to do something; it is *right* as 'freedom' or 'liberty'.[8]

3-09 One must be careful to distinguish this meaning of *right* from another sense of the word. *Right* can also be used to describe the situation where a person is entitled that another person either do or not do something. In that sense, the word *right* signifies that one person is entitled that another perform or not perform some act. Where used in that sense, it denies that the other person is free to perform the act or not as he or she wishes; it denies that the other person has, with regard to the conduct in question, a *right* in the sense of freedom or liberty to do or not to do the thing. If that person had a right to do or not to do that thing, that is, a right in the sense of freedom or liberty regarding it, then the first person would have no right, in the sense of an entitlement, that the other person perform or not perform the conduct. The presence of a 'right' in the sense of a 'freedom' or 'liberty' in one person regarding a particular conduct betokens the absence of any right in the sense of an 'entitlement' or 'claim' with others. If others can claim that a thing be done or not done, then a person has no freedom or liberty regarding that conduct.

3-10 It is with regard to such freedoms or liberties that Lord Diplock spoke when he used the words quoted above concerning a legislature's preparedness to restrict the liberties of individual citizens and deprive them of some of their freedom in order to achieve its policy objectives. It was the price, as he put it, that the legislature was prepared to exact from the citizen.

THE PRINCIPLE OF PROPORTIONALITY

3-11 If interferences and restrictions upon individuals' freedom and liberty constitute a price exacted by legislatures to achieve certain goals, the question arises of how high that price might be. One answer to that question is to say that the price should not be higher than is necessary to achieve the goal. The interference or restriction upon freedom or liberty should never be greater than is necessary. It should not be out of proportion to what is needed. For that reason, the measure of maintaining the balance between the loss of freedom and the achievement of the goal is sometimes described as the principle of proportionality. It is a cardinal principle of the legal system of the European Union, from where it has found its way into the domestic law of the countries of the United Kingdom.

[7] *Collins English Dictionary* lists fifty-one possible meanings for the word *right* in English.

[8] As noted above, §§1-53–1-54 and n. 18, public bodies and officials on the other hand have no *rights* in this sense unless given them by law.

In the context of European law, the principle of proportionality has been described as follows: 3-12

> the individual should not have his freedom of action limited beyond the degree necessary for the general interest.[9]

Its application in the field of EU law has led, for instance, to it being held by the courts that it is disproportionate to ban the sale of products on public health grounds when a less severe approach is capable of achieving the same result.[10] Thus, laws made by member states to carry into effect the policies of the European Union within their national territories can be set aside for breaching the principle. In other words, the means chosen for giving effect to the policies have to be proportionate. The question of whether the means chosen are proportionate will almost certainly require a comparison of various means of giving effect to the policy. In other words, the choice of the preferred option of means for carrying the policy into effect needs to be justifiable. The thoroughness with which options will have been identified, evidence gathered and rigorous analysis undertaken can thus prove crucial to the legal validity of the preferred option.

The principle has found its way from European law into the domestic law of England and Wales. This is unsurprising, as it would be anomalous if legislation made by government ministers to carry into effect European Union policies were subject to review on the grounds of proportionality whereas such legislation made by them to carry into effect their own policies was not. Therefore, as will be shown later, the principle of proportionality has become relevant to the judicial review of the manner in which government ministers and other public bodies, both in the UK and in Wales, exercise their functions, including their function of making subordinate legislation. The manner in which they are to exercise their functions is subject to the principle, and what they do is open to challenge by those who are adversely affected if it is thought that they have acted disproportionately.[11] 3-13

The principle, however, does not apply to legislation made by the United Kingdom Parliament given that it is legally sovereign, that is that it can make or unmake any law and that the laws which it makes cannot be overridden or set aside by other bodies. The courts have also indicated that they will not generally be prepared to review the legislation made by the devolved legislatures on such 3-14

[9] *Internationale Handelsgesellschaft mbH* v *Einfuhr- und Vorratsstelle für Getreide und Futtermittel* (11/70) [1970] ECR 1125.

[10] The principle is discussed, for instance, in *Steiner and Woods EU Law* (13th edn, by L. Woods, P. Watson and M. Costa, Oxford, 2017).

[11] It is submitted that it is highly unlikely that the proposed withdrawal of the UK from the EU will lead to an abandonment of approaches such as the principle of proportionality within the UK's legal systems. See further below, §§8-22–8-44 and nn. 37 and 40, on other such innovations adopted from EU law.

grounds.[12] Thus, it would appear that the means chosen by the National Assembly to give effect to policy goals by means of legislation will not be challengeable on this ground. The reason for not subjecting primary legislation to review on this ground is that the legislatures enacting it are representative of the people affected and directly accountable to those people through the ballot box. In the case of government ministers making subordinate legislation to implement either EU or domestic law, this is not so. Hence, the opportunity which the elected representatives of the people have to decide on the proportionality of the means adopted together with their ultimate accountability to the electors displaces the need for the courts to address the question. Political accountability ousts the need for legal review on this issue.

3-15 Having said that, the principle is nevertheless an excellent tool for use in deciding whether to adopt one means or another for giving effect to policies by legislation. Regardless of whether the proportionality of the means adopted will be open to legal challenge, those choosing the means should consider whether they are proportionate. Even where the means may not be open to challenge before the courts, they will need to be justified before the representatives of the people and in the media. The principle of proportionality will always prove relevant in the choice of means, which is – as Lord Diplock said – part of the choice of policy.

3-16 There is, however, one situation in which an issue of proportionality can arise in the making of primary legislation, at least primary legislation made by a devolved legislature. This became clear in the Supreme Court's ruling on the Recovery of Medical Costs for Asbestos Diseases (Wales) Bill, which had been referred to the Supreme Court by the Counsel General for Wales because of a doubt as to whether its provisions were within competence.[13] In that case, it was questioned, among other things, whether provisions in the bill allowing the Welsh Ministers to reclaim the cost to the Welsh NHS of treating victims of asbestos diseases could lawfully be recovered from the insurers of the victims' employers as well as from the employers themselves. It was argued that this was an interference with the peaceful enjoyment of possessions, a right protected under Article 1 of the first Protocol to the European Convention on Human Rights, a protection incorporated into the domestic law of the United Kingdom by the Human Rights Act 1998.[14] It is outside the competence of the National Assembly to pass legislative provisions

[12] See *AXA General Insurance Ltd* v *The Lord Advocate (Scotland)* [2011] UKSC 46, at ¶¶42–52 *per* Lord Hope, at ¶97 *per* Lord Mance, and at ¶¶135–53 *per* Lord Reed.

[13] [2015] UKSC 3. The legislative competence of the Assembly is discussed below in chapter four.

[14] Article 1 of the first Protocol [A1P1] reads:

> (1) Every natural or legal person is entitled to the peaceful enjoyment of his possessions. No one shall be deprived of his possessions except in the public interest and subject to the conditions provided for by law and by the general principles of international law.
> (2) The preceding provisions shall not, however, in any way impair the right of a State to enforce such laws as it deems necessary to control the use of property in accordance with the general interest or to secure the payment of taxes or other contributions or penalties.

which are incompatible with Convention rights.[15] In the case of a right such as the peaceful enjoyment of possessions, the protection is one that is qualified, in the sense that it is not absolute but can yield to interferences which are in the public interest. Taxation, monetary penalties and planning controls furnish examples of such justified interference. The question, however, is who is to determine whether an interference with a qualified protected right is justified.

In the *Asbestos* case, the Supreme Court was divided on the issue. The judgment of the majority was delivered by Lord Mance. He set out the general principles according to which a court would review legislation for compliance with the Convention rights. These are, he said: 3-17

> (i) whether there is a legitimate aim which could justify a restriction of the relevant protected right,
> (ii) whether the measure adopted is rationally connected to that aim,
> (iii) whether the aim could have been achieved by a less intrusive measure, and
> (iv) whether, on a fair balance, the benefits of achieving the aim by the measure outweigh the disbenefits resulting from the restriction of the relevant protected right.[16]

He was also clear that whereas the court would accept the legislature's judgment on the first point regarding what was in the public interest, provided that the legislature's judgment on the issue was not 'manifestly without reasonable foundation', the same was not necessarily the case with regard to the other three points and certainly not with regard to the fourth. There, he thought, an interference with a qualified protected right such as peaceful enjoyment of possessions had to strike a fair balance between the demands of the public or general community interest and the requirements of protecting the individual's fundamental rights.[17] There, the court would ask whether, weighing all the relevant factors, the measure adopted achieved a fair or proportionate balance between the public interest being promoted and the other interests involved. To do this, the court would weigh the benefits of the measure in terms of the aim being promoted against the 'disbenefits' to other interests. While, what Lord Mance termed, 'significant respect' might be due to the legislature's decision, the bar for intervention by the courts was not set at so high a level as to mean that they would only intervene if the decision exhibited 'manifest unreasonableness'.[18]

[15] GoWA 2006, s. 108A(2)(e), inserted by Wales Act 2017, s. 3, replacing s. 108(6)(c).

[16] [2015] UKSC 3, at ¶45.

[17] Ibid., at ¶48.

[18] Ibid., at ¶52. Two of the five justices who heard the case in the Supreme Court disagreed with this, believing that more than significant respect was due to the legislature's judgment on the issue. They believed that 'great weight' should be accorded to the legislature's determination: see ibid., at ¶¶118, 124 *per* Lord Thomas of Cwmgiedd LCJ.

3-18 Where, therefore, the means chosen to achieve a policy aim involves interference with a qualified protected right, the courts will be prepared to consider whether in making that choice of means the legislature has achieved a fair balance between the public interest involved in achieving the policy aim and the detriment to the protected rights of individuals affected. It is not only if the choice is manifestly unreasonable that the courts will be prepared to intervene. They will intervene whenever it can be shown that, in making the legislative decision, a fair or proportionate balance has not been achieved.

3-19 This gives rise to the question of how the courts are to determine whether the legislature has achieved such a balance, and, as a consequence, how much respect or weight should be accorded to its judgment. This issue was also addressed by Lord Mance in delivering the majority's judgment. He said that:

> if, … when the court is considering whether a measure strikes a fair balance, weight attaches to the legislative choice, then the extent to which the legislature has as the primary decision maker been in or put in a position to evaluate the various interests may affect the weight attaching to its assessment …[19]

To discover whether the legislature had been in a position or been put in a position to make such an evaluation satisfactorily, Lord Mance thought that the court could look at admissible background material. He quoted the words of Lord Nicholls in *Wilson* v *First County Trust Ltd (No. 2)* who had said that:

> as when interpreting a statute, so when identifying the policy objective … or assessing the 'proportionality' of a statutory provision, the court may need enlightenment

and that:

> sometimes the court may need additional background information tending to show … the likely practical impact of the statutory measure and why the course adopted by the legislature is or is not appropriate.[20]

Lord Nicholls believed that such additional background material could be found in published documents, such as government White Papers, ministerial statements made in the course of debate and in explanatory notes.[21] These are all documents and statements which would have been prepared by civil servants in the course of developing the policy behind the bill and in preparing for its introduction and presentation to the legislature. In the *Asbestos* case, which was a private member's

[19] Ibid., at ¶56.

[20] *Wilson* v *First County Trust Ltd (No. 2)* [2003] UKHL 40, at ¶¶63–4, [2004] AC 816, quoted by Lord Mance [2015] UKSC 3, at ¶55.

[21] Ibid.

bill, Lord Mance did not consider that the background to the bill evidenced that those responsible for promoting it had provided, nor that those responsible for passing it had been provided with, a full presentation and appreciation of its implications. Accordingly, he did not think that the fourth criterion, requiring a fair balance between the benefits of achieving the aim as against the interference with individuals' protected rights, had been satisfied.[22]

In doing this, and thereby assessing the sufficiency of the evidence before the legislature when it made its decisions, Lord Mance was aware that he was, to some extent, treating the primary legislation of the devolved legislatures as being more akin to subordinate legislation than primary legislation made by the UK Parliament. With regard to the Westminster Parliament, the Bill of Rights of 1689 provides in its article 9: 3-20

> That the Freedome of Speech and Debates or Proceedings in Parlyament ought not to be impeached or questioned in any Court or Place out of Parlyament.

Lord Mance did not think that this immunity extended to the law-making of other bodies, saying:

> there is a relevant distinction between cases concerning primary legislation by the United Kingdom Parliament and other legislative and executive decisions.[23]

The minority did not agree with this. While accepting that article 9 of the Bill of Rights did not apply to the devolved legislatures, the minority found it difficult:

> to make any logical distinction in the context of the United Kingdom's devolved constitutional structure between these legislatures and the United Kingdom Parliament in according weight to the evaluation of the different choices and interests in respect of matters which are within the primary competence of the legislatures.[24]

They felt that:

> the judgement of the Welsh Assembly in relation to social and economic policy underpinning primary legislation enacted by it should not be treated in any different way to the judgement of the United Kingdom Parliament underpinning primary legislation enacted by it,

and that that judgement should be preferred to a:

[22] [2015] UKSC 3, at ¶67.

[23] Ibid., at ¶56.

[24] Ibid., at ¶119 *per* Lord Thomas.

> judicial view of what it regards as being in the public interest and representing social justice.[25]

However, the view of the majority is the current legal position as decided by the Supreme Court.

LEGAL DUTIES

3-21 Legal duties are obligations which the law can enforce, and – again in the words of Lord Diplock – they often restrict the liberty of the individual. They are therefore one of the higher prices to be exacted as a means of achieving a policy objective.

3-22 As opposed to a freedom, a duty is something which one must do: one is obligated to perform it. The duty may be positive or negative in terms of its subject-matter. A positive duty is something that one is required to do: for instance, possess a valid driving licence before driving a motor vehicle. A negative duty, on the other hand, is something that one must not do: for instance, park one's vehicle on a double yellow-line. The existence of the duty negates one's freedom with regard to the conduct in question. Either one is free with regard to a particular conduct or one is not. If one is not, one is either under a duty to perform it or not to perform it. The presence of duty entails the absence of freedom with regard to the conduct in question. The presence of freedom with regard to that conduct entails the absence of duty.

3-23 The failure to perform a legal duty, whether that involves doing something one should not do (commission) or failing to do something that one should do (an omission), is a legal wrong.

ENFORCING LEGAL DUTIES AND CLAIM RIGHTS

3-24 Where the law has imposed a duty, there will be some means of enforcing that duty. The enforcement mechanism may involve some means of compelling the performance of the duty or of providing for punishment for the failure to perform. If there is no method by which the duty can be enforced, the duty is said to be imperfect. It is imperfect in the sense that it is incomplete or unfinished. What completes, or perfects, a duty is a means of enforcement. A duty which can be enforced is said to be perfect.[26]

3-25 For a duty to be perfect, it is necessary that someone or some body should be able to enforce it. A person who is able to claim that he or she is entitled to

[25] Ibid., at ¶¶123–4.

[26] This usage of perfect and imperfect is similar to that used by grammarians to classify verbs in the past tense. The past tense in which the action is over – completed – is the perfect tense; that in which it is continuing, unfinished and therefore incomplete, is the imperfect tense.

enforce another's duty is said to have a *right* in the sense of a 'claim' or an 'entitlement'. As has been shown, this sense of *right* must be distinguished from that used earlier of *right* in the sense of a 'freedom' or 'liberty'. Thus, the terms *claim-right* and *freedom-right* are sometimes used to overcome the ambiguity.

It is important, where it is intended to give effect to a policy by means of imposing duties upon persons or bodies, that the persons or bodies with the corresponding claim-rights are identified. This ensures that each duty is capable of being enforced. Likewise, if the policy goal is to be carried into effect by giving people rights in the sense of claim-rights or entitlements, it is important that the persons with the corresponding duties to meet those rights are identified so that the people with rights have someone against whom they can enforce them. It is useless, for instance, to give children living more than a certain distance from their school a right to free transport to and from their school unless someone else has a duty to provide that transport and the children or someone on their behalf the means of enforcing that duty. Thus, if A owes B £50, that is has a duty to pay B £50, it follows that B has a claim-right to that £50 and needs a means of enforcing his claim. If A has a right of way over B's land, B has a corresponding duty to allow A to pass over it, and A needs some method of ensuring that B is prevented, if it proves necessary, from interfering with his right of passage. Every duty has a corresponding claim-right, and every claim-right a corresponding duty. Failing this, the duty is imperfect. 3-26

Although it is important, when developing the legislative proposals which will deliver the means for giving effect to the policy, that one knows who has the claim-right corresponding to each duty, it may not be necessary in every instance to identify the relevant person or body expressly in the legislation. The reason for this is that there are some categories of duty, most notably duties placed upon the holders of public office, such as ministers, or public bodies, where the law may in advance have provided the means by which such duties can be enforced. Thus, while it may be necessary to provide expressly on the face of legislation how the duties placed upon private individuals are to be enforced and by whom, in the case of duties being placed on public bodies and officials, that may be implicit in the public nature of the duty. The principles, rules and remedies of the body of law which regulates public administration, that is administrative law, provides for such enforcement by means of mandating orders (to enforce the duties of public office holders),[27] prohibiting orders (to prevent actions which breach public duties),[28] and quashing orders (to invalidate actions or decisions which have been achieved in an improper manner).[29] The principles and rules of administrative law also identify the persons who can pursue such remedies, that is who have a legitimate interest or *locus standi* to enforce the duties in question. All three of the remedies mentioned 3-27

[27] Previously known by the Latin name, *mandamus*.

[28] Previously known as *prohibition*.

[29] Previously known by the Latin name, *certiorari*.

are orders used to ensure that public office holders and others with public duties carry out their functions, including their duties, in accordance with the law.

METHODS OF ENFORCEMENT

3-28 One of the policy choices, therefore, which will need to be made, is how any duties that are being imposed are to be enforced. This includes the duties that correspond to claim-rights or entitlements where the focus of the proposals is on creating or upholding rights in that sense. In making these choices, the five principles identified as key to good policy development will again be relevant: how does the choice fit in with the general programme of government; what will the impact and consequences of the choices be; what are the costs of choosing to adopt that approach; what are the mechanisms which will be employed; and will the choice made allow for effective implementation and evaluation of whether the method adopted is achieving the objectives of the policy. The preferred option must include the preferred method of enforcement, and the preferred method of enforcement must be justifiable on the evidence and its analysis. These issues must now be dealt with in justice impact assessments.[30]

3-29 Against this background, the method of enforcement chosen may be to make breach of the duty a criminal offence, or to make it a civil wrong, a tort, for which the person adversely affected may seek compensation in the form of damages from the wrongdoer or instead or additionally an order from the court, called an injunction, to prevent the duty from being broken or the continuation of a breach. Alternatively, a form of administrative control of the conduct may be preferred. This could, for example, require that a person obtain a licence before embarking on a particular activity, lay down regulations to govern the manner in which such an activity must be performed, or simply require those engaging in the activity to have regard to guidance or a code of conduct. In the past, when legislating for Wales was largely confined to the implementation of policies made elsewhere, such administrative approaches to enforcement may have dominated the choices available. With the advent of primary law-making powers, the choices available are no longer so limited, and the availability of the other options for enforcement need to be taken into account when deciding upon the preferred method of proceeding.

FUNDAMENTAL LEGAL CONCEPTS: THE STATIC SET

3-30 It has been seen that in relation to others, a person is either free to do or not to do something as he or she wishes, or else is constrained by a duty to do or not to do that thing, which duty one or more other persons can in some way enforce. The presence of a duty with regard to a particular conduct, therefore, entails the absence

[30] GoWA 2006, s. 110A, inserted by Wales Act 2017, s. 11.

of freedom with regard to it, and the presence of freedom entails the absence of duty. Duty and freedom are contradictory concepts: each implies the absence of the other. Either one is free to do or not to do a particular thing, or one is under a duty to do or not do it. Nothing else is possible.

It has also been shown that for the presence of duty to be complete, it is neces- 3-31
sary that someone or some body should be able to enforce it. That person would have a claim-right to enforce the duty in question. The presence of duty in one person requires the presence of a claim-right in another. The concepts of duty and claim-right of necessity go together; they have to correspond. The absence of a duty therefore means that no one can claim that a person perform the conduct in question. This is sometimes, a little artificially, described by saying that the presence of freedom regarding a particular conduct entails the presence of no-right or no-claim right in others to insist that one do or not do the thing in question.

These four concepts can therefore be arranged as two pairs of corresponding 3-32
concepts – duty and claim-right; freedom and no-right – or as two pairs of contradictory concepts – duty and freedom; claim-right and no-right. In each pair of corresponding concepts, the presence of one concept entails the presence of the other, while in each pair of contradictory concepts, the presence of the one entails the absence of the other. The four concepts are often set out as a diagram in which the corresponding pairs are placed vertically apart and the contradictory concepts horizontally apart to form a rectangle of four fundamental legal concepts.

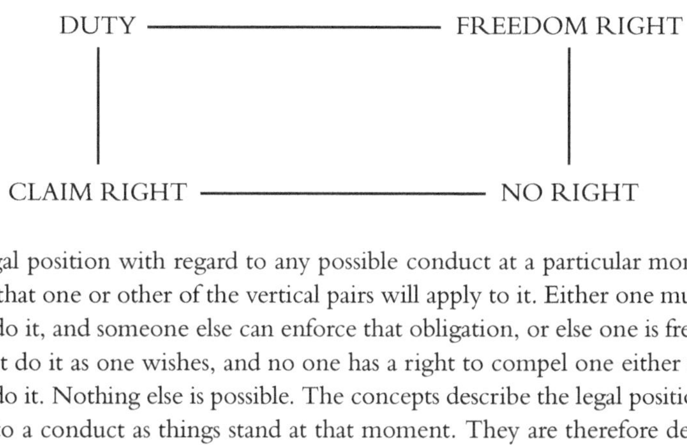

The legal position with regard to any possible conduct at a particular moment of time is that one or other of the vertical pairs will apply to it. Either one must do it or not do it, and someone else can enforce that obligation, or else one is free to do it or not do it as one wishes, and no one has a right to compel one either to do it or not do it. Nothing else is possible. The concepts describe the legal position with regard to a conduct as things stand at that moment. They are therefore described as being static legal concepts.

When legislation is made which changes the law, it may change the legal 3-33
position with regard to conduct. It may take away a freedom and replace it with a duty, or it may remove a duty so as to free the individual to do as he or she wishes. Either way, it can move the legal position with regard to conduct from one vertical side of the above diagram to the other. Those who have the authority to legislate have the power to do this. Their legislative power is a legal power which enables them to change the fundamental legal concepts that apply to others, the persons who are subject to that legislation. This brings us to the concept of a legal power.

THE CONCEPT OF A LEGAL POWER

3-34 A legal power in the sense used here is the power to make a change to the static fundamental legal concepts that govern the behaviour of others. Thus, a person with a legal power to do so can, as Lord Diplock said, restrict the freedom of another or deprive that other of the freedom altogether by the imposition of a duty. The holder of a legal power can also confer a claim right on some person to enforce others to perform their duties. He or she can also change the content of existing duties and claim rights, or remove the duty or claim right from one person and impose or confer it on another. It is the power to change the legal position of others.

3-35 The person who has a legal power to do such things may be free to exercise the power as he or she wishes or may be required to exercise it in a particular way at a particular time. In other words, the holder of a legal power may either be under a duty to exercise it or have freedom with regard to its exercise. Thus, a minister with responsibility for agriculture may have the power to ban the movement of certain animals in the event of a notifiable disease such as foot-and-mouth or avian 'flu' breaking out. The power, when exercised, takes away the freedom of farmers to move their animals and replaces it with a duty not to do so. The minister himself or herself, however, may be under a duty to make such an order if such a disease is notified.

3-36 On the other hand, there are powers where the power holder is free to exercise the power or not as they judge fit. Thus, motorists in Cardiff are free to drive down Westgate Street in either direction. However, the local Council has a power to close Westgate Street to traffic on days when there are major sporting events at the Millennium Stadium, the main entrance to which is situated in Westgate Street. It is up to the Council to decide whether to do so. It does not have to close the street to traffic whenever there is a big event there. It has a freedom to exercise the power or not. If it chooses to exercise the power, then motorists will lose their freedom to drive down Westgate Street on the day in question and instead find themselves under a duty not to do so.

3-37 Where one person or body, therefore, has the power to alter the legal position of others, those others are liable to have their freedoms, duties and claim-rights changed. Their legal position in this regard is therefore described as a liability. Their rights and duties are liable to be changed. Wherever one person or body has a power to make such a change, there will be others who are under a corresponding liability to have their rights or duties changed. The concepts of legal power and liability in this sense are another pair of corresponding legal concepts, but on this occasion they do not describe an existing legal relationship at a particular moment of time but rather the potential for such legal relationships to be changed by the exercise of a power. They involve changes to the legal position, and are therefore described as dynamic as opposed to static legal concepts.

3-38 There may, however, be persons whose rights and duties are not subject to change through the exercise of legal powers by others. Thus, for instance, although ordinary motorists may find their freedom to drive along Westgate Street taken away by the Council's exercise of its powers, the same may not be true with regard to the drivers of vehicles serving the emergency services. It may be that the freedom of fire appliances or ambulances to drive along Westgate Street cannot be changed by the actions of the Council. If that is the case, then the emergency services are said to have an immunity from having their freedom restricted by the Council, and therefore as against those persons the Council does not have a power but rather is under a disability. An immunity is the contradictory of a liability, and a disability is the contradictory of a power. Either one has the power to change the rights and duties of others, or one is under a disability in that regard. Nothing else is possible. Likewise, either one is under a liability to have one's rights and duties changed or one has an immunity. Nothing else is possible. Wherever someone has a power, someone else is under a liability, and wherever someone has an immunity, someone else is under a disability. Thus, we have two further pairs of corresponding concepts as well as two further pairs of contradictory concepts.[31]

FUNDAMENTAL LEGAL CONCEPTS: THE DYNAMIC SET

Once more, these can be set out as a diagram in which the corresponding pairs are 3-39
placed vertically apart and the contradictory concepts horizontally apart to form a rectangle of four further fundamental legal concepts.

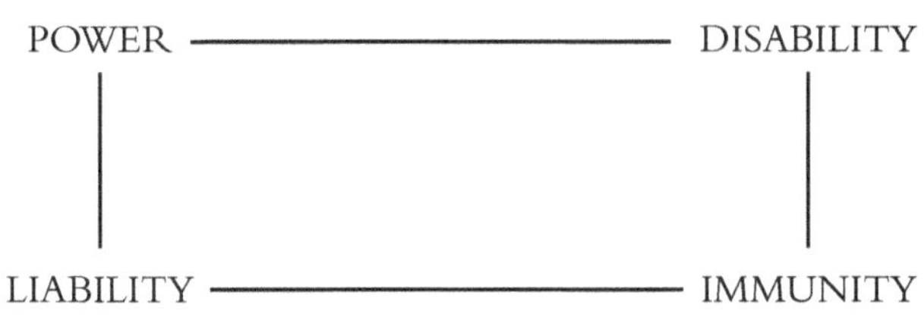

These are the dynamic legal concepts. They are described as dynamic because they are capable of changing the static concepts applying to others. Again, at any particular moment, the relationship between persons is either one of power and liability or of disability and immunity. They describe whether or not the static concepts of others can be changed.[32]

[31] It is worth noting here that the decision to grant an immunity to a person, class or group corresponds to that person, class or group having been identified earlier in the policy development process as persons who must not be affected by the change proposed or by the manner in which, that is, how, they must not be affected.

[32] See W. N. Hohfeld, 'Some Fundamental Legal Conceptions as applied in Judicial Reasoning' (1913) 23 *Yale Law Journal* 16. Hohfeld's analysis was perhaps inspired by atomic theory, seeking to analyse legal relationships into the equivalent of molecules and atoms. Hohfeld used the word *right* for what is here designated as a claim-right, and used the word *privilege* for what is here termed a freedom-right. Sir John Salmond later used the word *liberty* in preference to *privilege*: *Salmond on Jurisprudence* (12th edn, by P. J. Fitzgerald, London, 1966), § 40.

3-40 Legislators and legislatures exercise legislative power, that is the power to change the law so as to affect the freedoms, claim-rights, duties, powers and immunities of those subject to the laws they make. If there are freedoms, for instance, which the law-makers cannot change, then such freedoms may be described as basic or fundamental. In countries with written constitutions, the constitution as the fundamental law of the state may well guarantee the protection of such freedom-rights even as against the state's own legislative institutions. In such a case, the freedoms in question are subject to an immunity from legislative change, the state legislature having no power – that is being under a disability – to restrict or deprive the citizen of those rights. If the state attempts to do so, the citizen will be able to challenge the purported interference before the courts, and there will probably be a Constitutional Court which can declare the attempt invalid and thereby uphold the citizens' immunity. In the United Kingdom, the doctrine of the legal sovereignty of Parliament denies that any freedoms are immune from change by Act of Parliament. Other law-making agencies, however, do not enjoy such unfettered legislative power. Instead, their law-making powers are limited. The limits will have been set by the laws which gave them their legislative powers or competence. This is the case with the devolved legislatures in Scotland, Northern Ireland and Wales, and is also the case with regard to the subordinate law-making powers of both UK ministers and the Welsh Ministers. As the law-making powers of these bodies or persons are limited, the laws which they make are, unlike those made by the sovereign UK Parliament, open to challenge before the courts. Indeed, as has been discussed above, even the quality of legislative decisions made by the devolved legislatures is open to challenge before the courts when it comes to issues concerning the justifiability of interferences with protected human rights.[33]

3-41 Having decided what changes to the law it is necessary to make in order to provide the legal means for giving effect to the preferred option for promoting one's policy, that is having determined that the plan of action one has adopted is to be pursued by restricting freedoms through imposing duties, conferring powers or creating claim-rights, while possibly ensuring that some persons' freedoms and claim-rights are safeguarded by granting immunities with the corresponding disabilities, one must then determine which legislature or legislator has the legislative power to make the necessary changes to the law, and by what kind of legislation the change can or should be made. One must therefore examine the choice of law-making bodies and persons available and also the kinds of legislation and legislative approach that may be chosen.

[33] See the discussion of the *Asbestos Diseases* case above, §§3-16–3-20.

CLASSIFICATIONS OF LEGISLATION

Legislation can be classified in a number of ways. One of the most common classifications is according to the source of the legislation, that is by means of identifying the legislature or legislator responsible for its being made. Thus, with regard to Wales, one may distinguish laws made by the institutions of the European Union from those made by the United Kingdom Parliament, and those made by Parliament from those made by the National Assembly for Wales. Likewise, one would distinguish laws enacted by those legislative bodies from laws made by UK government ministers and the Welsh Ministers, distinguishing also laws made by the former from those made by the latter. 3-42

Distinguishing laws made by legislatures from those made by ministers leads to a second method of classifying legislation, namely according to a hierarchy of law-making authorities. Thus, the authority of some bodies to enact laws is derived directly from the constitution of the country in question or may be recognized as being inherent within them. That, for instance, would be the position of most parliaments. Other bodies, such as government ministers or local authorities have law-making powers which are given to them by enactments of the parliament of the state in question. Where legislative power has been given to a person or body by the enactment of a 'higher' legislature, the power to legislate will have been delegated, and for that reason the laws made by those persons or bodies are sometimes described as delegated legislation. Such powers are dependent for their exercise on the terms set out in the enactment of the higher legislature which conferred them, an enactment often referred to as 'the parent Act'. They are subordinate to the terms of the parent Act and are therefore also described as being subordinate legislation. In that the parent Act must be enacted first before the subordinate legislation can be made under the powers conferred, legislation made by the higher legislature is often described as being primary legislation, while the legislation made later under its terms is described as secondary. 3-43

Applying this distinction between primary and secondary legislation to the various sources of legislation made for or affecting Wales, one can immediately see that legislation made by the UK Parliament is primary legislation, because the law-making power of that parliament is not conferred upon it by any 'higher' law. Arguably, it is rather based on a political authority derived from the mandate given to the members of the House of Commons at elections. Equally, one can immediately see that the law-making power of UK ministers and the Welsh Ministers is secondary, as the former derive their law-making powers from statutes enacted by the UK Parliament and the latter from the enactments of that Parliament and of the National Assembly. In other words, in both cases, the ministers of the respective governments exercise law-making powers which have been conferred by a higher law-making body. 3-44

This raises some interesting questions about the other law-making bodies identified as sources of legislation for Wales.

The European Union[34]

3-45 Some laws made by the institutions of the European Union are immediately applicable in the United Kingdom and in Wales without the need for any further steps to be taken by the legislatures or governments in either place. Such laws are said to be directly applicable or to have direct effect.[35]

3-46 Other laws made by the European Union do not apply automatically in the member states but require those states to take the necessary steps to introduce them within their own jurisdictions. This is done by means of further enactments which ensure that the principles of the EU legislation when introduced are able to operate effectively in a manner which fits into the workings of the domestic legal system. This is usually achieved by requiring government ministers to produce subordinate legislation providing for the manner in which the relevant EU law is to be implemented in the United Kingdom or in Wales. Within the United Kingdom, UK government ministers have the relevant law-making powers to do this,[36] and in Wales, the Welsh Ministers can be given the power to fulfil this function, and they usually are where the EU law in question relates to a devolved subject.[37]

3-47 It may therefore appear as though, where the EU law is directly applicable, that law is a form of primary legislation, and that where it is carried into effect by subordinate legislation made by ministers in Whitehall or Cardiff, the relevant EU law is the parent Act. If, however, one asks by what authority the laws of the European Union become law in the United Kingdom, the path leads back to a statute of the United Kingdom Parliament, namely the European Communities Act 1972. It is this Act also which required the courts of the United Kingdom to give primacy to EU legislation over and above domestic legislation, creating an impression that in the areas where the EU institutions have competence to make law, Parliament is no longer sovereign.

3-48 However, if one remembers that the authority to apply EU law, even where it is given primacy over UK laws and enactments, is given to the courts by an Act of Parliament, it can be seen that this is not strictly speaking the case. The ultimate authority for according EU legislation the status of law in the United Kingdom is an enactment of the UK Parliament. This, however, in turn raises another interesting question, namely whether, if it derives its status as law from an Act of the UK Parliament, EU law is therefore a form of subordinate legislation, the validity of which depends on the terms of the parent Act. Opinions differ as to the answer to this question. In so far as the validity of EU law within the UK depends on a

[34] The discussion at this point proceeds according to the current legal position, namely that the United Kingdom is a member state of the European Union and will continue to be so until the terms of withdrawal have been finalized and approved by both the European and UK Parliaments.

[35] Whether or not this is the case is a question of interpretation ultimately within the jurisdiction of the Court of Justice of the European Union.

[36] European Communities Act 1972, s. 2(2).

[37] GoWA 2006, s. 58B, as inserted by Wales Act 2017, s. 20.

UK Act of Parliament, the answer is probably 'Yes'. However, the authority of the EU to make law is not delegated to it by Parliament. Whereas the UK enactment recognizes the authority of the EU institutions to make law which is applicable in this country, it is not that enactment which confers law-making authority upon the EU institutions; that is something which they have been given by the terms of the treaties made by the member states. The UK Parliament has not set the terms by which and under which the EU institutions legislate, but it is Parliament which has recognized that legislation as law for the UK. To that extent, EU enactments are a source of legislation within the UK and in Wales. Where, however, it does not have direct effect, but requires government ministers to provide for the form and method of its implementation, there can be no doubt that the powers of the ministers in question to do so derive from the parent UK Act, as does their duty to do so. This is distinct from the duty of the UK as a member state to provide for the implementation of such legislation.[38]

The National Assembly for Wales

The same question regarding classification as primary or secondary legislation can be asked about the laws made by the National Assembly. The answer here is even less straightforward. The power of the Welsh Assembly to legislate, its legislative competence, is derived from a parent Act of the UK Parliament, namely the Government of Wales Act 2006. Its powers are given to it, and it can only legislate in accordance with the powers it has been given. In that sense, Assembly Acts – and Assembly Measures before them – are subordinate to the enactments of the UK Parliament. Indeed, according to one statutory definition of what constitutes subordinate legislation, the laws made by all of the devolved legislatures are classified as subordinate.[39] 3-49

That definition, while it is specific to the Act in question, is nevertheless controversial.[40] Unlike, for instance, the subordinate legislation made by government ministers, Assembly Acts may, within the limits of the Assembly's legislative powers, make any provision which could be made by an Act of Parliament.[41] The equality, therefore, of the laws made by the Assembly with the enactments of the UK Parliament militate in favour of their being regarded as a form of primary legislation, and they are generally regarded as such.[42] It is also the case that they are not a means 3-50

[38] The legislative processes of the EU institutions are discussed below, §§9-54–9-86.

[39] See Human Rights Act 1998, s. 21(1).

[40] It certainly does not make for clarity or accessibility that there is no consistency as to the meaning of terms like primary and subordinate legislation across the statute book.

[41] Expressly stated in GoWA 2006, s. 108, now repealed by the Wales Act 2017, s. 3 and replaced with s. 108A which omits the statement, ostensibly on the basis that it is unnecessary.

[42] Indeed, the Wales Act 2017 specifically classifies Assembly Acts as primary legislation for certain purposes: see s. 69(8). It is also significant that they are stated to be 'Acts' by GoWA 2006, s. 107(1), and s. 107(3) goes on to say that their validity 'is not affected by any invalidity in the Assembly proceedings leading to [the Act's] … enactment' – whereas formal irregularity would invalidate subordinate legislation made by Ministers.

of giving effect in Wales to policies decided upon elsewhere, but are a means for giving effect to policies which are specific to Wales. Those who enact them do so within the limits of legislative powers derived from Westminster, but what they do within those powers is done in accordance with the mandate given to them by the Welsh people to whom they are ultimately accountable at the ballot box. Unlike government ministers, they are not accountable before the body that gave them their legislative powers. This again points to the propriety of regarding the laws they make as being a form of primary rather than secondary legislation. Assembly Acts are therefore considered to be a form of primary legislation in the remainder of this work.

CHOICES OF LEGISLATURE AND OF KINDS OF LEGISLATION

3-51 Legislation is needed to pursue the plan of action that has been adopted when the means chosen as the preferred option for giving effect to that plan of action requires a change in the law. The two classifications of kinds of legislation discussed above are relevant when choosing the kind of legislation to employ.

3-52 The classification according to source provides a choice of legislative body to enact or make the legislation required, while the hierarchical classification raises the question of whether one needs to employ primary or secondary law-making powers to do so. These questions are basically concerned with whether particular law-making bodies have the power to make the changes in the law required, that is whether they have the necessary legislative competence.

3-53 As well as the question of legislative competence to make the changes needed, there is also a question about the propriety of making the change by those means. This question recognizes the price in terms of deprivation or restriction upon freedom that the citizen may be required to pay for the change to be effected. Answering this question therefore involves not the application of legal rules but rather of democratic principles. Does the method to be employed to make the change give the democratically elected representatives of the people sufficient opportunity to consider and decide upon the change on their behalf?

Choice of legislature

3-54 In order to promote one's policy by means of a legislative proposal before a legislature, it is necessary that the proposal is introduced into that legislature for deliberation and decision. To introduce a legislative proposal, it is necessary that one has or has access to someone who has the legislative initiative in that legislature. They will then be able to introduce and promote the proposal in that place.

3-55 With regard to legislation made by the European Union, the legislative initiative is largely held by the European Commission,[43] which in turn is composed of

[43] The European Parliament can ask the Commission to initiate legislation and in practice this is a significant source of new legislation: see below, §9-62.

the commissioners appointed by the member states. Wales is not a member state in its own right, but rather part of a member state, namely the United Kingdom. It is therefore not possible for the Welsh Government to promote legislative proposals on its own behalf. Instead, it would be for the United Kingdom government to advance any such proposal on the Welsh Government's behalf. It is a highly unlikely scenario and will not therefore be pursued further here.[44]

It is, however, possible for the Welsh Government to introduce legislative 3-56
proposals before the United Kingdom Parliament. The Government of Wales Act 2006 expressly provides that the Welsh Ministers may introduce private bills at Westminster. Thus, the Welsh Ministers have a limited legislative initiative before the UK Parliament, but it is restricted to the introduction of private as opposed to public bills. They have no right to introduce a public bill.[45]

If, therefore, the Welsh Government wishes the UK Parliament to enact legis- 3-57
lation on its behalf for Wales, the most practical route is by persuading the UK government either to adopt the Welsh Government's proposals and promote them in a bill of its own, or to request their incorporation into an already existing legislative proposal of the UK government by inserting additional clauses relating to Wales into one of that government's own bills. The UK government has, from time to time, promoted legislation specifically for Wales. Such proposals are referred to as 'Wales only bills', which when enacted become 'Wales only Acts'. They are part of the law that generally applies only to Wales. Examples include, for instance, the Welsh Language Acts and legislation relating to the National Health Service in Wales. They are, however, few and far between. Given that Wales now has its own legislature for devolved matters in the National Assembly, it is likely that such Wales only legislation will become even rarer.

The attraction of proceeding by Westminster legislation is that the power 3-58
of the UK Parliament as the sovereign legislature to make law is unrestricted by any legal limits. It can legislate for Wales in relation to matters which are beyond the competence of the National Assembly. However, there are disadvantages too. While the Welsh Government might seek to persuade the UK government to promote a legislative proposal, there is no guarantee that the UK government would be willing to include a relevant bill in its legislative programme. Competition among UK government departments for places in the UK government's legislative programme is keen, and the Welsh Government would have to compete against them for a place, bearing in mind that the Whitehall departments may well be promoting manifesto commitments of the UK governing parties. It would almost certainly have to be the case politically that the UK government was supportive of the policy of the Welsh Government to which the bill was intended to provide the means for giving it effect.[46]

[44] The law-making processes of the European Union are described below, §§9-54–9-86.

[45] For the distinction between public and private bills at Westminster, see below, §9-12. For the introduction of private bills before the National Assembly, see below, §§7-86–7-88.

[46] This goes to the question of 'fit' mentioned earlier.

3-59 The chances may be better if the UK government is itself promoting legislation in relation to the same subject, for then provisions dealing specifically with Wales could be included in that bill. Again, the UK government would have to be willing and the Welsh proposals would have to be within the scope of the UK government's bill.[47] Even if the UK government were prepared to include Wales-only clauses in a bill of its own, the passage of those clauses into law could still not be guaranteed. Once incorporated into the UK government bill, the proposals would be under the control of the UK government as the promoter of the bill and of the UK Parliament with regard to its fate. The clauses containing the proposals could be amended in the course of the bill's passage through Parliament in ways which the Welsh Government would not wish, and the clauses could indeed be dropped from the bill altogether. Although enactment by a sovereign parliament has its attractions with regard to unrestricted competence, the political and legislative reality militates against that route being taken. Nevertheless, it exists, and needs to be borne in mind. Where the goals of the two governments coincide and the means are to hand, it can prove serviceable.[48]

3-60 The most likely route, however, by which legislative proposals relating only to Wales will be advanced is by enactment by the National Assembly. The powers of the Assembly to legislate are, however, limited. Those limited powers are referred to as the Assembly's legislative competence, and the question of whether the Assembly has the necessary competence to enact the provisions necessary to give effect to the policy proposals is an essential consideration in deciding how to pursue the plan of action adopted. Were the provisions of a piece of Assembly legislation to exceed its competence, they could be challenged before the courts and invalidated. Such challenges would constitute one kind of devolution issue to be adjudicated according to the special procedures set out in Schedule 9 to the Government of Wales Act 2006.[49]

Choice of kind of legislation

3-61 Not every change to the law needed to provide the means for giving effect to a policy requires that change to be made by primary legislation. It may be possible to make the necessary change by means of subordinate legislation. Such legislation may, for instance, be made by UK government ministers or by the Welsh Ministers, the latter being more likely if the proposed change to the law concerns a subject which is devolved. To make the change, however, requires in all cases that the person or body has the legal power to make the subordinate legislation. Whether the person or body does or does not have that power, frequently referred to as *vires*, is a

[47] For the meaning of *scope*, see below, §§7-24, 7-40 and n. 22, and 9-21. The scope of a bill is another way of describing what in Wales is termed its general principles.

[48] For the procedure by which such proposals would be advanced at Westminster, see below, §§9-01–9-49.

[49] These procedures are described below, §§4-79–4-91.

question of law. The question is answered by examining the relevant primary legislation which conferred the power on the person or body seeking to exercise it.[50]

3-62 The primary legislation which confers the power to make the subordinate legislation will have identified a number of factors concerning the exercise of that power. It will have identified the person or body entitled to make it. This may be a UK government minister, in which case the reference generally is to the power being exercisable by the Secretary of State, a phrase which is interpreted to mean, in the absence of any contrary intention, any one of Her Majesty's principal secretaries of state. In the case of the power being conferred on the Welsh Ministers, the conferral may be in a statute of the UK Parliament or in an Assembly Act or Measure, and the conferral is generally upon the Welsh Ministers. Occasionally, a specific Secretary of State may be identified, and in the case of legislation which applies to Wales, conferral can be upon the First Minister or the Counsel General. Occasionally, too, a power may be exercised either by a UK minister or the Welsh Ministers, in which case it is said to be concurrent, and more rarely it may be required that both act together to exercise the power, which is said to be joint.[51] Other persons or bodies may have the power to make subordinate legislation conferred upon them, such as government agencies or particular officials. Such exercise may or may not require confirmation or approval by an appropriate government minister, as for instance with the making of local authority byelaws in Wales prior to the Local Government Byelaws (Wales) Act 2012.

3-63 The mere fact that a power has been conferred does not give the recipient a free hand with regard to its exercise. The power will have been conferred for a particular purpose, and its use for any other purpose will therefore be unlawful. The parent Act may also have required the recipient to engage in a measure of consultation with the public or interested parties before exercising the power to legislate, in which case failure to consult or to consult properly can lead to the exercise of the power being declared invalid, together with the legislation made thereunder. Proper consultation requires that the process of consultation be conducted reasonably, the question of whether the process has been reasonable being for the courts to determine.

3-64 As well as requiring that certain procedures be followed prior to making the subordinate legislation, the parent Act may require that a particular procedure be used to make the legislation itself. Thus, it may require that the order, rules, regulations or other expressions of the legislative will be made in the form of a statutory instrument and laid before the legislature which passed the parent Act for approval

[50] In the case of Ministers of the Crown, the relevant power may arise from the prerogative, but this is not currently the case with the Welsh Ministers.

[51] Functions which are exercisable concurrently or jointly are now 'qualified devolved functions' as defined by GoWA 2006, Sch. 7B, para. 11(3), inserted by Wales Act 2017, s. 3 and Sch. 2. The *Local Government Byelaws* case (*Re Local Government Byelaws (Wales) Bill: Reference by the Attorney General for England and Wales* [2012] UKSC 53) concerned the removal of a concurrent function.

before becoming law – the so-called affirmative procedure.[52] More commonly, it will allow a ministerial recipient of the power to make the law by signing such an instrument but require it then to be laid before the parent legislature to allow the opportunity for its annulment – the so-called negative procedure.[53] In either case, failure to follow the appropriate procedure will render the exercise of the legislative power unlawful. Only non-controversial orders, such as the commencement orders which bring into force primary legislation already passed by the legislature, are likely to require no such procedure for their making.

3-65 The subordinate legislation itself may provide that certain procedures are to be followed: for example, if the subordinate legislation is concerned with the granting of licences to perform a particular activity there may be procedures set out for obtaining or renewing such licences, and for appeals against refusals to grant them. Such procedures will themselves have to be reasonable, and the question of whether they are reasonable is a matter for the courts to decide. Similarly, whatever the subordinate legislation requires to be done must satisfy the principle of proportionality described earlier, or else it can be declared to be unlawful.[54]

3-66 The power to make subordinate legislation is therefore a limited power, and where a power to legislate is limited, its exercise can be challenged by those with a legitimate interest in its exercise if it is thought that the limits have been exceeded. Thus, provisions made by subordinate legislation can be challenged if it is thought that the persons or body on whom the power was conferred have gone beyond the limits set by the parent Act, that is have acted beyond the powers given, or in legal parlance *ultra vires*. Likewise, the exercise of the powers can be challenged for having been exercised for a purpose other than that intended by the parent Act, or having been exercised unreasonably, or not in accordance with the proper procedures envisaged or promised, or with a lack of proportionality. Any persons who believe that they have a legitimate interest in the proper exercise of the powers can challenge what they believe to be an improper exercise before the courts. Such challenges will be heard according to the process known as judicial review. Judicial review is concerned with reviewing the legality with which the executive arm of government has exercised its powers, including its powers of making subordinate legislation. If it is found by the courts that the power has not been exercised lawfully, then the court will quash that exercise, rendering it invalid to the extent that it is *ultra vires*, unreasonable or disproportionate. The court is not concerned with whether it agrees with what the recipient has done with the power, that is the merits of its exercise. That is a matter for the recipient's political accountability. The court is solely concerned with whether the power has been exercised legally, in accordance with the terms of its conferral. If it has, the exercise is valid; if it has not, it will be quashed. It matters nothing that the provisions have not been annulled or that they have been specifically approved by the parent legislature.

[52] See §§1-59, 8-07–8-10.

[53] See §§1-59, 8-11–8-15.

[54] For the principle of proportionality, see above, §§3-11–3-13.

Applications for judicial review are heard in the Administrative Court, which is part of the Queen's Bench Division of the High Court.[55] The Administrative Court sits in Wales to hear applications relating to specifically Welsh matters.[56] An appeal from its decisions can be made to the Court of Appeal, which can and frequently does sit in Wales to hear cases which are specifically Welsh in nature. From the Court of Appeal, a final appeal on points of law is possible to the Supreme Court of the United Kingdom provided permission to make such an appeal has been granted. The Supreme Court has not yet sat in Wales. 3-67

There may be circumstances in which powers have been given to persons or bodies to make subordinate legislation where there is a duty to exercise that power in certain circumstances. Thus, the outbreak of an infectious disease among the human or animal population may require a legislative response from a government minister so as to attempt to halt the spread of the disease. In such circumstances, failure to perform that duty can be challenged by judicial review. The same is true if a failure to exercise the power to legislate amounts to incompatibility with the Convention rights incorporated into domestic law by the Human Rights Act 1998. 3-68

Where the question is one of whether the Welsh Ministers, as distinct from other public bodies, have a legislative power or whether they have exercised such a power lawfully, or whether they have failed to perform a duty placed upon them to legislate or whether a failure to act on their part is incompatible with Convention rights, that question constitutes a devolution issue within the meaning given to that phrase in Schedule 9 to the 2006 Act.[57] The procedures which apply to devolution issues about the legislative competence of the National Assembly, dealing with questions such as to which courts such questions can be remitted and the powers of the Attorney General and Counsel General to remove such litigation directly to the Supreme Court, also apply to devolution issues concerning the powers and duties of the Welsh Ministers.[58] 3-69

The availability of subordinate law-making powers to provide the means by which policy goals could be effected does not of itself justify the choice of secondary rather than primary legislation as the appropriate legislative vehicle for achieving those goals. While changing the law by means of subordinate legislation might be perfectly lawful, that does not mean that it will always be an acceptable route to take in terms of democratic principles. If the answer to the question: 'Can subordinate legislation make the changes to the law needed to provide the means 3-70

[55] For the work of the Administrative Court, see David Gardner, *Administrative Law and the Administrative Court in Wales* (Cardiff, 2016).

[56] The principle that cases with a Welsh dimension should be heard in Wales began with *Practice Direction (Supreme Court: Devolution)* issued by Lord Bingham LCJ on 30 June 1999: [1999] 1 WLR 1592. This was later incorporated into the Civil Procedure Rules as CPR PD 54, para. 3.1. The current rule is set out in CPR PD 54D. For a full discussion, see David Gardner, *Administrative Law and the Administrative Court in Wales* (Cardiff, 2016), ch. 2.

[57] This is one instance of devolution issues concerning the functions of Welsh Ministers. The matter is dealt with further below in chapter four.

[58] These are dealt with below, §§4-86–4-89.

for giving effect to the policy?' is 'Yes', the question remains 'Ought one to use subordinate law-making powers to make those changes?' The questions are distinct, even though the political pressure to insist that the answer to the first dictate the answer to the second may be immense. Proceeding by subordinate legislation will almost undoubtedly be quicker and less subject to compromise, because its making is not subject to the same level of scrutiny nor the same opportunity for amendment as that afforded by primary law-making processes. That is exactly why the second question always needs to be asked, for the question basically is whether what is being proposed deserves to be thoroughly scrutinized by the democratically elected representatives of the people with regard both to its general principles and its detail, with full opportunity for them to suggest and make amendments. Where there is a choice, it is the answer to the second question which should determine whether primary or secondary legislation be used.

3-71 Having said that, it must be acknowledged that the choice between the use of primary and secondary legislation, where both are lawful, is a free choice not governed by the application of legal rules. While one may disagree with the choice made, it cannot be challenged in the courts for failing to adhere to democratic principle. There are some countries where this would be possible: for instance, in Germany secondary legislation which purports to impose duties on citizens can be challenged and declared invalid. The same is not true of the United Kingdom.

3-72 It will be recalled that Lord Diplock commented in *DPP* v *Bhagwan* that legislation often involved imposing upon private citizens fresh obligations or restrictions on their liberties.[59] This he characterized as the price which Parliament was prepared to exact from the citizen in order to achieve its objectives. It is noticeable that Lord Diplock spoke of Parliament exacting such a price. Parliament has within it, in the House of Commons, the democratically elected representatives of those who have to pay the price, and so do other elected legislatures such as the National Assembly. In such legislatures, the representatives are directly accountable to and removable by those whom they represent through the ballot box. Government ministers, whether in Whitehall or Cathays Park, are neither accountable nor removable in the same way, and therefore it is arguable that they should not presume to make laws which exact such a price. Speaking extrajudicially after his retirement, another former Law Lord, Lord Oliver of Aylmerton, summed up the principle admirably when he said:

> the citizen … is entitled in a democratic society to have the rules by which his life is to be regulated properly debated and scrutinized by his elected representatives.[60]

From this, it follows that if it is proposed to restrict the existing freedoms of citizens by the imposition of duties, or for that matter to allow them to affect the freedoms,

[59] See above, §3-06.

[60] Lord Oliver of Aylmerton, 'A Judicial View of Modern Legislation' [1993] *Statute Law Review* 1 at 3.

rights or duties of others by conferring upon them powers or rights, the proposals should be properly debated and scrutinized by their elected representatives. In other words, primary legislation should be used. This includes proposals to confer on public officials, such as ministers, powers and duties which can, when exercised, affect the freedoms of citizens. Subordinate law-making should be confined to the making of rules which do not have such a substantial effect upon the freedom and lives of the citizen but rather seek only to implement how decisions already taken with regard to matters of such significance are to be effected. This would include, for instance, the provision or changing of matters of detail which do not go to the substance of the legislation, or adapting the means by which effect has been given to the policy in the light of experience gained through implementation while not changing the policy nor the means in any substantial way. It should never extend to matters which are so substantial or controversial that they merit full debate and scrutiny with the possibility of amendment.

These issues will also be relevant when deciding whether to include within 3-73 a legislative proposal provisions conferring subordinate law-making powers upon ministers or others. There, too, it will be seen that it is democratic principles rather than legal rules which should guide the choices to be made. Among the choices to be made at that point will be which, if any, procedures should be required for the making of subordinate legislation. In the present context of choosing whether to use existing subordinate law-making powers, that choice will already have been made when the parent Act conferring the powers was enacted. If a responsible choice, informed by democratic principles, was made at that stage, it should not really be possible to choose to abuse subordinate legislation at this point. The fact that the choice is available should not suggest that the use of subordinate legislation is justified. The choices made by governments when promoting legislative proposals before legislatures within which they have a working majority are not always as respectful of democratic principles as they might be. Comments on their choices in the reports of bodies such as the Delegated Legislation Committee at Westminster and the Constitutional and Legislative Affairs Committee of the National Assembly, who scrutinize both the proposals to confer such powers and the manner of their subsequent exercise, should be borne in mind when choosing whether to employ primary or secondary legislation. They provide powerful precedents for what is perceived to be appropriate – and inappropriate – by the democratically elected representatives of those whose freedoms they affect and whose lives they regulate.

If the choice is made to proceed by subordinate legislation, it will be neces- 3-74 sary to ensure that the intended legislator has the requisite powers. If the choice is made to proceed by primary legislation by introducing a bill into the National Assembly, it will be crucial to determine that what is to be proposed is within the Assembly's legislative competence. The legislative competence of the Assembly therefore falls for consideration.

Chapter 4

The National Assembly for Wales: Competence and Constraints

The competence of the National Assembly for Wales to make laws in the form of Assembly Acts is to be found in Part 4 of the Government of Wales Act 2006, and the Schedules to which Part 4 relates. Both Part 4 of the 2006 Act and the relevant Schedules have been amended by the Wales Act 2017. Until those amendments became operative, the legislative competence of the Assembly was based on Part 4 and Schedule 7 to the 2006 Act, together with decisions of the courts on how to interpret that Act. Since the amendments made by the 2017 Act have come into force, the Assembly's powers to legislate are governed by Part 4 as amended and the new Schedules 7A and 7B inserted into the 2006 Act by the 2017 Act, replacing the original Schedule 7. It should be borne in mind that questions regarding legislation enacted by the Assembly prior to the changes made by the 2017 Act coming into effect will be determined according to the competence which the Assembly enjoyed at the time that the legislation was enacted. To that extent, a knowledge of the previous competence remains important. 4-01

In terms of policy development and changes to the law, it also needs to be borne in mind that, on some issues, the Assembly's competence may have been greater under the previous competence than it is at present. Care needs to be taken therefore not to repeal provisions made before the new settlement came into effect where that might result in Wales losing its legal autonomy as a consequence. This is crucial particularly where the Welsh Ministers may have subordinate law-making powers and executive functions under Assembly Acts made before the change which could not be given to them by Assembly Acts under the new settlement. The same can be the case for other public bodies in Wales, such as Commissioners, and this could affect the rights of citizens as well. 4-02

The Assembly's competence will be analysed in terms of its territorial limits, its subject-matter limitations and other restrictions placed upon it. In each case, the competence given by the 2017 Act will be compared with that previously enjoyed under the 2006 Act, so that the danger zones where competence might be lost are identified. 4-03

TERRITORIAL LIMITATIONS

The Assembly may not legislate 'otherwise than in relation to Wales'.[1] This is unchanged by the new settlement. 4-04

[1] GoWA 2006, s. 108A(2)(b), inserted by Wales Act 2017, s. 3, replacing s. 108(4)(b).

4-05 Wales for these purposes consists of the area of the twenty-two Welsh local authorities, together with the sea adjacent to that area as far out as territorial waters extend. As territorial waters extend to a distance of twelve nautical miles, this means that there are some parts of the sea adjacent to Wales which are also within that distance of the coasts of England. The Government of Wales Act therefore provides that the Secretary of the State may make an order determining the boundary between the sea adjacent to Wales and the sea adjacent to England for the purposes of the Assembly's legislative competence. This power had been exercised so as to set the nautical boundaries between Wales in this sense and England for areas such as the Severn estuary in the south and the Dee estuary in the north.[2]

4-06 This definition of Wales is different from that which generally applies in UK legislation. According to the Interpretation Act 1978,[3] *Wales* means the land area of the Welsh local authorities, but not the adjacent sea. The Assembly's legislative competence can therefore be exercised in relation to a wider area than that usually taken to be the case in statutory references to Wales.

4-07 There is a further meaning which *Wales* sometimes has in legislation. This meaning is derived from the Welsh Church Acts, the statutes which disestablished the Church of England in Wales and subsequently made certain provisions regarding it. Wales for the purposes of those Acts[4] consists of the territorial area of the Welsh dioceses which form the ecclesiastical province created after disestablishment.[5] This ecclesiastical border is not identical to the secular land border formed by the local authority areas. The reason for this is that, at the time of disestablishment, there were some parishes along the border which were partly in Wales and partly in England. These parishes were given the choice of either remaining in the Church of England, and being part of an English diocese, or becoming part of the disestablished Church in Wales and being in a Welsh diocese. Some went one way, some another. The consequence is that there are some Church in Wales parishes and therefore dioceses which extend territorially into England and some Church of England parishes and therefore dioceses which extend territorially into Wales. *Wales* for ecclesiastical purposes has therefore a different meaning from that which it has for secular purposes. This is significant for the legislative competence of the Assembly in that, if these parishes have churchyards or burial grounds, the question arises of whether the Assembly's competence to legislate in relation to those subjects allows it to legislate in relation to Church of England burial grounds in Wales or Church in Wales burial grounds in England. It is at

[2] National Heritage (Territorial Waters Adjacent to England) Order 2002 (SI 2002 No. 2427).

[3] Interpretation Act 1978, Sch. 1.

[4] The Acts in question are the Welsh Church Act 1914, the Welsh Church (Temporalities) Act 1919 and the Welsh Church (Burial Grounds) Act 1945, together with some provisions of the Marriage Acts.

[5] The dioceses are six in number: Llandaff, St Davids, Bangor and St Asaph, which existed at disestablishment, and Monmouth and Swansea & Brecon, which were carved out of portions of the older dioceses in the decade following disestablishment in 1920.

least arguable that in both cases, such legislation would be 'in relation to Wales', although common sense would suggest that it should be one or the other and in that case probably the latter.

The latter because, according to the Supreme Court's interpretation of the phrase 'in relation to' in another part of the original section 108 of the 2006 Act, such legislation could 'fairly and realistically' be said to relate to Wales as it concerns the property and burial rules of the Church in Wales, and the connection would not be merely 'loose or consequential'.[6] Equally, with regard to Church of England burial grounds which are situated in Wales, as they are the property of and are subject to regulations made by the Church of England, it could fairly be argued that legislation concerning them would not 'fairly and realistically' be said to be 'in relation to Wales'.[7] 4-08

SUBJECT-MATTER COMPETENCE

The Supreme Court's ruling that 'in relation to' requires 'more than a loose or consequential connection' but has to 'fairly and realistically' satisfy the requirement was given when interpreting the meaning of the phrase with regard to the subjects 'in relation to' which the Assembly was able to legislate under the conferred-powers model of devolution provided by the original Part 4 of, and Schedule 7 to, the 2006 Act. The Wales Act 2017 has amended Part 4 of the 2006 Act and replaced the original Schedule 7 with two new Schedules 7A and 7B which provide Wales with a reserved-powers model of devolution. This is the most significant change to the legislative competence of the National Assembly made by the 2017 Act. 4-09

Subject-matter competence under the previous conferred-powers model

Under the conferred-powers model, the Assembly was able to legislate in relation to subjects listed under headings in Part 1 of Schedule 7 to the 2006 Act.[8] The Assembly could legislate in relation to any one or more of those subjects. It needed to be stressed that the Assembly's competence was in relation to the subjects and not the headings under which they were listed. It was common for this to be misunderstood. One frequently heard it said that the Assembly only had competence to legislate in relation to twenty subjects. This was incorrect. The Assembly's 4-10

[6] See *Re Agricultural Sector (Wales) Bill: Reference by the Attorney General for England and Wales* [2014] UKSC 43, at ¶¶50, 67.

[7] This issue may well be of relevance to the proposed Law Commission project on a modern framework for disposing of the dead: see Law Commission, *Thirteenth Programme of Law Reform* (Law Com. No. 377).

[8] There were originally twenty such headings, but this was increased to twenty-one by the Wales Act 2014, which introduced a new heading *16A Taxation*.

competence was to legislate in relation to the subjects listed under the headings, and these were many more than twenty or, later, twenty-one in number. Depending upon how one chose to enumerate them, they came to over a hundred in total. The Assembly's competence was quite extensive.[9]

4-11 The subjects, classified under the twenty-one headings, were the basis for the Assembly's legislative competence. They were descriptive of the areas within which executive functions had earlier been given to, and exercised by, first the Secretary of State for Wales, later the National Assembly and finally the Welsh Ministers. This did not mean that it was only in relation to the exact functions which had previously been transferred that the Assembly could then legislate. That view was advanced, but decisively rejected by the Supreme Court in *Re Agricultural Sector (Wales) Bill*. The pre-existing executive functions were the historical foundation of the subjects in relation to which the Assembly could legislate under the conferred-powers model, but they did not determine the meaning of those subjects in the original Schedule 7.[10]

[9] An example will help to illustrate this. The sixth of the twenty-one headings in Part 1 of Schedule 7 was *Environment*. Here are the subjects listed under it.

Environment

6 Environmental protection, including pollution, nuisances and hazardous substances. Collection, management and disposal of waste. Land drainage and land improvement. Countryside and open spaces (including the designation and regulation of national parks and areas of outstanding natural beauty). Nature conservation and sites of special scientific interest. Protection of natural habitats, coast and marine environment (including seabed). Biodiversity. Genetically modified organisms. Smallholdings and allotments. Common land. Town and village greens. Burial and cremation, except coroners' functions.

A casual glance is sufficient to reveal that there was more than one subject here. Even if one conservatively treats as one subject those items separated by full stops, one has twelve. More liberally, one can identify as many as thirty-one. While some, such as 'environmental protection', would be expected to fall within the description of *Environment*, topics such as genetically modified organisms, allotments or burial and cremation might not be things that shoot to mind when thinking of the environment. Nevertheless, they are subjects in relation to which the Assembly had power to legislate. Indeed, it was only under one heading, the last in the alphabetical list, *Welsh language*, that there was only one subject listed and that, 'Welsh language' identical to the heading itself.

[10] *Re Agricultural Sector (Wales) Bill*, ¶42. The Supreme Court said: 'The current legislative competence of the Assembly has to be determined by an interpretation of the terms of Part 4 and Schedule 7 and not by reference to the way in which functions may have been distributed between the UK Parliament and UK Ministers on the one hand and the Assembly on the other in the first and second phases of Welsh devolution.'

This question of how the meaning of those subjects was to be determined was faced by the Supreme Court in *Re Agricultural Sector (Wales) Bill.*[11] Dictionary definitions of the words used to describe the subjects were not determinative of their meaning in the statute. Rather each subject was to be interpreted as designating an 'object of legislative activity'.[12] Provided that the provisions of an Assembly Act could 'fairly and realistically' be held to relate to a listed subject, the provision was within competence. It did not matter that it might also relate to another subject not listed as being within competence provided that other subject had not been expressly excluded from the Assembly's competence. 4-12

This raised the question of how one determined whether a provision related to a subject. The Supreme Court took 'relates to' in this context to mean more than just 'a loose or consequential connection'. The test of whether a provision related to a subject was laid down in the 2006 Act itself. The original section 108(7) stated that: 4-13

> the question whether a provision of an Act of the Assembly relates to one or more of the subjects listed in Part 1 of Schedule 7 (or falls within any of the

[11] The case concerned a reference to the Supreme Court by the Attorney General of the United Kingdom to determine whether the provisions of the Agricultural Sector (Wales) Bill which had been passed by the Assembly were actually within the Assembly's legislative competence. The background to the case was that the UK government had introduced a bill into the UK Parliament which proposed the abolition of the Agricultural Wages Board for England and Wales which had, for half a century, amongst other things, set a minimum wage for agricultural workers. With the advent of a generally applicable minimum wage for workers in the United Kingdom, the UK government did not feel it necessary to preserve a separate scheme for agricultural workers. The Welsh Government disagreed. They wished to preserve the existing arrangements in Wales, and asked the UK government to leave Wales out of the proposed change and to limit the abolition of the Board to England. The United Kingdom government refused, and the Enterprise and Regulatory Reform Act 2013 was duly passed by the UK Parliament, s. 72 of which Act abolished the Agricultural Wages Board for England and Wales. The Welsh Government responded by introducing its own bill before the National Assembly, in effect reconstructing and thereby continuing the previously existing arrangements for Wales. The United Kingdom government challenged the competence of the Assembly to enact such a law on the basis that the bill's provisions did not relate to agriculture, a listed devolved subject, but rather to employment law, which was not listed as a devolved subject in the original Schedule 7. The Welsh Government defended its bill, arguing that the meaning of *agriculture* as a subject in Schedule 7 was sufficiently wide for it to be said that the bill's provisions related to it.

[12] The Supreme Court, having rejected the view that a term was to be interpreted as corresponding to the executive functions which had been earlier devolved, held that *agriculture*, and therefore every other subject listed in Schedule 7 was 'intended to designate a subject-matter which is the object of legislative activity'. It was not 'intended to refer solely to the cultivation of the soil or the rearing of livestock, but should be understood in a broader sense as designating the industry or economic activity of agriculture in all its aspects ... as it is to that broader subject-matter that legislative activity is directed" *Re Agricultural Sector (Wales) Bill*, ¶49.

The question, therefore, of whether the provisions of an Assembly bill were within the Assembly's legislative competence depended upon whether they related to one or more of the subjects listed in Schedule 7 in that broad sense of being, in the Supreme Court's words, 'objects of legislative activity'.

> exceptions specified in that Part of that Schedule) is to be determined by reference to the purpose of the provision, having regard (among other things) to its effect in all the circumstances.

Although sometimes referred to as the 'purpose and effect' test, strictly speaking it is the concept of *purpose* which is paramount, for the effect of a provision is only one thing, among others, to which regard should be had. It was the purpose of the provision, having regard amongst other things to its effect in all the circumstances, which determined whether it related to a devolved subject. Provided that the provision 'fairly and realistically' related to a devolved subject in more than a 'loose or consequential' manner, it was within competence.[13]

4-14 Given that the purpose of a provision is therefore likely to be decisive in determining whether it relates to a devolved subject and therefore whether it is or is not within competence, the question arises: how does one determine that purpose? The Supreme Court, once more, dealt with that issue, saying of a provision that:

> The clearest indication of its purpose may be found in a report that gave rise to the legislation, or in the report of an Assembly committee; or its purpose may be clear from its context.[14]

That being so, the importance of being clear as to the purpose of provisions, and indeed of their likely effects, when writing reports which prepare the way for legislation or when later providing written evidence or giving oral testimony which may be reflected in the reports of Assembly committees on the proposed legislation, is underlined.

Exceptions to subjects under the conferred-powers model

4-15 The 'purpose and effect' test as set out in section 108(7) of the Act was not confined solely to determining whether a provision related to a devolved subject but was also relevant in determining whether it 'falls within any of the exceptions listed' in Part 1 of Schedule 7. These exceptions, like the devolved subjects, were to be found listed under the twenty-one headings in Part 1 of Schedule 7. Thus, for instance, under the fifth heading, *Education and Training*, after the list of devolved subjects, one found an exception:

> *Education and training*
>
> 5 Education, vocational, social and physical training and the careers service. Promotion of advancement and application of knowledge.
>
> *Exception—*
>
> Research Councils.

[13] *Re Agricultural Sector (Wales) Bill*, ¶¶50, 67.

[14] Ibid., ¶50.

The exception helped to define the subjects. It clarified what was within competence. Having read that the promotion of the advancement of knowledge is a devolved subject, and realizing that knowledge can be advanced by research and that research is often made possible by funding from the Research Councils, one might sensibly conclude that the Assembly could, in legislating in relation to the promotion of the advancement of knowledge, enact provisions in relation to Research Councils. By excepting Research Councils, the limits of the devolved subject were made clearer.[15]

Noticeably, whereas the Assembly was given competence to legislate in relation to the devolved subjects, the limitations applied to provisions which were said to 'fall within' the exceptions. Whereas the Supreme Court has adjudicated upon the meaning of 'relates to', there has not so far been any judicial determination regarding the meaning of 'falls within'. What is clear is that the meaning was intended to be narrower than that of 'relates to'.[16] 4-16

[15] The exceptions reflected areas in which executive functions had never been devolved. Were it the case that the meaning of the devolved subjects was intended to be coterminous with areas in which executive functions had once been devolved, it would not have been necessary to include such exceptions as they would have been implicit in the meaning of the subjects. Their inclusion therefore supports the Supreme Court's view that it was not intended that the historical link with executive functions should define the limits of the devolved subjects.

Again, there were some common misconceptions about these exceptions. First, they were not an attempt to commence a list of subjects which had not been devolved. The conferred powers model in Wales proceeded by listing the subjects which had been devolved. The reserved-powers model in Scotland, on the other hand, listed the subjects which were not devolved. The function of the listed exceptions in Wales was to clarify the boundaries of the devolved subjects by expressly stating that certain other subjects did not fall within those boundaries.

A second common misconception was that the exceptions only related to the subjects listed under the particular heading where they themselves were listed. This was not so. The Act expressly stated that it was immaterial under which heading the exceptions were to be found (GoWA 2006, s. 108(4)(b)). The exceptions applied to all of the subjects listed in Part 1 of Schedule 7, other than devolved taxes under heading *16A Taxation* (GoWA 2006, s. 108(4A), inserted by Wales Act 2014, s. 6(3)(b)). The reason that they were listed under particular headings was that it was in relation to the subjects under that heading that they were thought to have the greatest relevance. Their location, however, did not determine the range of their application.

[16] A similar issue was discussed by the Roman jurist, Pomponius, see Digest L.16.181.

It is submitted that what must be borne in mind, in determining whether a provision falls within an exception, is the function of the exceptions. They indicate areas which might be thought to be within the meaning of a subject but are not, and are therefore expressly excluded. Therefore, in determining whether a provision relates to a subject, the meaning of that subject does not include any exception. Exceptions are not within the subjects. Thus, if a provision relates to a subject only if the excepted area is treated as part of the subject, the provision falls within an exception and as a consequence does not relate to the subject as defined for the purposes of the legislative competence of the Assembly.

Subject-matter competence under the new reserved-powers model

4-17 The most significant change to the Assembly's legislative competence wrought by the introduction of a reserved-powers model is to its subject-matter competence. Henceforth, the Assembly is permitted to legislate on any subject at all provided that its enactments do not relate to matters regarding which legislative competence is reserved to the UK Parliament. The new section 108A, inserted into the 2006 Act by section 3 of the Wales Act 2017 to replace the former section 108, states that a provision of an Assembly Act is outside competence 'if it relates to reserved matters'.[17] The reserved matters are set out in the new Schedule 7A, inserted into the 2006 Act by the 2017 Act replacing the former Schedule 7.[18] They are divided into General Reservations, set out in Part 1 of the Schedule, and Specific Reservations set out in Part 2.

General reservations

4-18 General reservations are made in relation to the Constitution, the public service, political parties, the single legal jurisdiction of England and Wales, tribunals, foreign affairs and defence.

4-19 With regard to the Constitution, the Crown (including succession to the Crown and regency), the union of England and Wales, and the UK Parliament are reserved matters. The reservation of the Crown does not, however, reserve the use of the Welsh seal, nor the monarch's executive functions – not including those conferred or imposed by legislation or the prerogative – or the exercise of such functions by persons acting on the Crown's behalf, other than with regard to the management of the Crown Estate and the functions of MI5, MI6 and GCHQ. The reservation does not include property belonging to the monarch in right of the Crown, the Duchy of Lancaster or the Duchy of Cornwall, nor property belonging to any person acting on the Crown's behalf or held in trust for the monarch by such a person. However, the hereditary revenues of the Crown, the royal arms, the royal standard and the compulsory purchase of property belonging to the monarch in right of the Crown, the two duchies or held or used by a Minister of the Crown or a government department are all reserved, but not property held by the monarch in his or her private capacity (other than that governed by the Crown Private Estates Acts 1800 to 1873).

4-20 The public service reservation reserves the Civil Service of the State, thus placing that branch of the civil service serving the Welsh Government outside the Assembly's legislative competence.

4-21 The registration of political parties, their funding and that of their members and officers, together with accounting requirements relating to them are all

[17] GoWA 2006, s. 108A(2)(c), inserted by Wales Act 2017, s. 3(1).

[18] The new Schedule 7A is to be found as Schedule 1 to the 2017 Act, and the substitution is effected by section 3(2)(a) of the 2017 Act. It is not surprising that there has been much criticism of the decision to effect these major changes by amending the 2006 Act rather than legislating afresh.

reserved, but this does not include the making of payments to political parties to assist AMs to perform their Assembly duties.

Reserved matters relating to the single legal jurisdiction are courts (including their creation and jurisdiction), judges (including their appointment and pay), civil or criminal proceedings (including bail, costs, custody pending trial, disclosure, enforcement of court orders, evidence, sentencing, the limitation of actions,[19] procedure, prosecutors and remedies), pardons for criminal offences, private international law,[20] and judicial review of administrative action. The reservation of prosecutors does not prevent the Assembly from legislating regarding the prosecution of offences which it is within the competence of the Assembly to create – called 'devolved offences' – nor regarding welfare advice to courts in family proceedings involving the welfare of children ordinarily resident in Wales, nor representation or the provision of support to such children and their families in such proceedings, nor regarding Welsh family proceedings officers. 4-22

Tribunals are a reserved matter, including their membership, members' appointment and remuneration, their functions and procedure, and appeals from their decisions. The reservation does not include so-called 'devolved tribunals' being those whose functions are exercisable only in relation to Wales and which do not relate to reserved matters. The Assembly may also legislate regarding the decision of appeals and applications on matters which are reserved by devolved tribunals but not with regard to the procedure of tribunals in so doing. A tribunal does not cease to be a devolved tribunal if the functions that it has other than in relation to Wales were within the legislative competence of the Assembly to confer or impose at the time of the enactment of the provisions conferring or imposing those functions. 4-23

International relations – including the UK's relations with other territories, with the European Union and its institutions, and with other international organizations – are reserved, as is the regulation of international trade and assistance and cooperation regarding international development. However, this does not prevent the Assembly from legislating regarding the observation and implementation of international obligations, obligations under the European Convention on Human Rights and obligations under European Union law, nor assistance to Ministers of the Crown regarding these reservations. 4-24

Finally, the defence of the realm, the armed forces (including reservists and visiting forces), international headquarters and defence organizations, trading with the enemy and enemy property, are all reserved matters. 4-25

[19] Limitation of actions is concerned with the time limits within which individuals may commence litigation before the courts following, for example, an injury.

[20] Private international law (sometimes referred to as the conflict of laws) is that part of the law of England and Wales which provides for how cases involving elements of the laws of other countries are to be determined in the courts of this country. It is different from public international law (sometimes simply referred to as international law) which consists of rules which are meant to be binding upon nation states.

Specific reservations

4-26 As well as the general reservations set out in Part 1 of the new Schedule 7A, Part 2 sets out additional specific reservations. Like the general reservations, these constitute reserved matters in relation to which the Assembly does not have competence to legislate. A provision of an Assembly Act which relates to any one or more of these reserved matters will therefore be outside competence and liable to be struck down by the courts.

4-27 The list of specific reservations is lengthy and complex. The Schedule lists 179 numbered reserved matters, grouped into 100 sections organized under 13 heads. Whereas under the conferred-powers model those requiring Assembly legislation to change the law in order to achieve their policy goal would have to ensure that their proposed provisions related to at least one of the listed devolved subjects, the task now is to ensure that no provision relates to any one or more of the reserved matters, general or specific. The task is therefore greater and more complex. Moreover, whereas under the conferred-powers model those challenging the validity of a provision in an Assembly bill or Act had to show that it did not relate to any of the devolved subjects while those defending their validity had only to show that the provisions related to one, under the new reserved-powers model those challenging Assembly legislation need only show that the provisions relate to one reserved matter to succeed in their challenge, whereas the proponents of the provision have to be clear that it does not relate to any matter listed. The advantage has shifted.

4-28 The thirteen heads in Part 2 of Schedule 7A are as follows, together with the number of sections and the number of reserved matters under each head.

	Head	**Sections**	**Matters**
A	Financial and Economic Matters	5	5
B	Home Affairs	22	45
C	Trade and Industry	17	31
D	Energy	6	7
E	Transport	6	27
F	Social Security, Child Support, Pensions and Compensation	5	10
G	Professions	1	1
H	Employment	3	3
J	Health, Safety and Medicines	6	14
K	Media, Culture and Sport	5	6
L	Justice	14	18
M	Land and Agricultural Assets	3	5
N	Miscellaneous	7	7

The matters listed are reserved if the sections under which they are listed apply to them, and a section applies to a matter described or referred to in it when it is read together with any exceptions or interpretation provisions in that section. The exceptions and interpretation provisions in a section apply only within that particular section and do not affect any other sections.[21] This last issue is markedly different from the approach taken in the old Schedule 7, where exceptions applied generally across all of the devolved subjects regardless of whether the exception was listed under the same heading as the devolved subject. In other words, where the exceptions limited the Assembly's legislative competence, they were of general application to the subjects, but now that they widen that competence by limiting reservations, their application is limited. The rule has been reversed, but the result is the same – in both cases it works to reduce the Assembly's legislative competence.

The straightforward rule is that, to be within competence, a provision must not 4-29
relate to a reserved matter. However, a matter is reserved only if a section applies to it, and in deciding whether the section within which the matter is listed applies to it, one must exclude matters which have been excepted within the section and interpret the matters within the section in accordance with any interpretation provisions provided within it. An example may make this clearer.

Under Head H – Employment, Section H3 is Job search and support. Only 4-30
one matter is listed under that section: it reads 'Arrangements for assisting persons to select, train for, obtain and retain employment, and to obtain suitable employees'. The Assembly accordingly cannot legislate about such arrangements if the section applies to the matter. However, the section will not apply to the matter if the arrangements to assist persons in the manner described are covered by the exceptions listed under H3, namely Education; Vocational, social and physical training; Careers services. Interpretation of the words 'Employment' and 'Employees' is also provided.[22]

[21] Schedule 7A, paras 12–14.

[22] This is how the Section appears in the statute:

H3 Job search and support

Arrangements for assisting persons to select, train for, obtain and retain employment, and to obtain suitable employees

Exceptions

Education
Vocational, social and physical training
Careers services

Interpretation

'Employment' includes
(a) work on a person's own account, and
(b) employment of a disabled person (including work on a disabled person's own account) under special conditions;
and 'disabled person' here has the same meaning as it has in the Equality Act 2010 as at the principal appointed day.
'Employees' includes partners and other business associates.

4-31 It will be recalled that under the conferred-powers settlement, the exceptions listed under H3 appeared as devolved subjects under heading 5 *Education and training*. There was, however, a further devolved subject under that heading, namely 'Promotion of advancement and application of knowledge'. In so far as this is not mentioned in the new schedule 7A, it is clearly not a reserved matter and therefore continues to be within competence. It will also be remembered that there was an exception set out under the *Education and training* heading, namely 'Research councils'. These continue to be outside competence, because they are the subject of reserved matters listed under Section C11. Therefore, they remain excluded from competence.

4-32 Previously, of course, they had been an exception to all of the subjects under the original twenty headings in the old Schedule 7, including 'Education, vocational, social and physical training and the careers service' under heading 5, to which they probably had the greatest relevance. In that 'Education; Vocational, social and physical training; Careers services' are now an exception under H3 and thereby have no purchase on C11, it is still not possible for the Assembly to legislate regarding research councils even when legislating about education, vocational, social and physical training, or the careers services.

4-33 Another very significant issue arises in this context. Under the conferred-powers settlement, to be within competence, the provisions of an Assembly Act had to 'relate to' a devolved subject, and would only not be within competence if they could be shown to 'fall within' an exception. It was generally thought that the meaning of 'falls within' was more restrictive than 'relate to'. In other words, to establish that a provision was not within competence, it would not be enough to show that it related to an exception. Many of the former exceptions under the conferred-powers model, such as 'Research Councils', have re-appeared in the new Schedule 7A as reserved matters, and provisions are now outside competence not if they 'fall within' them, but if they simply 'relate to' them. In other words, if the generally accepted view that 'falls within' was narrower than 'relates to' was correct, in each and every case that an exception has become a reserved matter, and there are a large number of such conversions, the legislative competence of the Assembly has suffered.

4-34 The inclusion of erstwhile devolved subjects as exceptions to reserved matters illustrates another aspect of the new settlement. The reason that 'Education; Vocational, social and physical training; Careers services' are listed as exceptions to the matter under section H3 is because otherwise the reserved matter would have decreased the legislative competence which the Assembly previously had in relation to those subjects. Indeed, wherever it has been necessary to include former devolved subjects as exceptions to reserved matters, it has been done to prevent a loss of competence. Equally, wherever the new reserved matter was not previously a listed exception to one of the former devolved subjects now re-emerging as an exception to a reserved matter, it follows that previously, when legislating in relation to that former devolved subject, the Assembly was not precluded from changing the law on what has now become a reserved matter. Competence has been lost.

The former ability of the Assembly to legislate so as to affect areas of the law not listed as devolved subjects, provided that the areas were not listed as exceptions, led to those areas being described as 'ghost areas' or 'silent subjects'. Until the unanimous judgment of the Supreme Court in *Re Agricultural Sector (Wales) Bill*, some believed that it was not open to the Assembly to affect such areas even when legislating in relation to a devolved subject. That view was rejected in terms by the Supreme Court. The Court held that provided the provision in question fairly and realistically related to a devolved subject, it was irrelevant that others might see it as dealing with a different subject, provided that that other subject was not listed as an exception. Specifically, in that case, the Attorney General had argued that the provisions of the bill related to employment and industrial relations rather than agriculture. The Supreme Court held that, provided they related to agriculture, it did not matter that they could also be regarded as relating to employment and industrial relations, as long as those topics were not listed exceptions. 4-35

Under the new reserved-powers settlement, the position is reversed. What one now has listed in the new Schedule 7A are the matters which are outside competence. Henceforth, if a provision relates to one of these matters, it is outside competence. That others might regard it as relating to subjects which are not reserved will be of no consequence, unless those subjects have been included as listed exceptions to the reserved matter. Employment and industrial relations are now reserved matters, being Section H1 of Head H – Employment. 'The subject-matter of the Agricultural Sector (Wales) Act 2014' is listed as the sole exception to the matters under that Section. This makes it abundantly clear, therefore, that, were it not for that exception, the competence to pass that legislation would have been forfeit under the new settlement. The only fragment of that competence which has been saved is the specific competence relating to the agricultural sector. The competence to legislate in similar fashion regarding other devolved subjects is lost. The silent subjects, whose ghosts were exorcized by the Supreme Court, have been powerfully resurrected. 4-36

One further question needs to be raised concerning the application of sections to the matters listed under them. It is arguable that, when applied to a matter, the title of the section may in itself, without any exceptions or interpretation provisions, narrow the meaning of the matter. An example of this may be Section B13 Dangerous items, under Head B – Home Affairs. Three matters are listed under this Section: the subject-matter of the Firearms Acts 1968 to 1997; the subject-matter of the Poisons Act 1972; and knives. The inclusion of 'Knives' as a specific reservation in the new settlement occasioned much criticism and indeed ridicule, particularly as the interpretation provision went on to include knife blades and razor blades; axes; and swords within the meaning of 'Knives'. If, however, one interprets the requirement that the Section 'Dangerous items' has to apply to 'Knives' for them to be reserved, and takes into account the other matters listed under the Section, the reservation may not be either as wide or as ridiculous as it might otherwise seem. The Assembly may only be prevented from legislating in relation to knives when the provisions relate to them as dangerous items, akin to firearms and poisons. 4-37

Legislating about their provision in restaurants or their sale as household cutlery may not therefore be caught.[23]

4-38 This brings the discussion back to the question of how under the new settlement one is to determine whether a provision relates to a reserved matter. The test for doing so is set out in the new section 108A(6), which provides that:

> The question whether a provision of an Act of the Assembly relates to a reserved matter is determined by reference to the purpose of the provision, having regard (among other things) to its effect in all the circumstances.

This is very similar to the purpose test in the old section 108(7), other than that there is no specific mention of how to determine whether provisions are covered by exceptions. It has already been noted that the ambit of what were once exceptions but are now reserved matters has been widened as a result of provisions being outside competence if they merely 'relate to' them rather than having to 'fall within' them. Given that several former devolved subjects re-appear as exceptions and that UK government ministers repeatedly denied attempting to roll back the boundaries of devolved competence, it is submitted that provisions should be within competence if they 'relate to' an exception to a reserved matter. Otherwise, even more competence would be lost over such subjects as education, training and the careers service. The continuing importance of the concept of purpose in determining whether a provision is within competence emphasizes yet again the importance of clarity regarding the legislative purpose when preparing reports and other background materials to which the courts may refer to discern what the purpose of a provision is.[24]

General provisions

4-39 As well as the General Reservations set out in Part 1 of the new Schedule 7A and the Specific Reservations set out in Part 2, the Schedule has a Part 3, which is headed General Provisions. In truth, this part of the Schedule contains what are in effect general exceptions to the reservations made in Parts 1 and 2, that is exceptions which operate in relation to all of the reserved matters and, unlike those set out in the earlier parts, are not applicable solely to the reserved matters or sections under which they appear. There are therefore some matters that would be reserved and outside the Assembly's legislative competence were they not saved for the Assembly under Part 3.

[23] Although other reserved matters may be relevant, such as those under Section C6 – Consumer protection.

There is also a question regarding the meaning of 'the subject-matter of' an Act. Does it mean the scope of the Act as a whole, or does it refer to the subject-matter of each and every provision within the Act?

[24] For the application of the 'relates to' test in the context of the Scottish reserved powers model, see *Imperial Tobacco Limited* v *The Lord Advocate (Scotland)* [2012] UKSC 61.

There are three categories of such matters. The first is the conferral, imposition, modification and removal of functions relating to the Welsh language,[25] while the second is council tax precepts.[26] 4-40

The third category is more complex. The Assembly is not prevented from legislating in relation to certain matters concerning devolved Welsh authorities and devolved tribunals.[27] Devolved Welsh authorities are one kind of public authority, public authorities generally being bodies, offices or office holders with functions of a public nature other than courts. 4-41

The concept of a devolved Welsh authority is dealt with in the new section 157A of the 2006 Act and the accompanying new Schedule 9A, both inserted into the 2006 Act by section 4 of the 2017 Act. In order to qualify as a devolved Welsh authority and thereby not be immune from the Assembly's power to legislate, a public authority must either satisfy the definition of a devolved Welsh authority set out in section 157A(2) or be listed as a devolved Welsh authority in the new Schedule 9A. To meet the requirements of the definition, a public authority must have functions which are exercisable only in relation to Wales, which functions must wholly or mainly not relate to reserved matters. Functions which are exercisable other than in relation to Wales are not to be deemed as not being exercisable only in relation to Wales if they are within the Assembly's legislative competence to confer or impose. The vagaries of the definition were clearly sufficiently recognized to lead to a further list of devolved Welsh authorities being set out in Schedule 9A. A body included on that list qualifies as a devolved Welsh authority regardless of whether it meets the requirements of the definition. In short, a public authority is a devolved Welsh authority if it either fits the definition or appears on the list. Section 157A provides procedures for the insertion of further bodies onto the list or the removal of bodies from it.[28] 4-42

With regard to devolved Welsh authorities, the reservations contained in Parts 1 and 2 of Schedule 7A do not prevent the Assembly from legislating in relation to the constitution of such an authority even if it has reserved functions, and the constitution of such an authority includes its establishment and dissolution, its assets and liabilities, and its funding and receipts. Nor is the Assembly prevented from legislating in relation to such an authority so as to confer, impose, modify or remove accounting or public procurement functions, nor so as to confer, impose, modify or remove functions specifically exercisable in relation to such an authority, other than functions specifically exercisable in relation to a particular reserved function of the authority. It is also specifically provided that the general 4-43

[25] GoWA 2006, Sch. 7A, para. 198, inserted by Wales Act 2017, s. 3 and Sch. 1.

[26] Ibid., para. 199.

[27] Ibid., paras 194, 196. Devolved tribunals are discussed above, §4-23.

[28] This is to be done by amending Schedule 9A by Order in Council, after a statutory instrument containing the Order has been approved by the National Assembly and both Houses of Parliament: s. 157A(5)–(7).

reservation of the Crown in paragraph 1 of Part 1 of Schedule 7A does not reserve an authority provided that the authority has no reserved functions and either its functions are exercisable only in relation to Wales or the authority is a devolved Welsh authority.[29]

4-44 Paragraphs 194–196 of Schedule 7A having granted the Assembly competence which would otherwise have been the subject of reservation, paragraph 197 then takes back some of that competence by specifically excluding some authorities from the Assembly's competence. These are any bodies which are reserved by name in the list of specific reservations in Part 2 of Schedule 7A, the postal service and post office companies reserved by Section C10 and the Research Councils reserved by Section C11 of that Part, the police and crime commissioners and the Commission for Equality and Human Rights. As a consequence, the Assembly cannot legislate in relation to the constitution of these bodies (including their establishment and dissolution, their assets and liabilities, and their funding and receipts), nor to confer, impose, modify or remove accounting or public procurement functions in relation to them, nor so as to confer, impose, modify or remove functions specifically exercisable in relation to them. This claw-back of competence does not, however, apply to the Assembly's competence to legislate in relation to them regarding Welsh language functions and council tax precepts.[30]

ENFORCEMENT

Enforcement under the conferred-powers model

4-45 Under the original Part 4 and Schedule 7, the competence of the Assembly to legislate so as to enforce or otherwise provide for the effective implementation of the laws it made was separate from the question of its subject-matter competence. While subject-matter competence was dealt with in section 108(4), enforcement was dealt with separately in section 108(5). That subsection provided that a provision of an Assembly Act was within the Assembly's legislative competence if it provided for the enforcement of a provision which was within the Assembly's territorial and subject-matter competence or was 'otherwise appropriate for making such a provision effective'. The provision to which the enforcement provision applied need not even have been in the same Act, but in any Assembly Act or Assembly Measure, provided always that the provisions being enforced were within the Assembly's subject-matter and territorial competence.[31] The Assembly therefore

[29] GoWA 2006, Sch. 7A, para. 195.

[30] Ibid., para. 197.

[31] GoWA 2006, s. 108(5)(a).

had very considerable power to provide for the manner in which its legislation was to be implemented.[32]

Provisions which are aimed at enforcing or otherwise making effective laws passed by the Assembly very clearly are concerned with the means for giving effect to a policy, and choosing those means, it will be recalled, is part of the choice of policy. In developing policy proposals, therefore, the question of how the legal changes being made are to be enforced has to be addressed. The key point with regard to the Assembly's legislative power under the conferred-powers model was that the full range of methods of enforcement described earlier could be utilised.[33] The choice of the method of enforcement was not constrained by any specific limitations upon the Assembly's competence. 4-46

Enforcement under the reserved-powers model

Under the new settlement, provisions which provide for the enforcement of provisions which are within territorial and subject-matter competence or are otherwise appropriate for making such provisions effective have been classified along with incidental and consequential provisions as being 'ancillary'.[34] Unlike their predecessors, which did not have to relate to a devolved subject but only to other provisions in an Assembly Act which were themselves within competence, the new ancillary provisions must not relate to reserved matters. They may, however, now be used to make such ancillary provision regarding the provisions of UK Acts of Parliament as they affect Wales. 4-47

Like their predecessors under the conferred-powers model, ancillary provisions may apply otherwise than in relation to Wales, but their application other than in relation to Wales has been subjected to a novel restriction; such ancillary provisions must not have any 'greater effect otherwise than in relation to Wales ... than is necessary to give effect to the purpose of that provision'. The same is the case with ancillary provisions relating to functions which may be exercisable otherwise than in relation to Wales.[35] 4-48

This gives rise to the question of who is to decide whether the effect which a provision has other than in relation to Wales is or is not greater than is necessary to give effect to its purpose. Given that the test is a statutory test, it would appear that it is justiciable, and that it is for the courts to make that determination in the 4-49

[32] The Assembly's competence to provide for the enforcement of its legislative enactments provided a particular example of the fear of 'ghost' areas within the conferred-powers settlement. *Criminal Law* was not a subject listed as devolved in Part 1 of the old Schedule 7, nor was the *Administration of Criminal Justice*. This led some to believe that it was not open to the Assembly to legislate so as to make changes to the criminal law as it applied in Wales, nor to the manner in which it was administered. This was simply not the case.

[33] See above, §4-45.

[34] GoWA 2006, s. 108A(7), inserted by Wales Act 2017, s. 3(1).

[35] GoWA 2006, s. 108A(3).

context of deciding a devolution issue under Schedule 9 to the 2006 Act. This would open the door to challenges from interested parties who will generally be outside Wales arguing that Welsh legislation affects them in a manner which is greater than necessary for its purpose to be achieved.[36]

4-50 If that is the case, it also begs the question as to what weight the courts will give to the fact that the Assembly, a democratically elected legislature, will have decided, in passing the legislation, that the challenged provision is necessary. The justification for allowing the challenge is undoubtedly that the views of persons affected outside Wales are not represented in the Assembly, creating a democratic deficit. It is not clear whether the courts in such a situation will, in revisiting the Assembly's decision, be prepared to override it if they simply disagree with the Assembly's assessment of the issue or whether they will intervene only if they hold the Assembly's assessment to be manifestly unreasonable. On analogy with the majority judgment in the Supreme Court in the *Asbestos Diseases* case,[37] the court may well be prepared to assess how well the Assembly considered the issues in coming to its decision. However, that case involved interference with a right protected under the Human Rights Act, and the courts may not be prepared to take so bold an approach where such rights are not in question. The minority judgment in the case argued forcibly that great weight needed to be given to the decisions of a democratically elected legislature, but again, in that case, the argument did not turn on there being a democratic deficit in the legislative process as regards those complaining of being unduly affected.[38] Either way, the courts in determining the issue may again make use background materials prepared for the Assembly's consideration of the issues in question, and the thoroughness of the treatment of those issues in the background materials may well prove crucial to the validity of the provisions called into question.

4-51 Ancillary provisions may be provisions which enforce legislative provisions made for Wales, or which are otherwise appropriate for making provisions effective or which are incidental to or consequential on such provisions. The question therefore arises as to how to identify such provisions. With regard to enforcement provisions, the question was considered in the Supreme Court in the *Asbestos Diseases*

36 Arguably, the appropriate test is whether the interference satisfies the principle of proportionality.

37 See above, §§3-16–3-20.

38 It is arguable that the issue of how great an effect is justifiable is one which should be determined politically rather than judicially. This could be argued to be an area where the appropriate remedy for an adversely affected citizen would be to raise the matter with their MP, who could take it up with the UK government in its responsibility for devolved matters in England. Thereafter, the matter could be addressed by the two governments, and, if necessary, the effect of the legislation other than in relation to Wales could be varied by, for instance, subordinate legislation made by the Secretary of State most appropriately by affirmative procedure in Parliament. A democratic solution would thus be provided for a problem about democracy. The judicial solution risks ongoing uncertainty concerning the validity of the operation of ancillary provisions in their applicability other than in relation to Wales, which is likely to manifest itself in timidity regarding proposals to make such ancillary provision. It also leaves the judiciary having to decide an issue which properly belongs to politically accountable legislators.

case. It was considered in the minority judgment delivered by Lord Thomas of Cwmgiedd LCJ. Lord Thomas suggested that the same approach could be taken to answering the question of whether a provision was an enforcement provision as had been suggested should be employed in earlier cases before the Supreme Court to answer the question of whether a provision was incidental or consequential, namely to ask whether the provision had an end or purpose of its own. The technique advocated to determine whether a provision was incidental or consequential was:

> to identify the primary purpose of the main provision of the Bill to which the provision in question is incidental or consequential and then to form a judgement on whether the provision in question is subsidiary to that primary purpose and has no end in itself.[39]

Lord Thomas thought that the same approach could be taken with regard to whether a provision was an enforcement provision or not:

> In the light of that approach to section 108(5)(b) [incidental and consequential provisions], it seems to me that a similar approach should be adopted in relation to section 108(5)(a) [enforcement provisions], namely to identify the primary purpose of the main provision and then form a view on whether the provision in question is intended for the enforcement of the main provision or to make it effective and has no end in itself.[40]

There seems much to commend this approach.[41]

INCIDENTAL AND CONSEQUENTIAL PROVISIONS

As well as stating that the Assembly had competence to legislate in order to enforce, 4-52
or otherwise appropriately make effective, provisions within its subject-matter and territorial competence, section 108(5) of the 2006 Act gave the Assembly competence to enact provisions which were 'otherwise incidental to, or consequential on,' such provisions. The meaning of these terms, *incidental* and *consequential*, was not judicially interpreted in the context of section 108(5), but they were subject to such interpretation in relation to the general restrictions and other limitations placed upon the Assembly's legislative competence by the old section 108(6). The case in which the meaning and application of these words was considered was

[39] [2015] UKSC 3, at ¶131.

[40] Ibid. The references are to GoWA 2006 prior to its amendment by Wales Act 2017.

[41] Indeed, it might be regretted that the opportunity was not taken in the Wales Act 2017 to incorporate such a test within the statute.

Re Local Government Byelaws (Wales) Bill.[42] The case arose following the passing of the very first bill promoted by the Welsh Government in the National Assembly following the coming into force of the Assembly Act provisions in 2011. The Attorney General on behalf of the UK government challenged the competence of the Assembly to enact certain provisions of the bill.[43] The provisions in question removed a power conferred on the Secretary of State to confirm byelaws made by local authorities in Wales, which power had existed before the Assembly Act provisions came into force. The power constituted therefore a pre-commencement function of a Minister of the Crown. Generally, such pre-commencement functions belonging to UK government ministers could not be removed by Assembly legislation without the Minister's consent, but consent was not required if the removal was incidental or consequential. The Welsh Government argued that it was. The Supreme Court unanimously found in favour of the Welsh Government. Judgments were delivered by Lord Neuberger and Lord Hope.

Lord Neuberger said:

[42] *Re Local Government Byelaws (Wales) Bill: Reference by the Attorney General for England and Wales* [2012] UKSC 53.

[43] The bill concerned the manner in which byelaws made by local authorities in Wales took effect. Prior to the creation of the Assembly in 1999, the power to confirm byelaws made by local authorities in Wales had been vested in the Secretary of State for Wales. Such confirmation was deemed necessary because local authority byelaws could affect people in a local authority area who were not electors in that area. Those making the byelaws therefore had the power to affect persons to whom they were not democratically accountable. Byelaws therefore needed to be confirmed by the Secretary of State, who was accountable for such confirmation to the representatives of the wider electorate in Parliament. With the creation of the Assembly, there came into being a body representative of that wider electorate in Wales, and the Assembly was therefore given the power to confirm Welsh local authority byelaws. However, the power of the Secretary of State to confirm byelaws was not taken away. Instead, local authorities were free to choose whether to go to the Secretary of State or to the Assembly for the confirmation of their byelaws. Without exception, after 1999 they went to the Assembly, and after 2007 to the Welsh Ministers, to whom the Assembly's power of confirmation passed with the separation of executive and legislative powers under the 2006 Act. The Secretary of State, however, retained the power to confirm byelaws for Welsh local authorities concurrently with the self-same power of the Welsh Ministers.

The Local Government Byelaws (Wales) Bill proposed a change to the regime for making byelaws. It proposed that, for the future, certain byelaws would not need to be confirmed by anyone, and further that the Welsh Ministers should have the power to withdraw the need for other byelaws to require confirmation if they saw fit. The effect of these proposals would be to remove the need for many byelaws to be confirmed by anyone. In such circumstances, both the Welsh Ministers and the Secretary of State would have removed from them the power to confirm such byelaws. The Secretary of State refused to consent to this removal of his pre-commencement function of confirming byelaws, but the Welsh Government and the Assembly believed that the removal of this function was a consequence of the introduction of the new regime for making byelaws and that therefore no consent was needed as this was an instance of such removal being 'incidental to, or consequential on' a provision otherwise within competence.

The Supreme Court accepted that the removal was incidental or consequential. In so doing, the meaning of the words *incidental* and *consequential* was considered.

> The answer to the question whether a particular provision … is 'incidental to, or consequential on' another provision … turns on the facts of the particular case. The answer may to some extent be a question of fact and degree, and it should turn on substance rather than form, although … in any well drafted Bill, the substance will be reflected in the form, at least in relation to that sort of question.[44]

Similarly, Lord Hope described how the question should be addressed:

> The words 'incidental to, or consequential on, any other provision contained in the Act of the Assembly' make it clear that the interpretative exercise to which it points is one of comparison. How significant is the removal of the pre-commencement function, when it is seen in the context of the Act as a whole? If the removal has an end and purpose of its own … it will be outside competence. If its purpose or effect is merely subsidiary to something else in the Act, and its consequence when it is put into effect … minor or unimportant in the context of the Act as a whole … it can then be regarded as merely incidental to, or consequential on, the purpose that the Bill seeks to achieve.[45]

Significantly, Lord Hope saw the question being answered in terms of the purpose of the provision, and considered whether the purpose or effect of the removal was subsidiary. Again, therefore, the concepts of purpose and effect acquire importance in determining whether a provision is within competence, and, having regard to the Supreme Court's later statement in *Re Agricultural Sector (Wales) Bill* that the clearest indication of purpose 'may be found in a report that gave rise to the legislation, or in the report of an Assembly committee', the importance of taking care to elucidate that purpose in documents produced when developing the policy and when presenting written or oral evidence regarding it to Assembly committees cannot be overstated.

Re Local Government Byelaws (Wales) Bill was concerned with the meaning of 4-53
the words *incidental* and *consequential* in paragraph 6(1)(b) of Part 3 of Schedule 7 to the 2006 Act rather than their occurrence in section 108(5)(b). However, given that the words occurred in the same enactment and in respect of the same issue, namely legislative competence, it is difficult not to conclude that the same approach should be taken with regard to the meaning of the words in both contexts. Indeed, as has been noted,[46] the test as to whether a provision was incidental or consequential was thought by Lord Thomas LCJ to be equally appropriate for determining whether or not a provision was an enforcement provision. Now that enforcement provisions and incidental and consequential provisions are grouped together as ancillary provisions in the new section 108A, it would appear to be all the more appropriate that they should be governed by the same test.

[44] *Re Local Government Byelaws (Wales) Bill*, ¶¶48–49 *per* Lord Neuberger.

[45] Ibid., ¶83 *per* Lord Hope.

[46] See above, §4-51.

GENERAL RESTRICTIONS

4-54 Under both the conferred-powers settlement and the reserved-powers settlement replacing it, General Restrictions have been imposed upon the Assembly's legislative competence. These restrictions mean that even when the Assembly is legislating within its territorial and subject-matter competence, or enacting permitted ancillary provisions, there are nevertheless some things which it is not permitted to do. They restrict therefore the Assembly's legislative powers even regarding what is otherwise within its competence. These general restrictions are now to be found in Schedule 7B to the 2006 Act, inserted by section 3(2)(b) of and Schedule 2 to the Wales Act 2017.[47]

The law on reserved matters

4-55 It might seem unnecessary to state that, as the Assembly cannot legislate *in relation to* reserved matters, it cannot legislate to change the law *on* those matters. However, on occasion, legislation which does not relate to reserved matters in terms of its purpose may require modification of the law on reserved matters in order to be effective.

4-56 The Assembly is not generally permitted to change the law on reserved matters, regardless of whether that law is to be found in legislation or any other source, such as binding decisions of the courts. However, it is permitted to modify the law on reserved matters in provisions which are ancillary to provisions which are otherwise within its competence, provided that the change made does not have a greater effect than is necessary to give effect to the purpose of the provision that is within its subject-matter competence.[48] This again gives rise to the vexed question of how and by whom is the determination to be made as to whether the effect is greater than is necessary. It is unclear how much weight will be given to the Assembly's decision of the issue, but certainly it will be important that the supporting background material from both the legislation's proponents and Assembly committees provides a full justification for the choice made.

Private law

4-57 The Assembly's legislative competence does not allow it to make changes to the private law of England and Wales, defined as being the law of contract, agency, bailment, tort, unjust enrichment and restitution, property, trusts and succession, although the Schedule specifically excludes intellectual property rights relating to plant varieties, thus confessing that the restrictions would otherwise have eroded

[47] Under the conferred-powers settlement, the restrictions were set out in Parts 2 and 3 of the former Schedule 7 to the 2006 Act; Part 2 basically setting out the restrictions, while Part 3 provided for exceptions to them.

[48] GoWA 2006, Sch. 7B, paras 1–2.

pre-existing competence in that regard. The restriction does, however, specifically include compulsory acquisition of property. Where, however, a provision modifying the private law has another purpose, and that other purpose does not relate to a reserved matter, the restriction does not apply.[49] Once more, therefore, clarity regarding the purpose of provisions assumes great importance.

Criminal law

In addition to not being able to change the criminal law relating to reserved matters, the Assembly cannot create criminal offences or change the criminal law regarding certain categories of crime. These are treason and related offences, homicide offences – such as murder and manslaughter – but also including offences relating to suicide, other offences against the person or offences involving violence or threats of violence which have to be tried on indictment in the Crown Court, sexual offences including crimes relating to indecency or pornographic images, and offences connected with perjury. The Assembly is also precluded from legislating about the defences relating to those crimes. Nor may it legislate to change the law of England and Wales regarding criminal responsibility and the capacity to commit crimes, the meaning of concepts regarding mental elements in crimes – such as intention, recklessness and dishonesty, the law relating to attempts to commit crimes and aiding, abetting, counselling or procuring their commission, or the sentences and other orders that can be made regarding criminal conduct. Outside these restrictions, the Assembly has the competence to create criminal offences and make changes to the law relating to them, although it should be noted that compensation for persons affected by crime or by miscarriages of justice are reserved matters.[50] 4-58

Acts of Parliament

Under the conferred-powers settlement, it was specifically stated that, generally speaking, within legislative competence, the provisions of Assembly Acts could make any provision that could be made by an Act of Parliament.[51] This statement has been omitted from the section dealing with legislative competence under the reserved-powers model.[52] Nevertheless, it remains the case that, within its limits, the Assembly's legislative competence includes the power to amend or even repeal Westminster Acts. However, there are some Acts of Parliament that the Assembly could not and cannot modify, nor give anyone else the power to modify by subordinate legislation. These statutes concern fundamental rights or are of constitutional significance. They comprise the European Communities Act 1972, the Human Rights Act 1998, the Civil Contingencies Act 2004, and section 100 of the Energy 4-59

[49] GoWA 2006, Sch. 7B, para. 3.

[50] GoWA 2006, Schedule 7A, Head L – Justice: Section L10.

[51] GoWA 2006, s. 108(1) as enacted.

[52] GoWA 2006, s. 108A, inserted by Wales Act 2017, s. 3(1).

Act 2008, together with regulations made under that section.[53] Certain provisions of the Government of Wales Act 1998 are similarly excluded from modification by the Assembly, as are various elements of the Public Audit (Wales) Act 2013.[54] Nor may the Assembly modify, or confer power to modify, any provisions within UK Acts of Parliament requiring sums needed to repay or pay interest on amounts borrowed by the Welsh Ministers to be charged to the Welsh Consolidated Fund.[55] Unsurprisingly, most of the Government of Wales Act 2006 is also beyond the competence of the Assembly to amend, although there are now a significant number of provisions which the Assembly can modify.[56]

Functions of UK ministers, UK government departments and other reserved authorities

Under the conferred-powers settlement

4-60 Under the general restrictions contained in the conferred-powers settlement, the Assembly was not permitted in its legislation to confer or impose any function upon a Minister of the Crown, unless the consent of the Secretary of State had been obtained. *Function* was and is defined in the Act as meaning any power or duty, so that the Assembly was barred from imposing duties on UK government ministers and from conferring powers upon them without their consent. The Act expressly provides that this includes the Treasury.[57] Nor could the Assembly, without consent, remove such functions from Ministers of the Crown nor modify them, if such functions pre-dated the coming into effect of the Assembly Act provisions, that is the enhancement of the Assembly's legislative competence following the referendum on its legislative powers in 2011. Such functions were referred to as pre-commencement functions. The Assembly was, however, entirely free to remove or modify Minister of the Crown functions created after that date without the need for any consent.[58]

4-61 There was, however, one circumstance in which a pre-commencement function of a Minister of the Crown could be removed or modified without the need for consent. That was where the removal or modification was incidental to, or

[53] GoWA 2006, Sch. 7B, para. 5(1). The Data Protection Act 1998 was included within the original restriction, but this is now covered by protection of personal data being listed as a reserved matter: Head L – Justice, Section L6; GoWA 2006, Sch. 7A, para. 170.

[54] The Public Audit (Wales) Act 2013 provisions which may not be modified are provisions taken from Schedule 8 to the Government of Wales Act 2006. These were themselves excluded from modification, but could be restated in the 2013 Act under the Assembly's power to restate provisions which are otherwise outside its competence: see further below, §4-74.

[55] GoWA 2006, Sch. 7B, paras 5(2)–(6), 6.

[56] GoWA 2006, Sch. 7B, para. 7. Many of the sections which the Assembly can modify are concerned with the powers which the Assembly now has regarding its name, elections to it, its committees and so forth.

[57] See the definitions in s. 158.

[58] The Assembly Act provisions came into force and effect in May 2011.

consequential on, a provision of an Assembly Act which was otherwise within the Assembly's competence. It was in this context that the courts considered the meaning of *incidental* or *consequential* in the *Re Local Government Byelaws (Wales) Bill*.[59]

What has been said in relation to provisions of Assembly Acts which sought to confer, impose, modify or remove Minister of the Crown functions applied equally to provisions which sought to confer the power to do those things by subordinate legislation.[60] Likewise, the Assembly could not make modifications to the functions of the Comptroller and Auditor General, or confer the power to make such modifications by subordinate legislation, unless the Secretary of State consented to the modification.[61] Nor could the Assembly make modifications to Acts of Parliament which require the repayment of money borrowed by the Welsh Ministers, or the interest due on such loans, to be charged against the Welsh Consolidated Fund, and the same applied to conferring power to make such modifications by subordinate legislation.[62] 4-62

The granting of legislative competence to the Assembly over certain taxes under the heading *16A Taxation* inserted into Part 1 of Schedule 7 to the 2006 Act by the Wales Act 2014 also involved allowing the Assembly to confer or impose, or to remove or modify functions of Her Majesty's Revenue & Customs (HMRC). The General Restrictions regarding the conferral, imposition, modification and removal of Minister of the Crown functions which already existed in Parts 2 and 3 of the old Schedule 7 were therefore extended to the conferral, imposition, modification and removal of HMRC functions – but with two significant differences. In the case of HMRC, the Assembly was prevented from ever legislating to confer, impose, modify or remove functions without consent. Unlike the previous provisions regarding functions of Ministers of the Crown, no distinction was made between the modification and removal of pre- and post-commencement functions, and no exception was made with regard to provisions which were incidental and consequential. All alike required consent, or else they were outside competence.[63] In terms of knowing when consent was needed, this was undoubtedly clearer. However, in terms of knowing whether the Assembly could legislate, it was equally clearly not an improvement, as tests governed by rules of law had been replaced with a discretion exercisable as an executive department deemed fit. 4-63

[59] *Re Local Government Byelaws (Wales) Bill: Reference by the Attorney General for England and Wales* [2012] UKSC 53.

[60] GoWA 2006, Sch. 7, Pt 2, passim.

[61] GoWA 2006, Sch. 7, Pt 2, para. 4, and Part 3, para. 7. No special provision is needed regarding the Comptroller and Auditor General under the reserved powers settlement as he will be a 'reserved authority' (see below) within the meaning of the new settlement.

[62] GoWA 2006, Sch. 7, Pt 2, para. 3. The Welsh Consolidated Fund is the money received from UK central government to finance Welsh Government expenditure.

[63] See GoWA 2006, Sch. 7, Pt 2, para. 4A and Part 3, para. 7A, as inserted by Wales Act 2014, s. 7(14).

Under the reserved-powers settlement

4-64 The move to a reserved-powers model of devolution has been accompanied by significant changes to the competence of the Assembly in this regard. The relevant provisions are now to be found in paragraphs 8–12 of the new Schedule 7B inserted in the 2006 Act by the 2017 Act. The new regime continues to distinguish between the competence to confer and impose functions on the one hand and to remove and modify such functions on the other. However, following the approach of the Wales Act 2014 with regard to Treasury consents for the modification or removal of HMRC functions, no distinction is any longer made between pre-commencement and post-commencement functions, nor is any allowance made for incidental or consequential modification or removal. In this regard, therefore, there has been some loss of legislative competence.

4-65 The greatest change, however, is undoubtedly the significant increase in the number of bodies to which the restrictions apply. In addition to Ministers of the Crown, the Treasury and HMRC, the 2017 Act has imposed restrictions on the competence of the Assembly to legislate with regard to a range of 'reserved authorities'. These are defined in the Act as being Ministers of the Crown and government departments generally – not just the Treasury and HMRC as previously – and public authorities which are not devolved Welsh authorities. Public authorities are broadly defined as being bodies, offices or office holders having functions of a public nature. Restrictions regarding the functions of such public authorities apply to all such bodies if they are not devolved Welsh authorities.[64]

4-66 The key issue with regard to the Assembly's legislative competence in relation to this new category of reserved authorities is whether consent is needed before functions, in the sense of powers and duties, can be conferred or imposed upon them, modified, or removed. Where consent is needed, that consent has to be given by 'the appropriate Minister', which in most cases is the Secretary of State, but in the case of HMRC is the Treasury. The appropriate Minister is required to consent to the provision regarding the function.

4-67 Where legislation is needed to provide the means for giving effect to a policy and the means chosen may or will involve conferring, imposing, modifying or removing functions of reserved authorities, it is therefore important that this be identified as soon as possible in the development of the policy, so as to discover whether any necessary consents are likely to be forthcoming or whether statute requires there to be consultation with the appropriate Minister. Failure to obtain such consent will require reconsideration of how to give effect to the policy, and could conceivably halt the proposed legislation or its development in its tracks. Where such consent is needed, the Assembly does not have competence to enact the provision without such consent. In other words, a provision enacted without it is outside competence, open to challenge and the possibility of being declared invalid by the courts. Where only consultation is needed, on the other hand, it is expressly stated that the making of provisions which require it are within

[64] For the concept of a devolved Welsh authority, see above, §§4-41–4-44.

competence.[65] While failure to consult, therefore, may lead to the invalidity of such a provision, UK ministerial disapproval will not. Whereas the need for consent, in effect, enables the appropriate Minister to veto a provision, the need for consultation does not.

UK ministerial consent is needed whenever it is proposed to confer powers or impose duties on Ministers of the Crown. There is no change here from the position under the previous, conferred-powers settlement. There is, however, a significant change to the position regarding the modification or removal of functions. Under the new settlement, consent is needed only in certain circumstances. These are defined in Schedule 7B as being, first, where the function relates to a qualified devolved function. A qualified devolved function is one which has been given by legislation to the Welsh Ministers, but the exercise of which requires the consent or agreement of a Minister of the Crown, or else can only be exercised after consultation with the UK Minister, or needs to be exercised jointly with him or her, or else is open to concurrent exercise – meaning that it can be exercised either by the UK Minister or the Welsh Ministers.[66] Consent is also needed to remove or modify a Minister of the Crown function exercisable in relation to the Welsh language, in relation to water supply, water quality, water resources management, the control of pollution of water resources, sewerage, rivers and watercourses, land drainage, flood risk management or coastal protection, certain functions of UK government ministers under the Marine and Coastal Access Act 2009, their powers under section 6 of the Railways Act 2005 regarding, for instance, financial assistance for railway services, and any Treasury functions regarding accounting by the Assembly Commission or the Welsh Ministers.[67] 4-68

With regard to Minister of the Crown functions which do not fall within the requirement for consent, it is now open to the Assembly to remove or modify them provided that the Welsh Ministers have consulted with the appropriate Minister – that is, the Secretary of State or the Treasury – about the provision. Regardless of the result of that consultation, provided it has taken place, the enacted provision will be valid. It is, however, important to ensure when developing the legislative proposal that the need for consultation is identified and time for it to take place allowed. That it has occurred will need to be notified to the Assembly, although – unlike the need for consent – its absence would not prevent the bill being introduced with a statement that it was within competence. 4-69

In relation to reserved authorities other than Ministers of the Crown, consent from the appropriate Minister is now required for the modification or removal of 4-70

[65] Schedule 7B, para. 12.

[66] This was, it will be recalled, the position in the *Local Government Byelaws* case [2012] UKSC 53. As the new settlement does not exempt incidental and consequential provisions from the need for consent, it is clear that the decision in that case would now go the other way were a similar situation to arise. Lists of such concurrent and joint functions are set out in the new Sch. 3A inserted, together with a new s. 59A, into the 2006 Act by s. 21 of and Sch. 4 to the 2017 Act.

[67] Schedule 7B, para. 11(1).

any of their functions. This is a new requirement, doubtless deemed necessary as a consequence of the potential enhancement of the Assembly's legislation competence in moving from a conferred-powers to a reserved-powers model. Consent, however, is not required for the removal or modification of the functions of the Electoral Commission, the Food Standards Agency, the Water Services Regulation Authority, any water or sewerage undertaker, the Consumer Council for Water, the Chief Inspector of Drinking Water for Wales (and any other such assessors for the enforcement of water quality appointed for Wales by the Welsh Ministers), the Joint Committee on Vaccination and Immunisation, the NHS Business Services Authority, NHS Blood and Transplant, or the Open University. Nor is consent needed for the removal or modification of traffic commissioners' functions relating to the registration of local bus services or the application and enforcement of traffic regulation conditions regarding those services. The funding of police and crime commissioners through council tax precepts is also free from the requirement of ministerial consent, as are the removal or modification of the devolved functions of courts, or the functions of tribunals involving or connected with making decisions relating to matters which are not reserved.[68]

4-71 Ministerial consent is also needed for Assembly legislation to modify the constitution of any reserved authority, including modifications which relate to its assets, liabilities, funding and receipts. This does not however apply to water or sewerage undertakers, the Consumer Council for Water, the Chief Inspector of Drinking Water for Wales and other such assessors for the enforcement of water quality appointed for Wales by the Welsh Ministers, nor to the funding of police and crime commissioners through council tax precepts. The same exclusions apply to the requirement which otherwise applies for Ministerial consent to confer, impose, modify or remove functions specifically exercisable in relation to reserved authorities.

4-72 With regard to conferring or imposing functions on reserved authorities, consent is generally required, but not, once again, in the case of the Electoral Commission, the Food Standards Agency, the Water Services Regulation Authority, any water or sewerage undertaker, the Consumer Council for Water, the Chief Inspector of Drinking Water for Wales (and any other such assessors for the enforcement of water quality appointed for Wales by the Welsh Ministers), the Joint Committee on Vaccination and Immunisation, the NHS Business Services Authority, NHS Blood and Transplant, or the Open University; the conferral or imposition of traffic commissioners' functions relating to the registration of local bus services or the application and enforcement of traffic regulation conditions regarding those services, the funding of police and crime commissioners through council tax precepts and the conferral or imposition of devolved functions on courts, or

[68] The explanation for this somewhat eclectic list of exceptions lies in the fact that under the conferred-powers settlement, the Assembly had competence to legislate regarding the functions of these bodies under headings such as *Food*, *Health and health services* and *Water and flood defence*, and would have lost that competence in moving to a reserved-powers model without these exceptions.

on tribunals where they are involved or connected with making decisions relating to matters which are not reserved.[69]

Wherever consent is a requirement for provisions which would in themselves confer, impose, modify or remove the functions of a reserved authority or modify its constitution, consent is also required for a provision which would confer a power to do any of those things by making subordinate legislation. 4-73

Restatements of the law and subordinate legislation

None of the general restrictions, however, prevents the Assembly from restating the law in an Assembly Act, repealing or revoking spent enactments, or conferring subordinate law-making powers to do these things. Where such restatements include laws on reserved matters, the Assembly may not at the time of restating or at any time thereafter modify that law other than is otherwise permissible. In other words, restating laws do not bring them into competence.[70] 4-74

Nor is the Assembly prevented by any of the general restrictions from modifying enactments, or conferring the power to modify enactments by subordinate legislation, in order to change the documents by which subordinate legislation may be made, confirmed or approved, the procedure if any to be followed by the Assembly in making such legislation, and the application of Assembly enactments to such documents. 4-75

Both of these provisions continue the position as it existed under the conferred-powers settlement.[71]

EXTENT

To be within competence, the Assembly's legislation must not extend 'otherwise than only to England and Wales'.[72] This limitation is not concerned with the territorial competence of the Assembly to legislate but with the legislation's jurisdictional extent. Territorially, as has already been discussed, the Assembly's legislation must not *apply* 'otherwise than in relation to Wales'.[73] *Extent*, on the other hand, refers to the legal jurisdiction within which the Assembly's legislation will be recognized as law. Within the United Kingdom, there are three jurisdictions: Scotland, Northern Ireland, and England and Wales. England and Wales is a single jurisdiction. Although some laws may apply only in England, some only in Wales and some in both countries, all of those laws are part of the law of the one 4-76

[69] Schedule 7B, para. 9.

[70] Thus, provisions in Sch. 8 to GoWA 2006 were restated in the Public Audit (Wales) Act 2013: see above, §4-59, n. 54.

[71] GoWA 2006, Sch. 7B, Pt 2, inserted by Wales Act 2017, s. 3(2)(b) and Sch. 2.

[72] GoWA 2006, s. 108(6)(b).

[73] GoWA 2006, s. 108(4)(b).

jurisdiction – England and Wales. The laws which apply only in England and the laws which apply only in Wales, all extend to England and Wales, as do those which apply in both countries. All Assembly legislation therefore extends to England and Wales, together with all of the subordinate legislation made to apply only in Wales. All such laws will be recognized and administered as law in the courts of England and Wales. Whereas the UK Parliament can enact laws which extend to all three of the jurisdictions or to any one or more of them, the Assembly can only enact laws for one. The same is true of the Scottish Parliament and the Legislative Assembly of Northern Ireland.[74]

COMPATIBILITY WITH EU LAW AND HUMAN RIGHTS

4-77 The final limitations placed upon the Assembly's legislative competence by section 108(6) of the 2006 Act concern the compatibility of provisions enacted by the Assembly with European Union law and the Convention rights, that is the rights derived from the European Convention on Human Rights which have been incorporated into UK domestic law by the Human Rights Act 1998. In both cases, if the provisions of an Assembly Act are incompatible with either body of law, the provisions are outside the Assembly's competence and therefore not law.

4-78 It is important to stress that the consequence for Assembly legislation of incompatibility with the Convention rights is different from that which follows a finding that the provisions of a United Kingdom Act of Parliament are incompatible. In the case of the latter, the courts make a declaration of incompatibility which does not affect the legal status of the enactment. It is then for the UK government or Parliament to take action if it is thought fit to do so.[75] In the case of the National Assembly's legislation, the consequence is more severe. Such provisions will be declared to have been outside the Assembly's legislative competence and therefore of no legal effect. This difference flows from the fact that the Assembly's legislative competence is limited, while that of the UK Parliament, as a sovereign legislature, is not. As has already been discussed, the courts are also prepared to examine the quality of the Assembly's decision making when legislating in relation to qualified protected rights, and they will not confine their intervention to instances where the Assembly's judgment on such issues is held to be 'manifestly unreasonable'. The courts are prepared to declare provisions as being of no legal effect because of incompatibility where they hold that the Assembly failed to achieve a fair balance

[74] It is sometimes said that laws cannot extend only to England or only to Wales as neither country is a legal jurisdiction. However, the Ecclesiastical Measures of the Church of England, which are enacted by Parliament, extend only to the Provinces of Canterbury and York, and there are provisions of the Marriage Acts which are stated in terms by those statutes not to *extend* to Wales.

[75] Human Rights Act 1998, ss. 4 and 10, dealing respectively with declarations of incompatibility and remedial action.

between the competing interests involved, possibly because of insufficient evidence having been put before it or evidence of insufficient quality.[76]

CHALLENGES TO LEGISLATIVE COMPETENCE

As has already been stated, where the power of a legislator or legislature to make law is limited, there will be mechanisms by which provisions can be challenged on the grounds that the law-maker did not have the power to make them. In that the legislative competence of the National Assembly is limited, it follows that its legislation is open to such challenge. Such challenges can occur in one of two ways: first, a bill passed by the Assembly can be challenged before it receives Royal Assent and becomes an Act; and, secondly, even after it has received Royal Assent, any person appearing in legal proceedings before a court in the United Kingdom can raise the question of whether the provisions of an Assembly Act are within competence. 4-79

Prior to Royal Assent

After a bill has been passed by the Assembly, a period of four weeks is allowed for the Attorney General of the United Kingdom or the Counsel General of the Welsh Government to refer it or any of its provisions to the Supreme Court of the United Kingdom for a determination as to whether the bill or the provisions in question are within competence. Two of the cases which have already been considered arose from references of this sort by the Attorney General. *Re Local Government Byelaws (Wales) Bill* was a reference on the basis that the Assembly lacked the competence to remove a Minister of the Crown function without consent, while the challenge in *Re Agricultural Sector (Wales) Bill* was on the basis that the Assembly had legislated in relation to a subject which was not devolved, so that there was no subject-matter competence. 4-80

Both these challenges failed, and the bills in question both went forward for Royal Assent. Had the challenges succeeded, the bills could have been referred back to the Assembly for reconsideration, thus giving an opportunity to bring the provisions within competence if that were possible. Following such a reconsideration, the bill as amended could again be passed, but there would be a further opportunity for either law officer to refer the amended bill as passed to the Supreme Court once again. Those responsible for amending the bill's provisions would in these circumstances need to undertake an analysis of the amendments required to assess whether and how they affected the achievement of the policy goals involved. They would have to reconsider the means chosen for giving effect to their preferred option, or even revisit their choice of that option. 4-81

It is, of course, possible for the lack of competence to go to the very heart of the bill's purposes, making it in practice impossible to rectify the defects. In 4-82

[76] See above, §§3-16–3-20.

such a situation, the bill – albeit having been passed by the Assembly – will fail to become law. This is what occurred with the Recovery of Medical Costs for Asbestos Diseases (Wales) Bill. The bill had sought to allow the Welsh Ministers to recover from liable employers and their insurers the cost of treating asbestos diseases suffered by former employees, on the basis that the Assembly had subject-matter competence in relation to 'Organisation and funding of national health service'. The majority of the Supreme Court did not consider that the bill's provisions could be interpreted so as to relate to this subject, even if the subject was interpreted so as to permit the raising of funds as opposed to the allocation of funding.[77]

4-83 In deciding whether the bill's provisions were within the Assembly's competence, the Supreme Court might be faced with alternative interpretations of provisions, according to some of which the provisions would be within competence and according to others not. In such an eventuality, the Government of Wales Act requires the Court to adopt the interpretation which is sufficiently narrow to bring the bill within competence.[78] No reconsideration by the Assembly is needed in such a case, but those responsible for the policy would still need to analyse the outcome and assess whether the restrictive interpretation imposed affected the likelihood of the policy goals being achieved.

4-84 It is open to the Attorney General and the Counsel General to notify the Presiding Officer that they have no intention to make a reference of this kind, in which case a bill can proceed to Royal Assent without needing to wait for the expiry of the four-week period.

4-85 It may be thought odd that the Counsel General should wish to challenge the competence of the Assembly to enact provisions. However, it should be remembered that not all legislative proposals come from the government, and that a government without a majority in the Assembly cannot necessarily prevent non-government bills from being passed. It is also the case that, if there is a genuine doubt as to whether provisions are within competence even if they are believed to be so, the Counsel General may well deem it wise to resolve the doubt before the bill becomes law, so as not to risk subsequent challenge before the courts even after Royal Assent. This is what motivated the Counsel General to refer the Recovery of Medical Costs for Asbestos Related Diseases (Wales) Bill to the Supreme Court.

After Royal Assent

4-86 Challenges to the competence of the Assembly to have enacted legislation are possible even after a bill has received Royal Assent. Such challenges constitute one kind of 'devolution issue', the determination of which is governed by Schedule 9 to the

[77] See *Recovery of Medical Costs for Asbestos Diseases (Wales) Bill: Reference by the Counsel General for Wales* [2015] UKSC 3, at ¶¶11–34 *per* Lord Mance. The minority (Lord Thomas of Cwmgiedd LCJ and Lady Hale) dissented from this view: see ibid., ¶¶82–83 *per* Lord Thomas.

[78] GoWA 2006, s. 154.

2006 Act. That schedule makes provision for the resolution of Welsh devolution issues before the courts of England and Wales, Scotland and Northern Ireland.

Any person may raise a devolution issue in the courts or in tribunals provided that he or she is involved in proceedings before them, whether as a claimant or a defendant. Devolution issues can be raised in either criminal or civil proceedings, civil proceedings being defined for these purposes as any proceedings which are not criminal. The courts, however, may choose to ignore issues that are raised frivolously or vexatiously, thus preventing the processes being used to protract or delay litigation.

If a devolution issue is raised in civil proceedings before a magistrates' court, 4-87 the court may refer it to the High Court for determination. If the issue is raised in the course of litigation before a County Court or the High Court, it can be referred to the Court of Appeal for determination, and if it is raised in the Court of Appeal, it can be referred to the Supreme Court for decision. Issues which have been determined by the High Court on the reference of a magistrates' court, or by the Court of Appeal from a County Court or the High Court, are subject to the possibility of appeal to the Supreme Court. This ensures that the highest court in the land is always ultimately the arbiter of questions regarding the Assembly's legislative competence. Further, both the Attorney General and the Counsel General must be notified of any devolution issue which arises in litigation and both have a right to become parties to those proceedings. It is then open to either to require that the devolution issue be referred directly to the Supreme Court for decision, and either can indeed forward devolution issues to the Supreme Court for determination even if they have arisen other than in the course of litigation.

Devolution issues which arise in tribunals must be referred to the Court of 4-88 Appeal if the tribunal is one from which no appeal lies, and where the tribunal is one from which an appeal is possible, the issue can be, but need not be, referred to the Court of Appeal.

In criminal proceedings, a similar set of provisions operates. A devolution issue 4-89 arising in a magistrates' court can be forwarded to the High Court for decision, while one arising in the Crown Court can be forwarded to the Court of Appeal. In both cases, a further appeal is possible to the Supreme Court, and if a devolution issue arises in criminal proceedings before the Court of Appeal it can be forwarded to the Supreme Court. Again, as with civil proceedings, the Attorney General or the Counsel General must be notified of such litigation and may become parties to it, being then able to require the immediate transfer of the devolution issue to the Supreme Court for determination.

There is no time limit following the enactment of Assembly legislation beyond 4-90 which such challenges may not be brought. Assembly Acts therefore are vulnerable to such challenges for as long as they remain law. This raises the spectre of Assembly Act provisions being found to be outside competence a considerable time after their enactment, with the consequence that their being declared invalid may have severe financial and other consequences for those who have in the meantime relied upon their validity, including the government and other public bodies, as well as ordinary citizens. Mindful of the problems that might arise, the 2006 Act gives the courts a discretion to remove or limit the retrospective effect of a determination that provisions were outside competence, or to suspend the coming into effect of a judgment to allow for the defects to be corrected. It must, however, be emphasized that the courts are not bound to do this, and have to take into account the possible adverse effects of such a course upon persons not before them as parties to the proceedings.[79]

4-91 Given the vulnerability of Assembly Act provisions to subsequent challenge by the citizen, one should not be surprised that the law officers may choose to raise any doubts by reference to the Supreme Court before a bill goes for Royal Assent. The Counsel General has indeed done this in *Re Recovery of Medical Costs for Asbestos Diseases (Wales) Bill*.[80]

SECRETARY OF STATE INTERVENTION

4-92 The grounds upon which the Attorney General or the Counsel General may refer an Assembly bill to the Supreme Court, and the grounds upon which a citizen may in legal proceedings raise the Assembly's legislative competence as a devolution issue, are legal in nature. The basis is not that the challenger disagrees with what the Assembly has done, but that he or she believes that, in doing it, the Assembly has exceeded its lawful powers. The challenge is a legal challenge to competence.

4-93 However, even if the bill passed by the Assembly is clearly within its legislative competence, it can still be prevented from proceeding to Royal Assent by means of an intervention by the Secretary of State under section 114 of the 2006 Act. The power to intervene is not limited to the Secretary of State for Wales; any one of Her Majesty's principal secretaries of state may exercise it.[81] Like the powers of the Attorney General and the Counsel General to refer provisions to the Supreme Court, the power of the Secretary of State to intervene must be exercised within a four-week period of the bill being passed by the Assembly, and notification by

[79] GoWA 2006, s. 153.

[80] Argued before the Supreme Court in May 2014, but for which no judgment was handed down until February 2015. The Counsel General's letter explaining his reference, stated:

> I am aware that bodies representing the insurance industry have consistently disputed the Assembly's competence to pass this Bill. I am of the view that this Bill is within the competence of this Assembly. I consider, however, it is appropriate in all the circumstances of this case, and in the public interest, to have the issue of the competence of this Bill clearly resolved before the Bill comes into force. I have therefore decided to make a reference to the Supreme Court to ensure this matter is put beyond doubt.

The full text of the Counsel General's letter can be seen on the Assembly website: *http://www.senedd.assembly.wales/documents/s22720/Response%20from%20the%20Counsel%20General.pdf*.

[81] This is the meaning of *Secretary of State* which applies according to the Interpretation Act 1978 unless a contrary intention has been expressed.

the Secretary of State that no such intervention is to occur brings the period to an immediate close.

In order to exercise this power, the Secretary of State must have reasonable grounds to believe either that the provisions will have an adverse effect on a matter which is not devolved, or that they may have an adverse effect on the operation of the law as it applies in England, or that they might be incompatible with the UK's international treaty obligations or the interests of defence or national security.[82] If the Secretary of State has reasonable grounds for such a belief, he or she may lay an order in the form of a statutory instrument before both Houses of Parliament, identifying the bill and its relevant provisions and stating the reasons for his or her belief, and prohibiting it from being forwarded for Royal Assent. If neither House of Parliament resolves to annul the order, it is made and the bill is stopped from becoming law. 4-94

It is important to emphasize that this process is not concerned with questions of legislative competence. It is a mechanism by which the UK government can stop a bill from being enacted even though it is within the Assembly's powers. Given that the 2006 Act requires the Secretary of State to have reasonable grounds for his or her belief, such an order could be challenged before the courts by judicial review, but the courts would be concerned solely with the legality, as opposed to the merits, of the Secretary of State's actions.[83] Further, the statutory instrument containing the order is subject to the negative, not the affirmative, procedure in Parliament, so that it takes effect unless action is taken in either the Commons or the Lords to annul it. If the UK government is able to mobilize a majority in the Commons, it is very unlikely therefore that the order will be annulled. 4-95

Putting aside the issues of international treaty obligations, defence and national security, no similar power is given to the Secretary of State under the devolution settlements for Scotland or Northern Ireland. There have been calls for its removal.[84] Nevertheless, while it remains in place, those who are promoting legislation 4-96

[82] Prior to 1 April 2018, the Secretary of State could also intervene on the reasonable belief that provisions could have a serious adverse impact on water resources, water supply or water quality in England. This ground for intervention has been removed by the Wales Act 2017, s. 52. Concerns regarding cross-border water issues are now dealt with under the Intergovernmental Protocol on Water Resources, Water Supply and Water Quality required by Wales Act 2017, s. 50, and the duty placed by s. 51 upon the Welsh Ministers to have regard to the interests of consumers in England when exercising their functions relating to water resources, water supply or water quality, and upon the Secretary of State to have regard to the interests of consumers in Wales when exercising his functions in that regard. The Secretary of State's power of intervention ceased when The Wales Act 2017 (Commencement No. 4) Regulations 2017 (SI 2017 No. 1179 (C. 111)) reg. 3(k) made under s. 71(4) brought s. 52 into force.

[83] This raises the vexed question of whether the courts can question the reasonableness of such a belief if it is not manifestly unreasonable.

[84] This was recommended in the second report of the Silk Commission – *Empowerment and Responsibility: Legislative Powers to Strengthen Wales / Grymuso a Chyfrifoldeb: Pwerau deddfwriaethol i gryfhau Cymru* (Commission on Devolution in Wales, 2014), 13.3.14 and recommendation R51 c.

before the Assembly need to be aware of its existence and, if possible, would do well to canvas the views of the UK government regarding proposals that might fall foul of the power's exercise. In this instance, unlike referrals to the Supreme Court, there is no argument that can be won over the Secretary of State's views. Provided the Secretary of State can show a reasonable belief, and unless a majority in either the Commons or the Lords can be mobilized against him, the cause is lost. If the power is exercised successfully, then the bill will return to the Assembly for reconsideration, meaning that, if it is to proceed successfully to Royal Assent thereafter, those promoting it will have to be ready to make the changes needed to prevent further intervention while still seeking to deliver on the policy goals intended.[85]

4-97 It should be noted that this power could be exercised during a four-week period commencing with a determination by the Supreme Court that a bill's provisions were within the Assembly's legislative competence, thus allowing the bill to be challenged first on the grounds of its legality and, failing the success of that route, by means of political intervention. Opponents of a bill within the UK government therefore have, in effect, two bites at the cherry.[86]

Having decided to proceed by introducing a bill into the National Assembly and having determined that the Assembly has the requisite legislative competence, it will now be necessary to pursue the adopted plan of action by expressing the relevant proposals in the form of legislative provisions. By whom this is to be done and how it is best done form the next topics for discussion.

[85] Were this power to be used in the run up to an Assembly general election, it could conceivably cause a bill to fall for want of time for its reconsideration. A late Supreme Court reference could have the same effect.

[86] In *Re Agricultural Sector (Wales) Bill*, the Counsel General responded to the Attorney General's argument that the Assembly was not intended to have power to make a patchwork quilt of employment law in the United Kingdom by pointing out that it was the Secretary of State's power of intervention which was meant to prevent undesirable consequences of that nature from arising – an appropriate but perilous *riposte* given the survival of the opportunity to intervene for four weeks following a verdict in favour of the Assembly.

Chapter 5

People and Preparation

Attention so far has been firmly fixed on the principles and practices needed to produce sound policy and good legislation. Little has been said about the people who undertake this work and their organization. This chapter serves to address that deficit. 5-01

THE BILL TEAM: ITS COMPOSITION AND FUNCTIONS

Introduction

No two bills are precisely alike in respect of their policy development, legislative development or handling issues, and for the same reason no two bill teams can be precisely the same. If a bill team is composed by slavishly adhering to the model that has been used successfully on any other bill, it will necessarily fail to perform its functions in the optimal way. As with all aspects of legislation, the only rule of legislative preparation and drafting is that there are no rules of legislative preparation and drafting. 5-02

No attempt will therefore be made to describe what an ideal bill team should look like, since there is no such thing. Instead, some of the principal issues to be considered in determining the composition of a bill team will be examined, by reference to the principal functions which it is typically required to perform.

Bill team manager

Having said that there are no fixed truths about the composition of the bill team, there is arguably one: a bill team requires a single bill manager, and that person is without doubt the single most important person for determining whether a bill will be enacted in an efficient and effective manner and form or not. 5-03

It is ironic that very often the bill team manager is one of the most junior officials involved in the preparation of a bill – ironic, but perfectly satisfactory. Seniority is not required, nor, oddly enough, is extensive experience of working on other bill teams. The attributes required are energy, perspicacity, efficiency, humility and a sense of humour. A bill manager who lacks any of these attributes is unlikely to be able to perform successfully. 5-04

The bill manager is not required to know anything about the policy or legislative intent of the bill, and it can be a positive disadvantage for the bill manager to have too much interest in these areas, or to be distracted from his or her essential administrative function by knowledge of and interest in the intricate details of the policy and execution. An intelligent bill manager will inevitably pick up a great deal about the policy and law surrounding the bill as it develops: but that will be a useful by-product that she or he will be able to deploy to good effect. It is not an initial requirement. 5-05

5-06 The bill team manager is essentially a coordinator. Some unwisely regard the function of coordination as an inexpert and easy function that can be carried out by anybody employed to do it, and that requires neither expertise nor seniority in any sense. That is why bill team managers have traditionally been appointed from junior ranks. It is also why the first job of bill team managers is to attract and maintain the respect of all their colleagues, both those directly and indirectly involved in the bill. Senior officials and ministers will often begin by assuming that the bill team manager is a junior functionary of no significant importance who is there to be ordered around in a peremptory fashion and who is there to follow rather than to lead. Unhappily, if a bad choice is made of bill team manager this will turn out to be a self-fulfilling prophecy, and the bill team manager will fail to control and the bill will suffer as a result. One of the traditional features of the United Kingdom Civil Service has been to provide a fertile spawning ground for junior officials in which they are able to acquire authority and exert increasing influence from a relatively junior position. This is perhaps no more true of any civil service position than it is true of the bill team manager. By the end of the process, particularly on a lengthy bill, from a relatively junior position the bill team manager will have acquired the respect of every member of the team and, 'I'll have to check with X' will be the constant refrain of senior officials, policy officials, Ministers, business managers and even the drafter of the legislation. The person drafting the bill – Parliamentary Counsel in the UK and Legislative Counsel in Wales – rightly considers himself or herself the driver of the bill: but a good bill team manager is the navigator, and the drafter will quickly learn to consult him or her at all stages and to lean as heavily on them as they have shown the will and ability to bear.

5-07 A bill is a project. That is to say, simply, that it is a lengthy process with a large number of stages through which it *must* pass and many stages through which it *may* pass, all with a single clearly defined aim. To that extent, therefore, the job of the bill team manager is project management. A bill team manager who wishes to acquire formal training for the task will derive greater benefit from formal training in time management and project management than from theoretical discussions about the nature of a bill and the process of its development. Of course, she or he will need to become familiar with the basics of the legislative process, but if they have the necessary energy and intellect they will be able to acquire that knowledge on the job, from published materials and with the necessary rapidity. Books and papers will inform them and prepare them to deal with the intricacies of legislative management, but they will not prepare them for the speed of thought required to react to the contingencies that will arise along the way and to constantly redesign the project template to react to changing events. Except in the case of the most excruciatingly boring bill that one can imagine, no bill runs according to plan: and the value of a bill team manager therefore lies less in the ability to plan than in the ability to change plans in midstream without losing overall course and direction.

5-08 If one had to write a job description for the bill team manager it would be something along the following lines: to coordinate the functions of all other officials involved in the preparation of the bill, to facilitate efficient communication between them, and to set, monitor and control delivery targets for each stage of the process in consultation with the appropriate officials.

Size of team

With the exception of the bill team manager the composition of the bill team will, for the reasons explained above, be specific to each bill. In size, in particular, it can and should vary enormously. 5-09

At one extreme, for a short and necessarily uncontroversial law reform measure expected to be welcomed by all parties and exposing no significant flank for amendment, and where the policy is and requires to be closely based on a report of an external organization such as the Law Commission or some other piece of published work, the bill team might consist of no more than four persons, each of whom might be giving only a very small part of their professional attention to that particular bill. 5-10

The personnel involved in this extreme case would be: the bill team manager, the policy lead, the departmental lawyer and the drafter. All other functions would be, in effect, 'contracted out' to relevant departmental officials, including at the stage of navigating through the legislature. 5-11

Even in this extreme case of a small bill and a corresponding small bill team, however, there is an advantage in having these four functions identified, ring-fenced and respected. It is still important to have someone whose function is to be responsible for the delivery of the project and its effective timetabling, even if that person is giving only an hour or two a week of their professional attention to that function. 5-12

It is for this reason, indeed, that the concept of the bill team is relevant not only to the production of Acts of Parliament or of the National Assembly. A wise department dealing with a statutory instrument of any significant length or importance establishes a team to handle it that is indistinguishable from a traditional bill team for handling a bill: indeed, as delegated legislation becomes responsible for a larger and larger share of the overall body of enacted law, there are many statutory instruments which cover precisely the same ground, and present precisely the same difficulties (including those of handling and process) as are required to be addressed by a bill team handling a bill. In particular, the growth of the formal super-affirmative resolution procedure for the handling of certain sensitive instruments,[1] and the greater use of consultation on one or more drafts of the instruments with a view to inviting comments, means that even in respect of amendments – which were always the key difference between primary and secondary legislation – the timing and handling considerations may be virtually indistinguishable. 5-13

At the other end of the spectrum from the four person mini-bill team, a team established to deal with a bill that is expected to run to two hundred or more clauses and deal with perhaps five or six distinct policy areas, and which is expected to attract significant difficulties of content and handling at all stages, might require a 5-14

[1] See below, §§8-16–8-18.

bill team of anything between twenty and thirty full-time officials. That this scale of resources is rarely allocated is just one of the reasons why so much legislation is produced in bad form, outside the desired timetable and having met undesirable and unnecessary complications along the way. A bill team that is constantly racing to catch up with itself to remedy errors or supply omissions in the original timetable will simply not be able to control the policy development of the bill and to steer it through the legislature in an efficient and effective way.

5-15 While it is pointless to try to describe the variety of numbers and natures of rôles that might be appropriate for a large bill team of this kind, it may be worth stating the obvious point that if the one fixed point of all bill teams is the bill team manager, and if her or his job is essentially a project management function, then a bill team of this kind is likely to require at least one assistant bill team manager whose job will be to support the project management functions of the bill team manager. In Wales, the bill manager's functions have come to be shared with a bill project board, and the somewhat inelegantly termed 'Senior Responsible Owner'.

5-16 Without trying to describe exactly what rôles might be found on a bill team that is appropriate for any particular bill, it may be helpful to adumbrate the functions that, in one form or another, they will have to allocate amongst themselves.

Policy officials

5-17 In terms of policy, the rôle of a bill team is distinctly problematic. On the one hand, there is no reason to expect that the members of the bill team will be experts in the substantive policy with which the bill deals. And there is every reason to expect that they will not be. Indeed, as in the case for the bill team manager, too great a knowledge of or interest in the details of the policy can lead to distraction from the efficient and effective delivery of the bill project. On the other hand, the bill team is required to have effective policy capability for two reasons.

5-18 First, there are few decisions about the development and handling of the bill that can be taken effectively without due consideration of the policy aims and objectives and, in particular, without a degree of practical understanding of how the policy will be operated, implemented and enforced once the bill receives Royal Assent. Indeed, one of the many mistakes commonly made by politicians and officials about bills is to regard them as a self-contained game the purpose of which is to achieve Royal Assent, at which point one goes off to find some other new toys to play with. In one sense it is salutary for the bill team constantly to remind themselves that there is no such thing as a bill, merely an incipient law; and its suitability and success must be tested at every stage of the way by reference to whether it is likely to be able to be made to work after Royal Assent in a manner that achieves its original policy objectives. So a degree of policy expertise, or at least understanding, is inseparable from the functions of an effective bill team.

5-19 The second, and in many ways yet more problematic, reason why a bill team requires a degree of policy expertise is that in almost every case the policy of a bill requires to be developed and refined at any or all of the stages from initial determination of the substance of the bill to the very last stages of its passage through the legislature (or beyond, in the case of a bill that requires significant commencement and transitional activity, as most bills of any size do). This aspect of the bill team's experience means that as well as understanding the policy they need to have the ability and authority to participate in its development.

What is required here is generally a fine balance between the rôle of the bill team and the rôle of the permanent policy owners within the relevant department, whose job it is to work permanently on the policy in question as opposed to those who may have been recruited specifically to work on the bill. In achieving this balance between these two constituencies, two temptations need to be avoided. 5-20

First, it is tempting for an overbearing bill team to take delivery of the policy and in effect to instruct the permanent owners to surrender it to the bill team for the duration of the bill, to react passively to requests for information or even clearance during the development of the policy and passage of the bill, and to prepare to receive back the finished product on Royal Assent and to take it forward. Apart from inevitably causing resentment and an attitude of leaving the bill team to make as big a mess as they feel inclined of the policy, this is not an effective way of maximizing the skills and deploying the experience of all those involved in the preparation of the bill. It can lead to serious inefficiencies from both sides and frequently result in significant misunderstandings that have the potential to undermine the entire fabric of the legislation. 5-21

The other temptation to be avoided is for the bill team to see themselves as a mere post-box passing messages between Ministers, politicians and others on the one side, and the permanent policy team on the other. This again leads to inefficiencies and fails to deploy each person's potential contribution to the process in the best possible way. In particular, while it is disastrous for handling decisions to be taken in ignorance of their policy implications, it is equally disastrous for policy decisions to be taken without a full understanding of the political and legislative context of the bill that is the vehicle for achieving them. 5-22

What is therefore required is a dialogue, in the process of which, as in the case of all the functions involved in the bill team, each participant understands and respects the contribution of each other participant. The permanent policy team needs to understand that the policy representatives on the bill team are a delivery mechanism by which their legislative objectives can be achieved, if they work with them to ensure that the policy is properly developed, understood, communicated and encapsulated in the legislation. The policy components of the bill team need to remember that they are temporary visitors in this particular policy area (even if in their pre-bill team capacity they had considerable knowledge and experience of the policy area) and that while they have and need to have considerable power during their period of occupation of the field, they fail to respect the permanent occupiers at their peril. They are essentially intelligent and empowered emissaries of the permanent policy officials and should see themselves in that representative capacity. With both sides respecting each other's rôles in this way, an efficient and effective dialogue can be established that is capable of resolving the most seemingly 5-23 intractable of substantive or procedural problems in a timely fashion so as to avoid derailing the delivery of the project as a whole.

Lawyers

5-24 In addition to the policy team the bill team will include one or more lawyers, whose rôle is distinct from that of the drafter.

5-25 The purpose of the lawyer on the team is sometimes perceived as being primarily to act as a conduit between the policy officials and the legislative drafter. In the cases of some bills, that is the most important function of the lawyer, and sometimes it is almost the only useful thing that she or he can bring to the process. But that is very rare. In the case of most bills, the lawyer exercises a degree of supervision and control over the broadest effect of the legislation of a kind that neither the policy officials nor the legislative drafter are able to exert.

5-26 In particular, the lawyer is aware of the relevant surrounding law that will affect, shape and reflect the operation of the legislation once enacted, in a way that even a thoroughly conscientious legislative drafter is unable to achieve. Apart from having oversight of the relevant statutory law, including subordinate legislation and quasi-legislation, the lawyer on the team will be thoroughly aware of relevant case law, and of the availability and practicability of traditional and other remedies in the area. Although some of this may be adumbrated to the legislative drafter in the course of the instructions to draft, there will inevitably be more than can sensibly be communicated to or absorbed by the drafter.

5-27 So although there is sometimes a temptation to regard the legal member or members of the team as something of a junior adjunct to the parliamentary drafter, it is generally a mistake for them to see themselves in that light or for others to assign that rôle to them. In Wales in particular, the lawyer will have to advise as to whether the proposals are within the legislative competence of the Assembly, an issue on which the advice of legislative counsel drafting the bill will also be important given their continual involvement in the work of legislation.

5-28 The legal adviser's rôle on a bill is also of crucial importance in another distinct and contingent way. Every bill of any length confers a range of powers to make subordinate legislation: although the balance between primary and secondary legislation is considered elsewhere,[2] and although it is certainly arguable that the balance of power has swung much too far towards the executive in the form of powers to supplement primary legislation by subordinate legislation, a degree of delegation is inevitable in the light of the complexity of modern legislation and the contexts within which it is required to operate within the real world. The legal member of the team should be keeping an eye not only on the proper division of material between primary and secondary legislation, as to which he or she should liaise with the legislative drafter who will also have a view, but they should be in effect preparing to exercise the delegated powers by drafting the subordinate legislation

[2] See above, §§3-61–3-73.

in due course. Whether or not it is actually the individual legal official on the bill team who will be personally responsible for doing that drafting, they should see themselves as in effect the representative of the ultimate drafter of the secondary legislation, ensuring that the *vires* are sufficient, the constraints properly expressed, and the nature and objectives of the delegation sufficiently clear to ensure that it can be drafted efficiently and effectively and is likely to be upheld by the courts in the case of challenge. As with the granting of executive functions generally, the risks of possible judicial review should be borne in mind when making choices.

Administrative functions

The largest class of functions of the bill team can be classified simply as administrative. That covers, of course, a multitude of different activities, the nature and extent of which will vary widely between bills. 5-29

Under the control of the bill team manager, the administrative team will be responsible for preparing, adjusting and monitoring the timetabling of each step of the bill's process. If timing is the secret of good acting, it is certainly the secret of good legislating. It can be taken as axiomatic that nobody will have sufficient time to perform their functions on a bill in the ideal way. Leaving aside the pressures of modern politics, it is simply the case that each part of the legislative process could be polished and perfected *ad infinitum*, and a certain feeling of time pressure is necessary to ensure that the best is not allowed to become the enemy of the good. 5-30

The timetabling function, therefore, has to start from the assumption that nobody will have quite as much time as they would like for the performance of their functions; and it must proceed to make as fair and sensible an apportionment of the inadequate amount of time available as possible. Extra time for developing the instructions and consulting is useless if the result is that the drafter has no time to absorb the results of the consultation process or the details of the instructions. Equally, allowing the drafter the luxury of extra time to consider the instructions will achieve nothing if sufficient time has not been given for the preparation of the instructions. It is a tricky balance, and perhaps here more than anywhere else experience of other legislation projects comes into its own. 5-31

In the course of the administrative function of the bill team one of the most time-consuming tasks will be that of preparing briefing. For the objective onlooker this can also often be one of the most agonizing experiences, as one witnesses vast amounts of time being spent on preparing briefing that everybody knows will never be read, leaving crucial briefing to be prepared as a matter of haste, sometimes by frantic scribbling at the back of the committee room itself. Manuals of legislative practice have something to blame for this. bill teams will frequently find examples and templates of notes on amendments produced in the context of other bills, and will be tempted to follow slavishly with the production of those notes for each amendment that is tabled or proposed to be tabled. In the context of Westminster bills, for example, one frequently observes quite literally full lever arch files of notes on amendments being prepared for material that is bound to be discussed 5-32 after the guillotine has come down under a programme motion and will therefore not be debated at all. Should earlier proceedings on the bill proceed unexpectedly rapidly, it is probable that the Minister will be able to make a reasonable fist of the amendments by reference to pre-existing explanatory materials. One of the key objectives of the bill team manager ought to be to ensure that the precious time of lawyers and administrators on the bill team is used only to good effect, and that material that is certain or likely to be unnecessary is not allowed to occupy time simply in order to satisfy precedent.

5-33 The final and largest part of the administrative functions of the bill team can be categorized simply as communication. Open and effective communication is the essence of good legislating. And misunderstandings are the most common cause of poor legislation. The bill team members need to ensure that they communicate effectively amongst themselves; they need to keep open effective channels of communication with all parts of the department outside the bill team, and with other government departments, whether within the Welsh Government, within Whitehall or, where appropriate, between the two. Moreover, they need to acquire rapidly a reputation for welcoming communication from outside, whether from politicians, from stakeholders and other interest groups, or simply from interested citizens. Time spent in satisfying interested parties that their concerns have been understood and, so far as possible within the constraints of achieving the policy, met in an appropriate way, will never be wasted. It will smooth the passage of the bill, and it is likely greatly to facilitate the smooth implementation of the bill once it is enacted.

5-34 In relation to amendments,[3] for example, it is agonizing to watch the game played where a non-government member tables an amendment, and the bill team proceed to guess as to what she or he is intending to suggest by way of an improvement or correction of the bill, and to brief the Minister accordingly. Subject to particular political sensitivities or departmental protocols, where there is any doubt it makes better sense to find out what the member has in mind by contacting their office and enquiring. In particular, where an amendment is a probing amendment designed to elicit information or to invite an assurance that a particular matter is dealt with by the bill or will be dealt with in other ways, advance notice of the point will enable the Minister to give a satisfactory reply on the record, which will both satisfy the member concerned and ensure that the resulting legislation is fully fit for the purpose for which it is intended.

PERSONS WITH AN INTEREST IN LEGISLATION

5-35 It is tempting for politicians and civil servants alike to regard a bill as a private game played for their own purposes, or at least played for public purposes but according

[3] As will be discussed below, §§7-40–7-62, the text of a bill is open to amendment by the legislature in the course of deliberation upon it.

to their own private rules. This is part of a wider temptation to think of a bill as a process that serves a purpose in itself, beginning when it is introduced into the legislature and ending with Royal Assent. A wise bill team constantly reminds itself and Ministers that Royal Assent is not the end of the process but the beginning, the moment at which a new law is imposed upon the world. The success or failure of that law will depend upon the way in which it is treated by those individual and commercial citizen stakeholders whose activities it concerns. Once one reminds oneself of that truism, it becomes equally obvious that the earlier and more thorough the engagement of those stakeholders in the preparation of the law, the more likely they are both to wish, and to be able to ensure, that it achieves its purpose.

In the modern world of government this has become associated with the mod- 5-36
ern phenomenon of consultation. Consultation as practised within government today, however, is often less about allowing policy and law to be informed by stakeholders and more about being able to assert that a stated proportion of stakeholders support a particular proposal. The constant streams of consultations that emanate from all arms of central, devolved and local government are rarely about asking open questions with a view to engaging the expertise and knowledge of stakeholders, and much more about conducting, in effect, mini referenda that will enable Ministers and others to cite a degree of support for what they propose to do. This may or may not be consultation as it is known within modern government; but it is certainly not effective stakeholder engagement in moving from policy proposals to effective legislative provisions and should not be confused with it.

Assembly committees have a significant advantage over public bill committees 5-37
in Westminster, in that the relevant subject committee of the Assembly follows a legislative proposal from its earliest stages before even draft legislation, all the way through to its passage through the Assembly.[4] Like public bill committees in Westminster, Assembly committees take evidence from interested parties, and this continuity enables them to engage stakeholders at a number of different points during the process. That is clearly one form of helpful engagement: but it is far too late to influence the fundamental structure and approach of the legislation. What is required is that stakeholders should be involved in the process of devising methods by which the policy objectives are to be converted into effective law.

In one sense, this is extremely easy to achieve. Representative bodies of all 5-38
kinds are falling over themselves to be of assistance to departments, bill teams and Assembly committees. The problem is not so much how to obtain help as how to filter out from all the help offered and available the help which is most likely to be useful.

It is sometimes assumed within government that the search for the help that 5-39
is most likely to be useful involves searching for independent parties who are most likely to give disinterested advice. This is, however, not likely to be the most useful approach. Truly independent bodies may be able to give sensible guesses as to how a particular proposed law will impact on particular sectors of society, but civil servants

[4] See below, §§7-23–7-24 and n. 14.

could do that to a greater or lesser extent themselves. What is wanted is not guesses but accurate predictions based on past experience and personal knowledge of the sector concerned. Independence and lack of interest are useful in determining policy, but they are neither necessary nor desirable when framing law to give effect to policy in the most effective and efficient way. In other words, there is nothing wrong with people with a clear interest in proposed legislation being involved in its preparation, and there are distinct advantages in that. What is wrong, is giving preferential treatment to particular stakeholders. So the bill team preparing a list of those to consult and engage in a positive manner in the preparation of legislation should not be looking for independence, but for balance. If legislation is designed to benefit one sector of society by controlling the activities of another, then both of those sectors must be adequately represented in deciding how to frame the law. A consumer protection measure designed to control the activities of estate agents will not work effectively if representative consumer organizations have not been given the opportunity to satisfy themselves that the developing proposals provide a practical solution to the problems previously encountered; but it will also not work effectively if it fails to take account of genuine concerns expressed by estate agents as to how to avoid drowning the commercially useful baby in the regulatory bathwater.

5-40 Traditionally within a Whitehall bill team, directly affected interest groups were held at arm's length. They would come along to standing committees – the precursor of public bill committees – and sit at the back of the public gallery, occasionally scribbling a note or two to backbench members who deigned to notice their existence. Such aloofness is still occasionally encountered within Westminster and Whitehall bill teams and it is, and always has been, gross foolishness. The bill team should ensure that any individuals and representative interest groups who have a significant interest in the proposed legislation have been contacted by the bill team themselves, long before any legislation is introduced into the legislature, and both have been given, and feel that they have been given, ample opportunity to make practical representations about how to make the law fair and effective.

5-41 A particular example of the need for this partnership is in relation to technical provisions in general and, in particular, transitional provisions around commencement of the legislation. The purpose of transitional provisions is to ensure a smooth transition from the old law to the new and to reflect the balance between allowing people necessary time to become acclimatized to new conditions and achieving an appropriately swift implementation of new law. The difference between fair and unfair law often lies in the arrangements made for its transitional implementation.[5]

[5] This is why including such transitional and technical provisions in commencement orders so as to require neither affirmative nor negative procedure with regard to their making is thought inappropriate by bodies such as the National Assembly's Constitutional and Legislative Affairs Committee when scrutinizing bills. The content of such provisions can have important effects on the lives of citizens and therefore deserve a measure of scrutiny from, and either the express or at least the implied consent of, their elected representatives.

For example, legislation that requires in practice the replacement of industrial machinery (for example, because the tolerance levels for effluent or some similar technical issue are changed by the law) needs to be designed so that it reflects the standard actuarial write-down arrangements of existing industrial machinery. Otherwise, those who happen to have changed their machinery relatively recently are significantly disadvantaged by the need to change it again, while those who happen to be about to change it in the ordinary course of events, receive, in effect, a free gift in terms of a competitive advantage against those other members of the same sector. A bill team that wishes to show regard for fairness in the implementation of the law will therefore engage the industry on the matter of transitional provisions at a very early stage. And by doing that, and being seen to be doing that, the industry as a whole becomes committed to the implementation of the new law, rather than beginning the new regime with a sense of injustice that encourages them to exploit any opportunities for circumvention.

Ample and early engagement with stakeholders also means that Ministers 5-42 can be accurately briefed as to what issues the industry is likely to raise during the passage of the bill through the Assembly, dealing with matters that it has not proved possible to resolve to the satisfaction of all in the preparation of the legislation. This enables Ministers to draw up an early and balanced strategy on possible concessions and it makes the process of the passage of the legislation through the Assembly altogether more constructive and orderly.

PREPARATION OF INSTRUCTIONS

Introduction

In the preparation of instructions to draft legislation, a number of possible 5-43 approaches can be taken. The traditional method operating in Whitehall in the early part of the twentieth century involved a rigid distinction between the development and analysis of policy and the preparation of instructions to change the law. That approach reflected the understanding of different rôles prevalent at that time, and, perhaps, a general tendency towards rigidity of distinction of rôles within the public service generally.[6]

[6] A tendency in the private sector for a more holistic and collaborative approach towards the deployment of different skills and expertise has not been carried through to the public sector in relation to the preparation of legislation as much as one might have expected from watching the tendency towards the adoption of private sector techniques in other areas of public administration. In particular, it is still noticeable that as a general rule departmental lawyers within Whitehall departments work in close communication, and even cooperation, with their policy counterparts, while maintaining a distinct working environment and a formality of division of rôles that is not commonly encountered in, for example, the in-house counsel rôle in private commerce, except in relation to technical governance matters. While there are variations and exceptions, this distinction of rôles in the public service has tended to preserve the essential formalities of the process of the preparation of instructions for legislation.

5-44 The practice may have its root in the method employed to draft legislation prior to the creation of posts for legislative drafters within the Civil Service towards the end of the nineteenth century. Before that time, instructions were sent to barristers in the Inns of Court to draft legislation, in much the same manner as they would have received instructions in order to commence litigation. The geographical separation of government departments in London from the office of specialist drafters, the Office of Parliamentary Counsel, has probably favoured the continuation of that historical approach. The greater proximity of the drafting offices to the policy departments in the devolved governments has led to a greater willingness to depart from the Whitehall-based precedent, given that neither the historical nor the geographical context is shared. This has been to some extent true of all of the devolved governments, including the Office of Legislative Counsel within the Welsh Government.

5-45 It is still taken as the working presumption from those involved in the preparation of legislation that there will be one or more documents amounting to 'instructions to the legislative drafter', and that this document will be prepared by lawyers with expertise in the substantive area concerned, based on one or more policy documents produced by administrators and other officials with expertise in that area. In one form or another, that model is deployed in the preparation of almost all legislation.[7]

Essence of instructions

5-46 Occasionally, a drafter will try to cut out the middle man by agreeing to draft on the basis of a range of policy documents without the benefit of anything identifiable as instructions to draft. As a general rule, and with the exception of tax law and other highly technical law already mentioned,[8] such experiments have not been noteworthy for conspicuous success.

[7] In Whitehall, there are time-honoured exceptions. It has always been the case, for example, that instructions for the drafting of provisions to be included in the annual Finance Bill are prepared not by departmental lawyers on the instructions of policy officials, but directly by those policy officials and communicated to the legislative drafter. There are obvious practical reasons for this. In areas of extreme technical complexity of which fiscal law is the predominant example, it is not to be expected that departmental lawyers could conveniently become sufficiently familiar with the complexities of the policy to convey them efficiently to the drafter, or at least not without an enormous commitment of resources and an inherent danger of a significant element of misunderstanding and error.

Similarly, there have traditionally been certain exceptions in the other direction, where the departmental lawyer has owned and developed the policy and therefore communicated with the legislative drafter without requiring policy instructions from within the department. A classic example of this was to be found in what was formerly known as the Lord Chancellor's Department, now the Ministry of Justice, where until the 1990s policy was developed in relation to civil procedure and other matters falling within the department's responsibilities by lawyers who were responsible for administering those areas.

[8] See above, n. 7.

Even in relation to subordinate or secondary legislation which is generally drafted by departmental lawyers themselves without the intervention of Parliamentary or Legislative Counsel or other full-time legislative drafters, some form of document is generally produced that endeavours to effect a transition between pure policy and instructions to draft of some kind. And, indeed, it is not unheard of for secondary legislation to be drafted on the basis of formal instructions produced by one departmental lawyer and transmitted to another, or even on the basis of a document produced by one departmental lawyer for his or her own use. The obvious advantage of that step in the case of a combined legal advice and drafting function, is that it allows a transitional document to be produced and circulated for approval internally, or for consultation with external stakeholders, before the drafting process is commenced and therefore before the draft is committed to particular legislative techniques and approaches. 5-47

It is that last concept that identifies the essential function or nature of instructions to draft, irrespective of how formal or informal the process is that leads to its production. 5-48

In moving from the development of policy to the drafting of legislation, one inevitably goes through a number of phases, which are often easier to enumerate in theory than to recognize as having independent and separate existence in practice. A good bill manager wishes to maintain a degree of separation between the documents embodying each of those different phases of policy and legislative development, irrespective of whether the functions involved in their production are separate or shared. This is partly for the purpose of efficient policy and legislative development and rigorous discipline in the application of the different techniques required at the different stages. It is also required or desirable for the purposes of producing an audit trail to explain, record and as necessary justify what is being done or what has been done. While the separation of the performance of these functions runs the risk of discontinuity, the practices it entails are conducive to achieving clarity of thought. 5-49

Development phases

As has been discussed in detail earlier,[9] the policy development phases include more or less distinct components. These include the identification of the fundamental mischief or problem at which the legislation is to be aimed (the social policy making the case for change); the political decisions required to steer officials between alternative and equally or similarly efficient ways of achieving that objective (political policy selecting the preferred option for achieving the desired goal); and the administrative or executive structures that will be deployed in order to give effect to the political decisions for the purposes of addressing the social policy (administrative policy, ensuring that the methods of implementation are identified and serviceable). 5-50

[9] See above, §§2-31–2-71.

5-51 In the same way, within the more legally focused parts of the process, there are at least two distinct stages.

5-52 First, a legal policy stage is required to identify how the law requires to be changed in order to reflect and deliver the social policy objectives identified in the administrative policy. That will require consideration of the law in a wide and inclusive sense. It will require consideration not merely of primary and secondary statute law, but also of relevant principles of common law, the potential application and reach of administrative law and frequently other issues as well (such as issues regarding the prerogative).

5-53 It is important that propositions about the required changes in the law in the widest possible sense are articulated long before the legislative drafter, whether or not the same person as is producing the legal policy document, comes to consider questions of legislative approach and structure. In the same way that consultation on a draft law is not an effective way of consulting on a policy that underpins it, because the skeleton is already too far advanced to admit of the necessary flexibility of attitude and adjustment, so too the lawyer considering the transition from policy development papers into potential legislation needs to start by asking himself or herself questions about the law in its widest and most holistic sense, before beginning to consider questions of legislative structure. Much of the worst law that one sees on the Statute Book is the result of this middle phase having been neglected entirely or undertaken incompetently.

5-54 Indeed, legislative drafters know well the dilemma in which they find themselves when the instructions are either wholly confined to policy proposals and have not been further developed through legal analysis of how the law can best be changed to achieve the desired results, or at the other extreme effectively amount to either draft legislative provisions or instructions on what to draft and how to draft it. In those circumstances, the drafter is torn between the temptation to develop legal policy himself or herself, and thereby lose the objectivity which is one of the key attributes that he or she brings to the process when it works as it should, or to resist that temptation and take the risk that the legislation as drafted will fail properly to reflect the wider legal considerations arising out of the policy objectives.

5-55 One of the few things that departmental lawyers generally remember about the protocol of producing instructions on legislation whether or not they have recently worked on a bill is that in writing to Parliamentary Counsel, one should always send two copies of the instructions (one for counsel and one for his or her junior);[10] and that it is more or less a capital offence to include or suggest a draft at any point in the process of instructing. Good Parliamentary Counsel have frequently pointed out to instructing departments over the years that this rule, which is one of the few rules of legislative preparation that is worth applying reasonably inflexibly, is not based on the *amour propre* of the drafter, or at least it should not be: it is based

[10] The concept of senior counsel working with junior counsel again reflects the influence of methods of working at the bar upon the practice of legislative drafting, harking back to its early history when it was undertaken by barristers at the Inns of Court.

on the simple proposition that the draft is not an effective way of conveying policy objectives to the drafter.

Components of instructions

When the process is carried out appropriately, instructions include the following elements. First, the drafter must be given the social, policy, and political and administrative backgrounds to what is proposed. In other words, the drafter needs to be informed of the case for change, the reasons for the selection of the preferred option and the reasons why particular methods have been chosen as the means to implement the change. This is always important, since readers of legislation including citizens and the court have always necessarily applied a contextual construction to legislation. As judges, and other readers of legislation, become more self-consciously purposive in their approach, inclusion of the background to the legislation in instructions becomes all the more important: the drafter needs to be aware of the considerations that courts and other readers will have in their mind, and will be encouraged to apply, when construing the legislative language. 5-56

After giving the background, which can frequently be most effectively achieved by incorporation of or reference to existing policy documents, the policy objectives identified at the administrative policy stage should be set out in a simple and straightforward form. 5-57

Having established the policy background and the administrative objectives, the instructions are ready to describe the law which is to be affected, and the surrounding statute law and common law that will affect an understanding of those parts of the law that are to be changed. 5-58

Finally, the drafter should be told what changes in that law are desired. Each change should be expressly linked to one of the administrative objectives and the relevant aspects of the social and political backgrounds should be referenced. When the work of writing the instructions has been done well, this final part of instructing the drafter will generally be short and simple. Indeed, if the work has been done by an expert, the legislative drafter will generally be able to work out what he or she is required to do before they come to the part that formally instructs them to do it. 5-59

Public access to instructions

It will be seen from the above that however formal or informal the distinction of rôles between policy-maker, lawyer and drafter is in the particular circumstances of the preparation of a particular piece of legislation, the resulting document that amounts to instructions to draft has the potential to be an enormously valuable record of what was intended to be done, what it was intended to achieve and for what purpose. 5-60

It is therefore to be regretted that this document, a prime source of evidence as to the legislative intention, is not routinely made available to citizens and others who have to understand and apply legislation. 5-61

5-62 In the middle and late twentieth century within the Parliamentary Counsel Office in Whitehall it was generally understood that outside stakeholders with a particular wish to consult instructions to counsel on particular legislation would be allowed to do so; and it was not generally required of enquirers to wait for the application of the thirty-year rule,[11] as it then was. With the exception of particularly sensitive or political pieces of legislation, including commercially sensitive documents such as instructions to draft in relation to provisions designed to counter tax avoidance attempts, an enquirer who could show a legitimate reason for needing to understand the provenance and development of a particular provision would be given access to the instructions.

5-63 One can imagine that nowadays as lawyers and other professionals, and indeed private citizens, become rightly more demanding in their access to and understanding of public administration, there might be resource considerations preventing the continuation of what was once a relatively informal arrangement for the consulting by the public of instructions to counsel. In fact, however, the real reason why this practice has largely diminished, except in relation to documents of antiquity and non-sensitivity, is one other aspect of the way in which the introduction of a freedom of information law in the Freedom of Information Act 2000 has, predictably, reduced the public access to information of various kinds. Applications to see instructions addressed to the Parliamentary Counsel Office in Whitehall today, even if framed as informal requests to consult papers, are treated as formal applications under the Freedom of Information Act and are routinely refused on grounds that they engage the legal advice exceptions.

5-64 The reality is, however, that instructions to counsel very rarely contain anything significant in the way of legal advice within government and on occasions where they do this could easily be removed or redacted. Indeed, if there were a real desire to enhance the freedom of information and to ensure that professionals and others have ready access to the legislative intent, instructions could be prepared in such a way as to ensure that content that could reasonably be perceived or described as internal government legal advice could be isolated in a separate part of the instructions that could readily be removed when making them available for inspection on application.

THE STRUCTURE OF A LEGISLATIVE PROPOSAL

5-65 The earlier passages on what instructions are required to provide should make it reasonably clear what is expected in the way of the structure of a legislative proposal.

5-66 In essence, the legislative proposal consists of simply two propositions: what the law presently is; and what the law is to become.

[11] This was the rule that government papers were not usually released for public inspection until thirty years had passed from the date of their creation. After that length of time, they became available to the public at the Public Record Office, now the National Archives.

While everything else discussed is essential in preparing an orderly proposal, providing the necessary background to enable it to be fashioned effectively and providing the necessary involvement of stakeholders to ensure that it achieves what is intended in terms of social policy, there is a great deal to be said for the bill team and others constantly reminding themselves of what the core legislative proposal is, in terms of those two factors. 5-67

In the case of green field legislation, the answer to the question what is the law now may simply be that there is no law at present. Where an unregulated field is to be regulated, the existing law is *laissez faire*, subject to any relevant propositions of general application, and the new law is regulation. In most cases, however, there is already a certain amount of law in the field which it is desired to regulate; provided the bill team keep their eye firmly on the core transition from the previous propositions to the new propositions of law, they will not go far wrong. While they constantly need to refer back to the social policy documents, the background documents and representations made by relevant stakeholders, these must always be seen in the light of commentaries and guidance relating to achievement of the core legislative proposals moving from the old law to the new. 5-68

In essence, the bill manager will wish to report to Ministers at the end of the process that the mission has been accomplished in the sense that the key legislative proposal of moving from the old law as stated to the new law as stated has been achieved, in a manner which takes account of representations received and the social policy background and purposes. 5-69

RESPONDING CONSTRUCTIVELY TO DRAFTS

Members of a bill team can make two kinds of mistake when it comes to dealing with the draft produced and circulated by the legislative drafter. The first mistake is to treat them with an extremity of deference and to assume that the drafter not only must be right about all matters of law and legislative technicality, but must also have a monopoly of wisdom in relation to matters of style and presentation. The second mistake is to assume that the drafter, being a relative outsider in terms both of policy and political strategy and presentation, has no appreciation for the necessary nuances and subtleties of language required in the context and that the entire process will be shortened if she or he is simply instructed how to present provisions and what words to use, and simply falls into line. 5-70

The first approach results in bad law and is very likely to result in serious but natural misconceptions on the part of the drafter being encoded into the legislation for all time, not because those commenting did not see the mistakes but because they mistrusted their own judgement and did not draw them robustly to the attention of the drafter. 5-71

The second approach will also lead to bad law because the misunderstandings on the part of the bill team of the way in which legislation is applied by the courts will not be properly rectified and balanced in the course of the normal constructive 5-72 discussion between drafter and bill team, because the bill team do not really want to listen to what the drafter has to say. The correct approach, which lies between these two mistaken extremes, is for the bill team and the drafter to engage in a constructive dialogue with humility and a wish to learn on both sides. That can be a frustratingly time-consuming process. The bill team can console themselves, however, with the knowledge that any attempt to shorten it will certainly lengthen it in the long term.

5-73 One of the many ways in which the growth of modern communications technology has damaged effective communication is by encouraging rapid knee-jerk reactions to drafts to be sent off by e-mail almost as soon as the draft is received. Before the advent of e-mail people were forced to take the draft slowly, roll it around the mind and prepare a considered response. Now that communication has almost entirely taken the place of thought in modern society, this is increasingly difficult to reconcile with modern working practices. One way in which the drafter can ensure that he or she is receiving a properly considered reaction is to consolidate responses received from different members of the bill team or on different subjects, and then arrange one or more meetings at which the responses can be discussed and tested to see whether they are fully thought through and considered. As a general rule, where an aspect of the draft has been improperly understood by one or more members of the bill team, an exchange of rapid-fire e-mails is unlikely to be the most effective mechanism for resolving the misunderstanding. A meeting at which points can be advanced, rebutted, rephrased and discussed can take the place of, and be more effective than, an exchange of dozens of e-mails recording increasingly entrenched misunderstandings. And the same point holds good for misunderstandings on the part of the drafter.

5-74 The drafter is the ultimate arbiter of the appropriate choice of language to convey the material to the target audience.[12] Only one person can drive the engine and make decisions in the light of the overall navigation strategy, and that has to be the drafter. But the crew members need to have confidence in the drafter as the captain of the vessel and, in particular, need to feel that they are being given a genuine opportunity to influence decisions taken on language and structure as well as on policy. Very often, there will be presentational and political considerations relating to language and structural choices on which the drafter should, while making the ultimate decision, pay a great deal of attention to the instincts and experience of the bill team. If there is not a feeling of mutual respect and influence then the system will fail to work in a constructive manner and it is unlikely in the extreme that good and effective law will emerge. With that in mind, drafters should take an early opportunity of communicating to the bill team, particularly those among them who are new to the experience, the importance of their feeling free to make comments on all matters of the draft; she or he should also set out informal rules as to how those communications are most likely to be effective in the context of the particular bill and the working practices of the drafter and the bill team.

5-75 Ultimately, if the bill team loses confidence in the wisdom of the legislative drafter there is a real problem that needs to be resolved. The bill manager, or

[12] The rôle of the drafter in framing the legislative proposals is discussed below in chapter six.

currently in Wales the Senior Responsible Owner, should not hesitate, once he or she comes to the view that relations with the legislative drafter are not conducive to constructive dialogue, to raise the matter with the drafter's manager, who will generally be the head of the legislative drafting office. If this is done in a constructive manner it need not be seen as a nuclear option, although hopefully it is not one to which bill teams will often have recourse. At the end of the day, the legislative product is more important than individual feelings, and the head of the legislative drafting office will want to know sooner rather than later if there is a communication difficulty. The process of legislative drafting can sometimes be both intense and pressurized in terms of timing and otherwise, and this can place its own strains on personalities both at the drafting end and within the bill team. This can feed through and prevent the development of what would otherwise be productive relationships. The quality of the legislation is too important to allow personality clashes to destroy it and, where minor interventions to clear the air or to re-establish good working practices are insufficient, the head of the legislative drafting office will not hesitate to move a drafter to another project to which she or he may be better suited. Many stories could be told of UK bills prepared in circumstances in which the drafter and the bill team have fallen out to such an extent that there was virtually no communication by the end: although these instances are relatively rare, it should be borne in mind that the ultimate victim of these and lesser breakdowns in communication is the citizen, and all the public servants involved have an obligation to try as hard as possible to prevent damage of that kind.

In terms of timing, it is often helpful to layer responses to drafts. An instinctive 5-76
reaction to the overall style and approach of a draft, provided that it is explained that that is what it is, is a helpful thing for the drafter to receive as an immediate response to producing draft provisions. In particular, it provides her or him with a steer that will enable them to continue producing other provisions, pending receiving detailed comments on the first set of drafts, while avoiding any of the high level presentational or structural issues that the bill team have spotted immediately on seeing the first set of drafts. Where this approach is thought to be useful, the first set of reactions should state that this is what they are, and should set a timescale for the production of detailed comments on the drafts.

Where the bill team are not satisfied for one reason or another with a particular 5-77
aspect of the draft presented to them, it is important that they indicate the nature of the problem rather than simply suggesting solutions. Alternative drafts or forms of words are not an unhelpful thing to offer to the drafter, but they must be a supplement to exposing the issues that concern the bill team and not a substitute for it. Equally, simply criticizing an approach without indicating the kinds of alternative that are likely to find favour and the reasons why, reduces the likelihood that the drafter's second shot will be any more successful than the first.

Subject to pressures of time, the bill team should conduct appropriate informal 5-78
consultations with key stakeholders on aspects of the draft before coming back to the drafter with their comments. The overall timetable will be considerably reduced if the drafter is enabled to respond, in effect, to a single set of consolidated

comments incorporating the external perspective, rather than having to respond first to a set of internal government comments and then at a later stage to a set of external comments, some of which may falsify assumptions underlying the first set of reactions. As with all aspects of the process this is something that must be tailored to fit individual circumstances and timetables, but bill teams should at least routinely consider the extent to which informal consultation with stakeholders on the drafts will facilitate their provision of first responses to the drafter.

THE CONTENT OF A LEGISLATIVE PROVISION

5-79 Since the only purpose of legislation is to change the law, it follows that the core content of a legislative provision is a declaration of how the law is changed.

5-80 That may at its simplest involve the imposition of a new obligation on one or more classes of citizen. But it may be a great deal more subtle than that: at the most extreme, a piece of aspirational legislation may have real-world effects only in the most indirect of ways – such as by setting a series of targets that affect how a class of public authorities are to approach their pre-existing functions – but in one way or another it will change the legal environment within which citizens operate and thereby in the widest sense change 'the law'. Anything that does not contain within it a proposition changing the law in one of these extreme ways or to an extent that lies somewhere between the two extremes is not a valid legislative proposition.

5-81 In terms of the substantive content of a law and the appropriate structure for the disposition of that content, it is most helpful to think of the drafter as telling a story, the subject of which is how the law is being changed as a result of the provision. In this respect the art of storytelling in a legislative context is no different from the art in other contexts. The aim is to set out the material as clearly and simply as possible, and in a form which tells the reader what she or he needs to know in order to understand the entire proposition, in an order which reduces the number of questions that they need to ask along the way in order to secure comprehension.[13]

[13] When one understands this, one immediately understands how questions like 'should definitions come at the beginning or at the end?' are not susceptible to a helpful answer in a hypothetical context. In terms of storytelling, legislative definitions fall into one of two classes. At one extreme, they are technical provisions included not as part of the key content but simply in order to avoid actual or mischievously pretended confusion as to the purport of the provision. Everybody knows what a dog is: but in case somebody mischievously pretends to believe that a hound is not a dog for the purposes of the prohibition against hunting with dogs, it is necessary to include a provision expressly designating hounds as dogs. But that is not part of the key storytelling context. And it should therefore be relegated to the end, along with other material which is necessary for technical or legal purposes or for the avoidance of doubt or confusion, but which is not necessary in order to understand the key effect of the law. At the other end of the spectrum, a provision about the taxation of dividends on oil futures will not be fully comprehensible even to someone within the industry key target audience, unless the question of what kinds of transaction are included for the purposes of that legislation in the concept of oil futures and profits from oil futures is settled at the outset.

Chapter 6

From Proposals to Provisions

When it has been determined that the plan of action which has been adopted to achieve the policy goals requires a change or changes in the law to be effected, it becomes necessary to provide for those changes by proposing legislation. The process of legislating, that is *legislation* in the sense of the activity of making a law in consequence of a proposal to do so, is about to be set in motion. The manner in which it is proposed to change the law as the means chosen for giving effect to the policy will need to be provided through expression in legal provisions. The legal provisions provide the legal means, the purpose of which will be to change the existing law so as to give effect to the policy. Where such proposed changes affect the rules of conduct which regulate the lives of citizens, according to Lord Oliver of Aylmerton's dictum quoted earlier,[1] the proposed changes to those rules should be placed before the citizens' democratically elected representatives for their consideration, and ultimately for their approval or rejection. That at least is what one would expect if the society in question is in truth a democracy, as opposed to one which so classifies itself in its own self-regarding utterances. In the case of the United Kingdom Parliament and of the National Assembly for Wales, as with many other legislatures, the proposed provisions are presented in the form of a bill. 6-01

A bill therefore presents the legislature with proposals for changes in the law in order to achieve the promoters' underlying policy goals. It is for the legislature to decide whether the changes required to the rules by which the citizens it represents lead their lives is a price worth paying to achieve the policy goal. The legislature must also decide whether the particular changes proposed are to be supported, or whether the goal might be better or more fairly achieved by changes other than those proposed. The legislature in other words must approve the principle of changing the law to achieve the goal and also the particular changes proposed. 6-02

LONG TITLE AND SHORT TITLE

The proposal that the law should be changed to achieve the policy goal is set out at the beginning of a bill in what is called its long title. It is called the long title to distinguish it from the bill's short title, which is the name given to a bill so that it can be referred to concisely in discussions, identified concisely in later items of legislation and other documents, and cited concisely before the courts. 6-03

Long titles of bills before the Assembly are required to begin with the words: 'An Act of the National Assembly for Wales to …'. Even though a bill has not been enacted, its long title refers to it as an Act, as that is how it will appear if and when 6-04

[1] See above, §3-72.

it is enacted. It sets out the purpose of the bill and is required to do so in terms which are factual and neutral with regard to the desirability of making the change proposed. Language which seeks to promote or justify the policy goals underlying the bill's proposals or which exaggerates their effects, has to be avoided, and this is the case with the short title as well.[2] An example of a long title is that of the Mobile Homes (Wales) Act 2013. It reads:

> An Act of the National Assembly for Wales to reform and restate the law relating to mobile home sites in Wales.

It proposes that the law relating to mobile home sites in Wales should be reformed and restated. This was the purpose of the bill, the general principle of which the Assembly was asked to approve on behalf of the people it represented. How exactly it was intended to change the law followed in the detailed provisions of the bill.

THE BILL'S PROVISIONS

6-05 The provisions of a bill place before the legislature for scrutiny and debate the details of how it is proposed to change the law to give effect to the underlying policy. If and when the bill is enacted, as an Act it changes the law in the manner set out in its provisions. The bill as enacted is also a record of the legislature's decision that the law is to be changed in that manner, which is why Acts are also referred to as statutes, from the Latin *statutum est* – 'it has been decided'.

6-06 The changes to the law which it is therefore proposed to make need to be placed before the legislature in a form which allows the legislature to scrutinize, debate and decide whether those changes should be made or whether they should be rejected, including offering the opportunity to the legislature of amending the changes proposed so as to improve upon the proposals. It is important to emphasize that this is the purpose of a bill, as it is the purpose of an Act to make those changes and, as a statute, to record the decision. It is not the purpose of any of these to set out the law relating to the area under consideration. Unless it is intended to restate or consolidate the law on a particular topic in the legislation, the legislation is intended to do no more and no less than make the changes to the existing law which it is believed is necessary or desirable to provide the means for giving effect to the policy. It is sometimes complained that it is difficult for the reader of legislation, particularly a reader with no legal background or qualifications, to understand what the law is from reading the legislation. The complaint is in a sense misplaced. It is not the function of legislation to set out the law on a given topic, unless it breaks entirely new ground and is setting out for the first time an entirely new legal regime with regard to a topic, and even then it is highly unlikely that it will not be taking for granted a great deal of legal context. More usually,

[2] These requirements are to be found in the Presiding Officer's Determination on Proper Form: Structure ¶¶10–12.

the legislation will assume the background of existing law and confine itself to the changes which need to be made to it, for that is what the legislature is required to scrutinize, debate and either approve or reject. It is in the explanatory materials which accompany the bill that the wider context should be explained, and the effect upon that wider context which the bill's changes are intended to deliver. Thus, the existing state of the law regarding the policy area needs to be explained in the Explanatory Memorandum, which must be presented to the Assembly at the same time as the bill is being introduced, together with a full explanation of why the changes are being proposed. The Explanatory Notes for the bill, on the other hand, are intended solely to explain the legal changes which are being proposed.

As the purpose of the bill therefore is to allow the legislature, on behalf of 6-07
those it represents, to consider the proposed changes to the law, it is of paramount importance that the proposed changes are set before it in a way that allows it to carry out that task efficiently and fairly. Each change needs to be capable of being scrutinized, debated, possibly amended, and finally either agreed or rejected. To enable this to be achieved, bills before the Assembly are required to be set out in numbered sections, each section proposing a particular change to the law. As has been discussed, these changes may involve the imposition of duties, the granting of rights or entitlements, or the conferral of powers, and it is necessary to know who is and who is not to be affected by these changes, how they are or are not to be affected, in what circumstances – when and where – they are or are not to be so affected, and how these changes to the law are to be enforced or otherwise appropriately implemented, together with any consequential or incidental changes to the existing law which the changes proposed entail. The time has arrived to express the conclusions of the policy development process in the form of legal provisions.

This is usually accomplished in two discrete stages, and even if the stages are 6-08
not formally separate, there are two discrete functions to be performed. The first involves the policy proposals being analysed to determine whether legislation is needed, that is whether there is a need to change the law to effect the policy goals. If it is decided that it is necessary to do so, then as part of this function it needs to be determined which legislative body can make those changes and which legislative body is appropriate to make them. These questions will turn on the legal competence of the legislative body and the requirements of democratic principle respectively. Once it has been determined what changes are needed and who must be invited to make them, the proposals must then be set out in the form which allows the legislative body to consider them and come to a decision as to whether to agree to them. If these two functions are performed separately by means of a written process, which they traditionally have been when proposing such changes to legislatures in the United Kingdom, the policy proposals will be forwarded to lawyers in the form of policy instructions, asking them to advise as to what changes in the law are needed, and the request for those changes to be made will be forwarded by the lawyers, with the agreement of those who instructed them regarding the policy, to legislative counsel or drafters, who will frame the provisions that the legislature needs to approve if the changes are to be enacted.

Who is to be affected and how?

6-09 Those who are to be affected by the legislative provisions and how they are to be affected should, in constructing the bill, be the focus of its principal provisions. They may be affected by having duties imposed upon them, having rights in the sense of claim-rights or entitlements given them, or may have powers conferred upon them. The following provisions of the Government of Wales Act 2006 illustrate the manner in which provisions impose duties and confer rights and powers. The Act's long title gave it a broad purpose – 'to make provision about the government of Wales'.

Duties

6-10 The Act imposes a variety of duties on amongst others the Welsh Ministers. Section 78 of the Act provides that:

> The Welsh Ministers must adopt a strategy ('the Welsh language strategy') setting out how they propose to promote and facilitate the use of the Welsh language

and goes on, in section 78(6) and (8) respectively, to impose a duty to publish the strategy and report on its implementation and success:

> The Welsh Ministers must publish the Welsh language strategy …
>
> After each financial year the Welsh Ministers must publish a report of—
>
> (a) how the proposals set out in the Welsh language strategy were implemented in that financial year and how effective their implementation has been in promoting and facilitating the use of the Welsh language, …
>
> and must lay a copy of the report before the Assembly.

The manner in which each provision is expressed reveals that it imposes a duty. The Welsh Ministers *must* do as required. They have no choice or freedom in the matter; the provisions remove their freedom regarding such a strategy and replaces it with obligations – duties – to do so. The use of the word *must* is an indication that duties are being imposed.[3]

[3] It is the word used by the Assembly and the Welsh Ministers in legislating for Wales, where traditionally UK legislation had used the word *shall*. *Shall* is still used in some UK legislation, although the use of *must* is becoming more common. It is significant that in the Government of Wales Act 2006, the UK Parliament followed the Welsh practice. The use of *must* in Welsh legislation was influenced by the need for parity of expression in the Welsh and English versions of legislative text: see Keith Bush, 'Approaches to UK Legislative Drafting: the Welsh Perspective' (2004) 25 *Statute Law Review* 144–50.

Claim-rights

As has been stated earlier, wherever there is a duty, there must be a corresponding claim-right, although the existence and location of that right may not need to be spelled out on the face of the legislation if the legal context within which the duty is being imposed will serve to identify it by necessary implication. In this instance, a failure by the Welsh Ministers to fulfil this duty would constitute a devolution issue which could be litigated under the provisions of Schedule 9 to the 2006 Act.[4] Successful litigation could lead to the courts issuing a mandating order requiring the Welsh Ministers to carry out their duty.[5] 6-11

Examples of claim-rights being expressly conferred can be found in section 134 of the 2006 Act, giving the Auditor General for Wales rights to see accounts of subsidiaries acting for the Welsh Ministers. It states: 6-12

> the Auditor General—
>
> (a) has a right of access at all reasonable times to every document relating to the accounts of any subsidiary of the Welsh Ministers ...
> (b) is entitled to require from any person holding or accountable for any of those documents any assistance, information or explanation which the Auditor General reasonably thinks necessary for those purposes, and
> (c) may require any subsidiary of the Welsh Ministers to provide the Auditor General ... with accounts of ... the subsidiary's transactions ...

The section illustrates three different ways in which the conferral of a claim-right can be expressed: 'has a right'; 'is entitled to'; 'may require'. It therefore also illustrates that it is the substance of the provision and not its form which determines its content. In each case, there is a duty on another person, usually here the subsidiary, corresponding to the claim-right given.

Freedoms

In the same way as the word *must* indicates the imposition of a duty, so the word *may* is a useful indicator that a power is being conferred. However, *may* is not as reliable a guide as *must*, as it can be used to indicate a freedom to do something, in the sense of there being no obligation to do or not do the thing in question, or even a claim-right as in paragraph (c) above.[6] One example of this in the 6-13

[4] See GoWA 2006, Sch. 9, para. 1(1). See above, §§3-27, 3-69.

[5] The most obvious person who might seek to enforce this duty by applying for a mandating order would now be the Welsh Language Commissioner, a position created by the Assembly's Welsh Language Measure 2011. Placing the responsibility on such a public official allows members of the public to pursue such issues without incurring costs as private litigants.

[6] The word *may* in essence indicates a discretion as to whether one does or does not do a thing. If the choice does not affect the legal position of others, it is a freedom; if it involves a change to their legal position, it is a power, and if it is a choice allowing one to require them to do or not do something, it is a claim-right.

Government of Wales Act 2006 is the freedom given to Welsh Ministers to retire from office as and when they choose, without anyone having a right to prevent them. Section 48(4) states:

> A Welsh Minister … may at any time resign.[7]

Powers and corresponding liabilities

6-14 This use of *may*, to emphasize freedom, has to be distinguished from the more usual use of *may* to indicate the conferral of a power to alter the rights, duties and freedoms of others. Numerous examples of this usage can be found in legislation, such as this from the 2006 Act.

> The Secretary of State may make an order prohibiting the Presiding Officer from submitting the bill for Royal Assent.[8]

Ordinarily, the Presiding Officer is under a duty to submit bills passed by the Assembly to the Queen for Royal Assent, but the power quoted above allows the Secretary of State to prohibit that from happening in certain circumstances and its exercise has the effect of removing the Presiding Officer's duty to forward the bill for Royal Assent and substituting for it a duty not to do so. The exercise of the power changes the legal position of the Presiding Officer.[9] The Presiding Officer, therefore, is subject to a liability to have her duty changed, the liability corresponding to the Secretary of State's power.

Disabilities and immunities

6-15 Provisions can also be used to indicate the absence of a power to change rights and duties, that is the presence of a legal disability corresponding to the immunity to such change enjoyed by those possessing the rights or duties in question. Thus, for instance, whereas the Welsh Ministers enjoy considerable powers with regard to making subordinate legislation and performing executive functions, they cannot exercise those powers in a manner which is incompatible with the Convention rights incorporated into UK domestic law by the Human Rights Act 1998. The 2006 Act specifically sets out this disability:

> The Welsh Ministers have no power—
> (a) to make, confirm or approve any subordinate legislation, or

[7] It might be thought unnecessary to include such a provision, as it merely states rather than alters the legal position. However, as Ministers of the Crown at Westminster in theory need to request permission to resign, the provision clarifies the different position of Welsh Ministers – a simple illustration of legislating being desirable even though no change to the law is needed.

[8] GoWA 2006, s. 114(2), as amended by Wales Act 2017, s. 12(2)(c). Prior to the amendment, the duty to submit had been that of the Clerk of the Assembly, not the Presiding Officer.

[9] The circumstances in which this power may be exercised were discussed above, §§4-92–4-97.

> (b) to do any other act,
>
> so far as the subordinate legislation or act is incompatible with any of the Convention rights.[10]

Therefore, all those who enjoy the Convention rights concerned also enjoy an immunity from having those rights affected by the exercise of functions by the Welsh Ministers.

Focus of provisions

In all of the instances cited so far, the focus of the provision has been on the person 6-16
who enjoys the right or power being conferred or who is under the duty being imposed. Sometimes, however, the focus will be on the right, power or duty rather than on the person, in which case the structure of the provision will be altered to reflect this. This is basically a matter of emphasis which does not affect the legal result, although it does serve to highlight the issue for consideration by the legislature. Thus, in dealing with the question of who may exercise the legislative initiative within the Assembly and introduce legislative proposals in the form of bills into it for consideration, section 110(1) of the 2006 Act provides:

> A Bill may … be introduced in the Assembly—
>
> (a) by the First Minister, any Welsh Minister … any Deputy Welsh Minister or the Counsel General, or
>
> (b) by any other Assembly member.

This could quite as easily have been drafted to read:

> The First Minister, any Welsh Minister … any Deputy Welsh Minister, the Counsel General, or any other Assembly member may … introduce a Bill in the Assembly.

It is only the focus of the provision which is different.[11]

Where and when are the persons affected in this manner to be affected?

Frequently the conferral of a right or a power or the imposition of a duty is lim- 6-17
ited to certain circumstances. It is necessary therefore to state these circumstances in the provision so that they are open to scrutiny. Legislative provisions therefore often begin by setting out the circumstances in which the duty in question will apply or the right or power concerned may be enjoyed. The description of the

[10] GoWA 2006, s. 81(1).

[11] Many modern drafting manuals advocate a preference for active rather than passive constructions on the grounds of clarity. It is submitted that clarity should be judged according to the context in each case and not according to any dogmatic approach.

relevant conditions is frequently presented in a phrase beginning with 'When …', 'Where …' or 'If …'. Section 82 of the 2006 Act furnishes an example.

> If the Secretary of State considers that any action proposed to be taken by the Welsh Ministers would be incompatible with any international obligation, the Secretary of State may by order direct that the proposed action is not to be taken.[12]

This power of the Secretary of State is a considerable one. Stripped of the words defining the circumstances in which it may be exercised, its significance becomes clear:

> The Secretary of State may direct that any action proposed to be taken by the Welsh Ministers is not to be taken.

The definition of the circumstances in which this considerable power may be exercised achieves two things: it both limits the possibility of its lawful exercise, and thereby also introduces a test according to which the lawfulness of any exercise can be questioned. When limiting the circumstances in which a person may exercise a power, it should therefore be remembered by those seeking the limitation that it opens the door to challenging the lawfulness of the power's exercise. In the case of public bodies, such challenges would be made by judicial review. The circumstances as defined will constitute the test of the lawfulness of the power's exercise, so that it is crucial that the circumstances be clearly defined in the provision.

6-18 Again, the circumstances can be stated at the start or at the end of the provision depending upon the focus or emphasis which is preferred. The Control of Horses (Wales) Act 2014 provides an example of the latter approach.

> A local authority may seize and impound a horse which is on any highway, or in any other public place, in the local authority's area if the local authority has reasonable grounds for believing that the horse is there without lawful authority.[13]

Where there are several requirements to which the exercise of the power, the enjoyment of the right or the imposition of the duty is subject, it may be preferable to set them out in discrete subdivisions of the text. This may be done as part of the text creating the power, right or duty, or in succeeding subdivisions of the text. For example:

> A local authority may seize and impound a horse which is on any other land in the local authority's area if the local authority has reasonable grounds for believing—

[12] GoWA 2006, s. 82(1).

[13] Control of Horses (Wales) Act 2014, s. 2(1).

(a) in the case of land of which the local authority is the occupier, that the horse is there without the local authority's consent, or
(b) in the case of other land in the local authority's area, that the horse is there without the consent of the occupier of the land and that the occupier consents to the local authority seizing and impounding it.[14]

Divisions of the text

The sections which form the principal divisions of the text of a bill can be divided into numbered subsections, which in turn can be subdivided into paragraphs and if necessary sub-paragraphs. Such subdivision is a useful device to make what might otherwise be a complicated and lengthy provision manageable and accessible, and is particularly useful as a method of isolating distinct issues which the legislature may wish to debate and amend. The following numbering convention is used in both UK and Assembly legislation.[15] 6-19

1 **Section**
(1) Subsection
(a) Paragraph
(i) Sub-paragraph

Excessive subdivision should however be avoided, as it can in itself complicate the text and render it difficult to understand.

Who is not to be affected – how, when and where?

The circumstances in which a provision is to apply set out the general criteria for its application. If there are to be exceptions to the application of the provision even in those circumstances – for instance, by their not being applicable to particular persons or in particular circumstances – the exceptions need to be clearly stated so that they can be identified by the reader and subjected to scrutiny and debate by the legislature. This was at one time done by the insertion of provisos towards the end of the relevant text, but this practice has largely been abandoned in favour of their statement in a separate provision or subdivision of a provision. Thus, section 82(2) of the Government of Wales 2006 provides that: 6-20

> If the Secretary of State considers that an action capable of being taken by the Welsh Ministers is required for the purposes of giving effect to any international obligation, the Secretary of State may by order direct the Welsh Ministers to take the action.

[14] Ibid., s. 2(2).

[15] The word *section* is used for the principal subdivisions in both Assembly bills and Acts, while at Westminster the word *clause* was traditionally used in relation to bills.

This, like the power in section 82(1) quoted earlier, is a very considerable power and can indeed be used to require the Welsh Ministers to introduce a bill into the Assembly.[16] Even where the condition for its exercise is met, however, the Secretary of State is not permitted to use the power without first consulting the Welsh Ministers. Section 82(9) provides that:

> No order is to be made by the Secretary of State under subsection (2) … unless the Secretary of State has consulted the Welsh Ministers.

The use of a separate subsection highlights the requirement and, in this case, also allows it to operate with regard to two other subsections as well as avoiding the need for its repetition.[17] If the exceptions are numerous or complicated, it is sometimes necessary to place them in a separate section or even sections, so as to enable their detailed scrutiny and debate. Such provisions are particularly suited to highlight immunities from the exercise of powers and the corresponding disabilities which limit the range of powers. They can also be useful in setting out exceptions to the general imposition of duties, whether with regard persons, places or circumstances.

ENFORCEMENT AND IMPLEMENTATION

6-21 Whenever a duty is imposed, it is necessary to ensure that it can be enforced, otherwise its imposition can prove pointless. Unless there already exist mechanisms for enforcing such duties generally – for instance, as will be the case with duties placed on public officials or public bodies – the proposed legislation will need to make provision for that enforcement. Likewise, where claim-rights are being conferred, provision will need to be in place to secure their delivery. It is for those who are promoting the policy to which the Act will give effect to choose the method of enforcement.

Criminal law

6-22 The chosen method of enforcement may be the creation of a criminal offence. The provisions will need to make it clear that such an offence is being created as the courts will not ordinarily imply that criminal liability is being imposed on citizens

[16] See GoWA 2006, s. 82(15).

[17] It could – and perhaps would in earlier enactments – have been stated as a proviso within the relevant provision itself, which would then read:

> If the Secretary of State considers that an action capable of being taken by the Welsh Ministers is required for the purposes of giving effect to any international obligation, the Secretary of State may by order direct the Welsh Ministers to take the action, provided that no such order is to be made by the Secretary of State unless the Secretary of State has consulted the Welsh Ministers.

without express provision to that effect. Section 18 of the Mobile Homes (Wales) Act 2013 provides an example of enforcement through the criminal law.

> (1) An owner of land who has been served with a compliance notice which has become operative commits an offence if the owner fails to take the steps specified in the notice … within the period specified in the notice …
> (2) A person guilty of an offence under subsection (1) is liable on summary conviction to a fine.

The Assembly has competence to legislate to enforce provisions which are otherwise within its competence, and its powers to introduce criminal offences are not limited to those which can be punished by fine. Terms of imprisonment can also be imposed.[18] Section 60 of the Holiday Caravan Sites (Wales) Bill[19] proposed the creation of a number of offences relating to harassment, and section 61(3) proposed that:

> A person guilty of an offence under section 60 is liable—
> (a) on summary conviction, to a fine or to imprisonment for a term not exceeding 12 months, or to both, or
> (b) on conviction on indictment, to a fine or to imprisonment for a term not exceeding two years, or to both.

Such punishment should, of course, always be proportionate, and the punishment chosen must not contravene the Convention rights set out in the 1998 Human Rights Act. It should also be borne in mind that criminal sanctions involve additional work and cost for the police, the courts and, in the case of imprisonment, the prison service. Occasionally, the power to prosecute may be given to a specific body such as a local authority,[20] or the consent of an official such as the Director of Public Prosecutions may be required in order to prosecute.[21] Again, such limitations

[18] Its competence to enact enforcement provisions is part of its competence regarding the making of ancillary provisions as defined in GoWA 2006, s. 108A(3), inserted by Wales Act 2017, s. 3(1). Such provisions must not have a greater effect otherwise than in relation to Wales than is necessary to give effect to their purpose. The Assembly's competence to create criminal offences is also restricted by GoWA 2006, Sch. 7B, Pt 1, para. 4, inserted by Wales Act 2017, s. 3(2) and Sch. 2: see above, §4-58.

[19] The Holiday Caravan Sites (Wales) Bill was a backbench member's bill, introduced by Darren Millar AM. It failed to complete its passage through the Assembly before the end of the Fourth Assembly term prior to the Assembly General Election in 2016. As a consequence of its running out of time, it fell in accordance with SO 26.77.

[20] Thus, s. 63 of the Holiday Caravan Sites (Wales) Bill proposed, with regard to offences it was intended to create under Part 5 of the Bill to protect against harassment, that: 'Proceedings for an offence under this Part [Part 5] may be instituted by any local authority'.

[21] Thus, s. 12 of the Human Transplantation (Wales) Act 2013 provides that: 'No proceedings for an offence under section 10 [prohibition of activities without consent] may be instituted except by or with the consent of the Director of Public Prosecutions'.

reflect policy choices which need to have been considered and chosen ahead of the provisions being drafted.

Civil law

6-23 Wherever an Act places a duty on a person not to do something, then if that person threatens or is likely to breach that duty, those affected by the anticipated breach may seek an injunction from the courts to prevent the breach. As this remedy is already available, there is no need for the legislation to make provision for it. The same is true where a duty is imposed on a person to do something; a mandatory injunction may be sought to compel the duty's performance. Where a duty of either kind is breached, persons adversely affected by the breach may seek compensation in the form of damages in the courts. Where the duty is a new one, the liability to compensate for such harm may be specifically set out in the legislation. The Animals Act 1971 provides several examples of such provisions. For instance, sections 2(1) and 3:

> Where any damage is caused by an animal which belongs to a dangerous species, any person who is a keeper of the animal is liable for the damage …
>
> Where a dog causes damage by killing or injuring livestock, any person who is a keeper of the dog is liable for the damage …

While the Assembly has not as yet legislated to create such a general liability to compensate for harm done or loss suffered,[22] it has been proposed that its enforcement competence be used to provide for orders and payments to be made in the courts. Thus, section 56(3) of the failed Holiday Caravan Sites (Wales) Bill proposed that:

> If the owner of a holiday caravan site fails to comply …, the occupier may apply to a county court for an order requiring the owner to comply with those terms

and section 44(2) of the Mobile Homes (Wales) Act 2013 provides that:

> Where the court by virtue of this section suspends the enforcement of an order, it may impose such terms and conditions, including conditions as to the payment of rent or other periodical payments or of arrears of such rent or payments, as the court thinks reasonable.

[22] The Recovery of Medical Costs for Asbestos Diseases (Wales) Bill attempted to impose liability on the former employers of victims of such diseases and on the employers' insurers for the cost to the Welsh NHS of treating the victims, but the Supreme Court found the bill's provisions to be outside the legislative competence of the Assembly: see *Recovery of Medical Costs for Asbestos Diseases (Wales) Bill: Reference by the Counsel General for Wales* [2015] UKSC 3.

It is interesting that both of these instances of the use of civil law, as opposed to public or criminal law, mechanisms for enforcement occurred in legislation promoted by backbench Assembly Members rather than the Welsh Government, suggesting perhaps that the policy options considered by the latter still tend to focus on administrative controls and redress.[23]

Administrative law

Administrative mechanisms, of course, remain a viable and proper option. They can include controlling activity by licence or regulation, or influencing its conduct by means of guidance or codes of conduct. Where licences are to be granted, the legislation will need to provide for applications to be granted them, a procedure for considering such applications, possibly criteria for determining the suitability of persons to receive them, a procedure for appealing against a refusal to grant one, some mechanism for reviewing the grant from time to time, opportunity for complaint against a licence holder, and procedures for withdrawing licences and for appeals against such withdrawals. Some or all of this will need to appear among the principal provisions of the legislation, while the detail of the procedures involved may suitably be placed in a Schedule to the bill, as might the detailed terms upon which a licence is granted. In the Mobile Homes (Wales) Act 2013, for instance, the details of the terms to be implied in mobile homes agreements are to be found in Schedule 2 to the Act. The duty to obtain a licence and the criteria for its grant, on the other hand, would appear among the principal provisions of the bill, together with the consequences of indulging in the activity without a valid licence. Section 7 of the Holiday Caravan Sites (Wales) Bill furnishes an example: 6-24

> **Prohibition on use of land as regulated site without site licence**
>
> (1) The owner of a regulated site must not cause or permit the site to be used as a regulated site unless the owner holds a licence under this Part in relation to the land (a 'site licence').
>
> (2) A person who contravenes subsection (1) commits an offence.
>
> (3) A person who is guilty of an offence under subsection (2) is liable on summary conviction to a fine.

The use of schedules to provide the detail with regard to procedures and forms is also well illustrated by the Food Hygiene Rating (Wales) Act 2013, where the creation of an offence and the issue of a fixed penalty notice are dealt with among

[23] The restriction placed upon the Assembly's competence to legislate so as to modify the private law of England and Wales does not prevent it from doing so where the purpose of the modification does not relate to a reserved matter, provided always that the effect of the change otherwise than in relation to Wales is not greater than is necessary to give effect to the purpose of the provision: GoWA 2006, Sch. 7B, para. 3, inserted by Wales Act 2017, s. 3(2); and GoWA 2006, s. 108A(3), inserted by Wales Act 2017, s. 3(1).

the principal provisions in sections 9 and 21 respectively, while the Schedule sets out both the procedure for those notices and their form and content.

6-25 In framing all of these provisions, it needs to be remembered that the decisions made under them will be challengeable by judicial review with regard to their legality, reasonableness, propriety and compliance with human rights.

Procedures for making regulations – affirmative and negative

6-26 If an activity is to be controlled by means of regulations, the Act will need to grant the power to make such regulations to an appropriate body. Again, it needs to be remembered that the making of such regulations and their content will be subject to challenge by judicial review. Once in place, it may also be the case that their implementation will automatically fall within the purview of an already existing disciplinary or regulatory body: for example, the General Medical Council in the case of doctors. Where the power to make such regulations is conferred upon the government, the legislation will need to provide for their scrutiny by the legislature, either giving the legislature the power to approve or reject the regulations made by means of affirmative procedure or the power to require the annulment of the regulations by means of negative procedure. The following provisions are typical of such provision, requiring the power to be exercised by statutory instrument and then distinguishing between those requiring affirmative and negative procedure.

> **Regulations**
>
> (1) Powers to make regulations or orders under this Act are exercisable by statutory instrument.
>
> (2) Regulations under sections … may not be made unless a draft of the instrument has been laid before, and approved by a resolution of, the National Assembly for Wales.
>
> (3) Other regulations made under this Act are subject to annulment pursuant to a resolution of the National Assembly for Wales.

It can be seen from the need to cite specifically those that require affirmative procedure that negative procedure is taken to be the norm.

'Soft law' approaches

6-27 Conduct may also be influenced, as opposed to controlled, by means of the issuing of guidance or a code of conduct. The power, or even the duty, to issue such guidance can be provided for on the face of the Act. For example:

> **Guidance by Welsh Ministers**
>
> (1) The Welsh Ministers may issue guidance … as to the performance of … functions under this Act.
>
> (2) [Those performing those functions] must have regard to any guidance issued under subsection (1).

Whether or not such regard has been had to the guidance will be relevant if the performance of the functions is challenged by judicial review. 'Having regard' does not require exact compliance with the guidance, but the manner of performing the functions should not undermine its principles.

MULTI-PURPOSE LEGISLATION

The achievement of a policy may well require more than one change to the law. The legislation that provides the means to effect the policy will in such cases have to change the law in more than one area. Where this can conveniently be done within the scope of a single bill, it may be necessary to divide that bill into a number of distinct parts, albeit that those parts are connected by the underlying policy. 6-28

The multi-purpose nature of a bill may be signalled by the length and content of its long title, although this will not always be the case.[24] The bill which became the Housing (Wales) Act 2014[25] provides an example of a long title that signals its multi-purpose scope. It reads: 6-29

> An Act of the National Assembly for Wales to provide for the regulation of private rented housing; to reform the law relating to homelessness; to provide for assessment of the accommodation needs of Gypsies and Travellers and to require local authorities to meet those needs; to make provision about the standards of housing provided by local authorities; to abolish housing revenue account subsidy; to allow fully mutual housing associations to grant assured tenancies; to make provision about council tax payable for empty dwellings; and for other housing purposes.

The several objectives of the bill are then manifested in the presentation of its provisions in eight parts, reflecting the several changes to the law needed to deliver the policy objectives as a whole. These are respectively:

> REGULATION OF PRIVATE RENTED HOUSING
> HOMELESSNESS
> GYPSIES AND TRAVELLERS
> STANDARDS FOR SOCIAL HOUSING

[24] Both the Holidays Caravan Sites (Wales) Bill and the Mobile Homes (Wales) Act 2013 had condensed long titles focusing on their intention to reform and restate the law relating to their respective subjects.

[25] The bill underwent substantial amendment prior to enactment as the Housing (Wales) Act 2014. The examples in §§6-29–6-31 are taken from the bill as introduced, which better illustrate the issues discussed.

HOUSING FINANCE
ALLOWING FULLY MUTUAL HOUSING ASSOCIATIONS TO GRANT ASSURED TENANCIES
COUNCIL TAX FOR EMPTY DWELLINGS
MISCELLANEOUS AND GENERAL

and their correlation to the items in the long title is obvious. It may even be (as was the case with the second of the parts in the Housing Bill – HOMELESSNESS) that a change to more than one area of the law is needed to effect the policy goals in that area, in which case (as was the case with Part 2 of the Housing Bill) the Part is further subdivided into Chapters. Each one of these Parts or Chapters, with the exception of those intended to have a general application over all the others (as with Part 8 – MISCELLANEOUS AND GENERAL in this instance), could be a bill in its own right.

6-30 Within such parts or chapters, or within a bill which has not been subdivided, the provisions expressed in sections may then be grouped under italic cross-headings, indicating the content of the sections contained in them. Thus, Part 1 of the Housing Bill, dealing with the regulation of private rented accommodation, grouped its thirty-five sections under eight italic cross-headings:

Introduction
Prohibition of letting and management without registration and licence
Registration
Licensing
Enforcement
Powers of the Welsh Ministers
Supplementary
General

These self-explanatory headings guide the reader into the sections which contain the legislative provisions themselves. The *Introduction* has an Overview of Part 1 (section 1) and a definition of the key terms contained in it (section 2), before the scheme of the proposals becomes apparent. The letting and management of private rented accommodation is to be prohibited unless the landlord is registered and licensed. Those who are not to be affected are also defined. The manner in which registration and licensing is to be accomplished is then covered, followed by the methods to be used to enforce the provisions. These sections include the relevant procedures and mechanisms for appeal. Finally, the Welsh Ministers' powers regarding the scheme are set out, followed by provisions relating to supplementary matters such as the charging of fees and general interpretative provisions. The whole structure is aimed at presenting the contents in an accessible, understandable manner. Each section has its own cross-heading describing briefly the content of its provisions. Thus, Part 1 was presented in the bill's Table of Contents as follows:

PART 1

REGULATION OF PRIVATE RENTED HOUSING

Introduction

1 Overview of this Part

2 Meaning of key terms

Prohibition of letting and management without registration and licence

3 Requirement to be registered and licensed: landlord

4 Landlord's requirement to be registered and licensed: exceptions

5 Requirement to be registered and licensed: agent or responsible person

Registration

6 Duty to maintain register in relation to rental properties

7 Registration by a local housing authority

8 Duty to update information

9 Revocation of registration

Licensing

10 Licence application requirements

11 Fit and proper person requirement

12 Training requirement

13 Determination of application

14 Licence conditions

15 Duty to update information

16 Duty to show licence number

17 Amendment of licence

18 Revocation of licence

19 Expiry and renewal of licence

20 Licensing appeals

Enforcement

21 Rent stopping orders

22 Impact of rent stopping order

23 Procedure for rent stopping orders

24 Appeal against rent stopping order

25 Withdrawal of rent stopping order

26 Power to require documents and information to be given

27 Offences by bodies corporate

Powers of the Welsh Ministers

28 Code of practice

29 Guidance

30 Directions

Supplementary

31 Regulations about fees

32 Information about applications

OVERVIEW PROVISIONS

6-31 Section 1 of the bill provided a descriptive overview of Part 1, usefully describing how the various component parts were to deliver the changes required. Section 1 read as follows:

1 **Overview of this Part**

(1) This Part provides for regulation of the letting and management of certain kinds of residential property; the 'rental property' in respect of which regulation arises and other key terms are defined in section 2.

(2) Section 3 makes it an offence for landlords—

(a) to let rental properties without being registered, and

(b) to manage rental properties without being licensed;

section 4 provides for exceptions to the requirement for landlords to be registered or licensed.

(3) Section 5 makes it an offence for persons acting on behalf of landlords ('agents' and 'responsible persons' – for definitions of these terms see section 2) to manage rental properties for those landlords without being registered and licensed.

(4) Sections 6 to 9 and Schedule 1 provide for the system of registration, including—

(a) a requirement for local housing authorities to keep a register of—

(i) persons who let and manage rental properties in their areas, and

(ii) the rental properties in their areas;

(b) a requirement to make certain information kept on that register available to the public upon request (see section 6 and Schedule 1).

(5) Sections 10 to 20 provide for the system of licensing; in order to be licensed a person must meet certain criteria, including being a fit and proper person (see section 11) and having undertaken training (see section 12).

(6) Sections 21 to 25 provide for enforcement of registration and licensing requirements, including a power for local housing authorities to issue rent stopping orders where landlords fail to comply with licensing requirements.

(7) Section 28 provides for the Welsh Ministers to issue a code of practice setting standards to be followed when managing rental properties and provision is made for guidance (section 29) and directions (section 30).

(8) Sections 31 to 34 make supplementary provision.

(9) Section 35 makes further provision about interpretation and indexes the defined terms used in the Part.

The Housing Bill showed a clear appreciation of how overview sections can be used regularly throughout a lengthy enactment to introduce the content and structure of either Parts or Chapters, demonstrating a discriminating use of overview provisions where they assist in elucidating the enactment for the reader. Nevertheless, controversy exists regarding the inclusion on the face of enactments of material which seeks to provide the reader with the purpose of the legislation or to give an overview of its structure as well as its contents. Some drafters are very much in favour of doing this, and others equally opposed. Some believe that it is in explanatory notes and memoranda that such material rightly belongs, not on the face of an Act. However, the National Assembly has in large measure embraced these techniques enthusiastically, so that Overview sections at the start of bills are now a common feature.[26]

PURPOSE PROVISIONS

Much the same is true of purpose provisions. While some hold to the view that such statements, explaining why the changes to the law contained in the bill are being proposed, rightly belong in accompanying explanatory materials, others emphasize the usefulness to the reader of their being present on the face of the legislation. In the past, a device commonly used to provide a statement of the purpose of an enactment was the Preamble, but these have fallen out of favour. Some would argue that the inclusion of purpose sections in contemporary legislation is a reflection of the loss sustained through abandoning preambles, and would favour a return to their use. Preambles are still used at Westminster to explain the need for legislation in private as opposed to public bills. Preambles were, however, used to explain why, in policy terms, it was proposed to change the law. Purpose provisions in modern legislation are meant to explain why the changes are being made in terms of how it is proposed to change the law. 6-32

As with overview provisions, purpose sections are becoming common in Assembly legislation. Sometimes the two functions are confused. Both of the following are described in the respective texts as Overviews, but it is submitted they are in truth purpose provisions – and good ones too. The first is from the Control of Horses (Wales) Act 2014. 6-33

> This Act makes provision for local authorities to seize, impound and dispose of horses which—
> (a) are in public places without lawful authority, or
> (b) are on other land without the consent of the occupier of the land.

[26] Other good examples of effective Overview provisions can be found in the Food Hygiene Rating (Wales) Act 2013 and the Renting Homes (Wales) Act 2016.

The provision does not describe the structure and content of what follows, but states what it is intended to achieve by legislating. It is a purpose provision. The same is true of the purported overview at the start of the Recovery of Medical Costs for Asbestos Diseases (Wales) Bill.

> This Act—
> (a) imposes liability on persons by whom or on whose behalf compensation payments are made to or in respect of victims of asbestos-related diseases to pay charges in respect of National Health Service services provided to the victims as a result of the diseases;
> (b) makes provision for the certification of the amount of the charges to be paid, for the payment of the charges, for reviews and appeals and about information;
> (c) extends insurance cover of liable persons to their liability to pay the charges.

The provision states what the legislative changes made by the bill will achieve; it does not describe where the changes are delivered in the proposal.

6-34 Purpose provisions in Assembly Acts may be both useful and dangerous. They may be useful in that they can assist the courts in determining the purpose of provisions if the Assembly's competence to enact them has been challenged.[27] While the courts will not accept at face value that the purpose of a provision is within competence merely because the enactment claims that it is so,[28] it would be bizarre if they were to entirely discount such statements, particularly as the statements have been enacted formally by the legislature.[29] Where it could be shown that provisions which could be read as going beyond the competence of the Assembly could also be read as being entirely within competence if their effect was limited to the purposes set out in a purpose provision, then the usefulness of such provisions would be immense.[30] However, this is what also makes them dangerous. If a provision of an Assembly Act, where no question of competence arises, could be interpreted as having a wide effect or a narrow effect, the purpose provision might be deployed to argue for the narrower interpretation. This could be restrictive on those who have to implement the enactment's provisions. In particular, if the Act gave powers to make subordinate legislation or to take executive action, those granted the powers might find them to be circumscribed by the Act's statement of purpose more than would have been the case if no such section had been included, and therefore

[27] They can also be useful in the interpretation of other provisions when the courts adopt a purposive approach: see below, §§8-33–8-44.

[28] See *Re Local Government Byelaws (Wales) Bill* [2012] UKSC 53 at ¶49 *per* Lord Neuberger.

[29] Surprisingly, little was made of the statement in section 1 of the Recovery of Medical Costs for Asbestos Diseases (Wales) Bill in the judgments of the Supreme Court. It was generally accepted that the purported purpose of the bill was to fund the NHS in Wales, even though the subject is not mentioned in the opening section of the bill, which though headed 'Overview' reads more in the nature of a purpose provision.

[30] GoWA, s. 154 requires a provision 'to be read as narrowly as is required for it to be within competence … if such a reading is possible, and is to have effect accordingly'.

susceptible to challenge by judicial review for having gone beyond the powers granted when considered in the light of the stated purpose.

Given the potential for purpose provisions to be used to interpret the provisions of Assembly Acts and limit their effects, there is also a danger that those developing policy and drafting provisions may seek to rely on that fact to avoid the difficult work of determining exactly the limits of the proposed provisions, relying on the courts to limit the effects of enactments in individual cases through application of the purpose section rather than spelling out the exact limits in the legislation itself. This is a danger which attends law-making in a legal culture that allows purposive interpretation, and is one of the differences between the traditional style of legislation in England and Wales and that in the civil law jurisdictions of mainland Europe. It is submitted that such a change in legislative style and judicial responsibility should not be made to arise by the practices of policy development and legislative drafting. Unless and until there arises a consensus among the various branches of government that such a change is desirable, policy proposals should be developed and legislative provisions framed with a view to thoroughness. 6-35

INTERPRETATION

It is not only with regard to the purpose of provisions that the question of how the text of an enactment is to be interpreted is of importance. The same is true with regard to the meaning of all its provisions. In order to ensure that the words and expressions employed in a statutory enactment are given the precise meaning which the legislature intends when it comes to their being applied and interpreted by the courts, it is customary to include within the enactment provisions that define the meaning to be given to certain terms within it. This may be done in the particular section where a term occurs, or the terms to be defined may be collected and presented in an interpretation section towards the end of the bill or, if the bill has been subdivided into parts, at the end of the relevant part. Which approach to adopt will depend partly on how best to assist the reader and partly on whether the definition is to apply to the use of the term throughout the enactment or only in a particular part or a particular section or sections within it. Where definitions are distributed within an enactment, it is a useful practice to include an index of defined terms towards the end of the enactment.[31] The following is a typical interpretation section: 6-36

[31] It is customary to place interpretation sections towards the end of Acts, whereas they are usually placed at the beginning of items of subordinate legislation. The difference is held to be a consequence of the fact that the scrutiny of bills proceeds from their start to their finish, and that it would be unwise to settle the meaning of terms before their use in the text has been examined. As subordinate legislation is not subjected to such scrutiny, it is convenient for the reader to be told the meanings at the outset. The explanation implicitly recognizes that bills are structured for the benefit of those who consider whether to enact them, and not necessarily for those who will refer to them after their enactment. It is becoming customary to place interpretation provisions relating to key terms, essential to the understanding of an enactment, towards the beginning of an Act or its relevant part.

> In this Act—
>
> 'horse' ('*ceffyl*') includes a pony, donkey or mule or any other equine animal;
>
> 'local authority' ('*awdurdod lleol*') means the council of a Welsh county or county borough.[32]

It is customary for the definitions in interpretation sections to be set out alphabetically. In a bilingual text, this poses the problem that, as in the example above, the terms will not appear in the same order in both languages. The practice of placing the equivalent term in the other language in parentheses immediately after the term is therefore followed to allow for ease of cross-reference. The equivalent provision in the Welsh version therefore reads:

> Yn y Ddeddf hon—
>
> ystyr 'awdurdod lleol' ('*local authority*') yw cyngor sir neu fwrdeistref sirol yng Nghymru;
>
> mae 'ceffyl' ('*horse*') yn cynnwys merlen, asyn neu ful neu unrhyw anifail ceffylaidd arall.

This is not generally done in the case of single definitions or in lists which are numbered rather than alphabetical as the problem does not arise, although there seems no reason why it should not be done as the apparent inconsistency can confuse readers.

6-37 Definitions within single sections follow this pattern, but can be put to another use. It is often the case that a subject or concept within a provision requires careful, perhaps lengthy, definition, and that it would be inconvenient to repeat the whole of that on each occasion the concept is to be employed. In such circumstances, terms are frequently coined for use in those contexts, which terms are then defined elsewhere in the provision or group of provisions. The following is an example of such use from the Control of Horses (Wales) Act 2014:

> The 'relevant day' means—
>
> (a) if the local authority gives notice under section 3(4), the day on which that notice is given, and
>
> (b) otherwise, the day on which the local authority places the notice under section 3(1).[33]

The use of 'relevant day' avoids the need to repeat a formula such as 'either the day on which the local authority gives notice under section 3(4) or otherwise the day on which it places the notice under section 3(1)' each time the concept is employed.

[32] Control of Horses (Wales) Act 2014, s. 9.

[33] Section 5(2).

Referential interpretation

Occasionally, the intended meaning for a term has already been ascribed to it in another enactment. In such circumstances, the interpretation provision may simply refer to the earlier definition. For instance, in the interpretation section of the Government of Wales Act 2006 one finds: 6-38

> 'the Convention rights' has the same meaning as in the Human Rights Act 1998.[34]

While such a referential provision is hardly helpful to the reader, it indicates clearly that no change is being made to a meaning already enshrined in law and that any interpretation placed upon the expression in that context by the courts can be applicable in the new context as well, although whether that will be the case is a question of interpretation for the courts on each occasion. The usage underlines the function of enactments as changers of the law rather than as presenters or explainers of it. Where an enactment is one of a series of statutes relating to a particular subject, the number of such referential definitions may be considerable to ensure that consistency of terminology and meaning is achieved throughout the series as a whole.

The Interpretation Act

The creation of a common canon of interpretative provisions across a range of statutes brings one to the statute the entire object of which is to provide a corpus of settled meanings for use throughout the statute book, or at least in the absence of a contrary intention. That statute is the Interpretation Act, the current version in force for England and Wales being that of 1978. The meaning of many terms and expressions used repeatedly in legislation is set out in the provisions of this Act, thus making it unnecessary to reproduce them on every occasion that they are relevant to a piece of legislation. While objectionable as a potential pitfall for the uninformed reader, it undoubtedly circumscribes the need for regular repetition of the definition of commonly used terms. What is important is that the definitions are provided in accompanying explanatory materials, and modern techniques of electronic production should make it possible to allow for such terms to be identified in the text and their definition accessed by means of hyperlinks. Scotland now has its own Interpretation Act, and it has been suggested that Wales should follow 6-39

[34] GoWA 2006, s. 158(1).

suit, particularly as the 1978 Act has no equivalent corpus of definitions for Welsh legal terms to that contained for English terms.[35]

Presumptions

6-40 In drafting the provisions of a bill, legislative counsel will be aware of the existence of such background interpretative material and will draft the provisions accordingly. They will advise against duplicating definitions which are already implicitly present courtesy of the Interpretation Act. They will also be aware of certain presumptions that the courts will make when interpreting legislation, advising whether the presumption needs to be rebutted in the proposed law to achieve a different effect or whether it is unnecessary to include material on the face of a bill because it is safe to assume that the courts will achieve the desired interpretations of the provisions courtesy of the presumptions.

6-41 These presumptions are not rules of interpretation which the courts must follow. They are presumed interpretations to which the courts will adhere unless a contrary intention has been expressly indicated or must be deduced by necessary implication. They include, for instance, the following:

- a presumption against retrospectivity: the courts will presume that the legislation is not meant to apply other than to conduct following the legislation's coming into force and effect;
- a presumption against strict liability: the courts will presume that no one is to be civilly or criminally liable for breach of any duty contained in the legislation unless they are blameworthy for that breach;
- a presumption against taxation: the courts will presume that it is not intended to impose a tax or duty in the absence of a clear, express intention to do so;
- a presumption against creating rights and duties: the courts will presume that there is no intention to create entitlements or to impose duties in the absence of a clear, express intention to do so;
- a presumption against removing rights and duties: the courts will likewise presume that there is no intention to remove entitlements or duties in the absence of a clear, express intention to do so;

[35] This was suggested in 2012 by the then Counsel General, Theodore Huckle QC. The Law Commission has subsequently recommended that 'the Welsh Government and the National Assembly consider, and keep under review, the practical benefits of introducing an Interpretation Act of the Assembly': Law Commission, *Form and Accessibility of the Law Applicable in Wales / Ffurf a Hygyrchedd y Gyfraith sy'n Gymwys yng Nghymru* (Law Com. No. 366), 10.44–10.65, and Recommendation 25. The Welsh Government has since held a consultation on the issue: see *Interpreting Welsh Law: An Interpretation Act for Wales*, WG33701, December 2017 (version 2), and published a draft Legislation (Wales) Bill for consultation (March 2018).

- a presumption against ousting the jurisdiction of the courts: the courts will presume that their jurisdiction to administer the law is not affected by the enactment.[36]

Canons of construction

Legislative counsel will also be aware and take account of certain canons of construction used by the courts when interpreting – construing – legislative provisions. These again are not hard and fast rules but principles which guide the courts' interpretation. Unlike presumptions, they do not indicate a definite result in the absence of a contrary intention but suggest what may be a sensible interpretation in the light of experience. Many of them are encapsulated in brief Latin expressions, particularly in cases dating from more than a generation ago. They include, for instance: 6-42

> *eiusdem generis* – literally 'of the same kind'. Where a legislative provision contains a list of things which are similar to one another, the court may take this to mean that it is meant to include other similar things even though they are not expressly mentioned. For instance, the definition of 'horse' from the Control of Horses (Wales) Act given above listed ponies, donkeys and mules as being within the definition. Even if the words 'or any other equine animal' had not been added, it is likely that the courts would have interpreted the term to include such animals.
>
> *noscitur a sociis* – literally 'it may be known by its friends', a legal equivalent of 'birds of a feather flock together'. Where there is a doubt as to the meaning of a term in a provision or group of provisions containing other terms which exhibit common characteristics, an interpretation of the doubtful term will be adopted which recognizes the likelihood that it was meant to share those characteristics.
>
> *in pari materia* – literally 'in like materials'. This approach recognizes that a term or an expression has an accepted meaning in legislation dealing with the same or a similar subject and therefore suggests that the same meaning is likely to be the one intended in the provisions being considered.
>
> *expressio unius, exclusio alterus* – literally 'the expression of one excludes the other'. In a sense, this principle contradicts the *eiusdem generis* approach, for it suggests that if a thing has been omitted from a list while similar things have been included, the omission will be taken to have intended that the thing was not to be included. It illustrates perfectly that these canons of construction are

[36] For a full treatment of the relevant presumptions, see Daniel Greenberg (ed.), *Craies on Legislation* (11th edn, London, 2017), ch. 19.

not hard and fast rules, but that their purpose is always to assist in finding the legislative intention.

The context alone determines which, if any of them, is a useful tool of construction. This is why legislative counsel prefer to avoid relying on them to achieve a desired interpretation but rather to make the intention and the required meaning plain. Hence the inclusion of 'or any other equine animal' in the definition of 'horses' mentioned above.[37]

PROVISIONS AMENDING OTHER LEGISLATION

6-43 As a general rule, the provisions of an Assembly Act can amend or even repeal provisions in other legislative enactments, including Acts of the UK Parliament. Where this is done in order to effect the policy goals which the Assembly legislation aims to achieve, the amendment or the repeal will form the subject-matter of a section or sections in the bill before the Assembly. Sometimes this will involve the insertion or deletion of a whole section, subsection, paragraph or sub-paragraph in an earlier Act, while on other occasions it may require the insertion, substitution or deletion of only a few words. Either way, the amendment will be drafted so as to accord with the structure and phrasing of the Act being amended.[38]

6-44 In the interests of ensuring that legislation which applies only in relation to Wales is to be found in Assembly Acts rather than scattered across the UK statute book and in the interests of ensuring that such legislation can be found in both languages, the Assembly and the Welsh Government have, as a matter of policy, preferred to repatriate legislative provisions by means of including them in Assembly Acts rather than placing such provisions in Westminster statutes by amendment. This is a sensible and commendable approach, well exemplified by the Human Transplantation (Wales) Act 2013. Indeed, the Assembly is permitted to re-enact provisions relating to matters outside its competence where that does not change the law.[39] This allows relevant legislative provisions to be gathered together in one place in the interests of accessibility, and can be of immense value therefore in

[37] Once more, a fuller treatment of the canons can be found in Daniel Greenberg (ed.), *Craies on Legislation* (11th edn, London, 2017), ch. 20.

[38] Frequently, where several new sections are being inserted into an earlier Act, these will be drafted so that each section to be inserted forms the content of a section in the bill making the amendment. Strictly speaking, this is not necessary as one section in a bill could make all the insertions. However, as scrutiny and amendment of the bill before the Assembly proceeds on a section by section basis, allotting each new section to be inserted to a distinct section in the bill makes for a more manageable process of scrutiny. This again illustrates how it is the legislative process that shapes – even dictates – the structure and expression of proposals.

[39] GoWA 2006, Sch. 7B, Pt 2, para. 13. Prior to the insertion of the new Schedule 7B by the Wales Act 2017, the restatement provision was in GoWA 2006, Sch. 7, Pt 3, para. 8.

the process of consolidating or codifying legislation on a topic.[40] It also allows for provisions to be consistently available in both Welsh and English, rather than some being bilingual and some English only.[41]

Existing legislation can be amended in different ways. Most often, amendment is effected by altering the text, but other methods can be employed. 6-45

Textual amendment

This is done by altering the earlier enactment by means of insertion, substitution or deletion. The extent of the change can be considerable in terms of the amount of text altered, but even a small alteration in the text can produce a major change in the legislation's effect. The following examples of textual amendments, taken from section 15(4) of the Human Transplantation (Wales) Act 2013, illustrate how changes are made by insertion and substitution. Deletion does not require illustration. 6-46

> In section 29 (approval of codes)—
>
> (a) after subsection (1) insert—
>
> '(1A) Where a code of practice to which subsection (1) applies deals with a matter relating to the carrying on in Wales of a transplantation activity (within the meaning of the Human Transplantation (Wales) Act 2013) the Authority may not issue the code unless—
>
> (a) a draft of it has been sent to and approved by the Welsh Ministers and laid by them before the National Assembly for Wales, and
>
> (b) the National Assembly has approved the draft by resolution.';
>
> (b) in subsection (2)(a) for 'National Assembly for Wales' substitute 'Welsh Ministers';

Textual amendment results in changes being made to the earlier Act so that, when it is read in its amended form, the effect of the amendment is clear on the face of the legislation. Its disadvantage is that, other than in the case of the insertion of a significant amount of new text, the effect of the amendment is not clear on the face of the bill proposing the amendment. Paragraph (b) above, amending the text of section 29(2)(a) of the Human Tissue Act 2004 illustrates this perfectly: there

[40] The Law Commission has recommended that the Welsh Government pursue a policy of codification and institute regular programmes of codification: see Law Commission, *Form and Accessibility of the Law Applicable in Wales / Ffurf a Hygyrchedd y Gyfraith sy'n Gymwys yng Nghymru* (Law Com. No. 366), Recommendations 1 and 14, and generally 2.1–7.46, and Recommendations 1–18.

[41] This would, however, give rise to questions about the equal standing of the two language versions of such 'repatriated' texts, given that some provisions would not have originally been enacted in both languages, and no change to the interpretation of such provisions would have been intended.

is nothing to explain to the reader what the effect is of deleting the reference to the National Assembly and substituting the Welsh Ministers. The effect of such an amendment therefore needs to be explained in the accompanying materials, and many advocate the use of so-called Keeling schedules to make the effect of the amendment clear by reproducing the text as amended, or even with the text to be amended with the amendment tracked upon it.[42] The amended paragraph would then be shown to read:

> (2) Before approving a draft code of practice sent to him under subsection (1), the Secretary of State shall—
>
> (a) if the code relates to Wales, consult the ~~National Assembly for Wales~~ Welsh Ministers, … .

Non-textual amendments

6-47 The intention behind an amendment is often clearer when the method used is to gloss the text of an earlier enactment rather than to alter the text itself. An instance of this can be seen in section 20 of the Education (Wales) Act 2014, which states how an earlier enactment is to be read as a consequence of the new legislation being made. It reads:

> (1) Chapter 2 of Part 2 of the 2013 Act (intervention in local authorities) has effect in relation to duties imposed and powers conferred by virtue of section 17 as if references to the local authority included—
>
> (a) the governing body (within the meaning given by section 90(1) of the Further and Higher Education Act 1992) of a further education institution, and
>
> (b) an appropriate body other than a governing body of a school maintained by a local authority, the governing body of a special school not so maintained or a local authority.

While such 'glossing' amendments make clear what is being achieved on the face of the amending bill, they in turn however leave no trace of the amendment made on the face of the earlier enactment which has been amended. Both methods therefore have their disadvantages as well as their advantages. With electronic publication of statutory enactments, it is technically possible to indicate by means of a footnote reference where text has been subject to a non-textual amendment, although not necessarily easy to determine where such amendments have occurred.

[42] The schedules are called Keeling schedules because the suggestion that a Bill amending or applying an existing enactment by reference should contain a Schedule setting out the enactment as it would read when amended by the Bill was put forward in 1938 by Sir Edward Keeling MP. The Assembly now requires a schedule of that sort to be included in the Explanatory Memorandum accompanying a bill if there is a significant amount of such textual amendment: SO 26.6C.

Consequential amendments

The amendments considered thus far are those which appear among the principal provisions of a bill, as they are concerned with changes being made to the existing law in order to give effect to the policy goals it is hoped will be achieved. It may, however, be the case that these changes will necessitate changes in other existing pieces of legislation, albeit that these are not directly concerned with the achievement of the policy goals. It may be, for instance, that the new enactment being made needs to be added to the text of other statutes or to replace the short titles of enactments being repealed, or that a new body being created in the proposed legislation needs to be included in already existing provisions. As such consequential amendments need to be made only if the principal provisions are approved, and approval of those principal provisions requires their being made, consequential amendments of this kind are usually set out in a Schedule to the bill. They are therefore subject to scrutiny and can be amended, as they will need to be if the principal provisions which they facilitate are rejected or amended in a way which affects them. An example of such a schedule can be seen in the Mobile Homes (Wales) Act 2013. 6-48

SCHEDULE 4

(introduced by section 58)

CONSEQUENTIAL AMENDMENTS

Caravan Sites and Control of Development Act 1960 (c. 62)

1 (1) The Caravan Sites and Control of Development Act 1960 is amended as follows.

(2) In section 1, after subsection (1) insert—

'(1A) Subsection (1) does not apply in relation to a regulated site within the meaning of the Mobile Homes (Wales) Act 2013.'

(3) In section 23—

(a) in subsection (1), after 'any land' insert 'in England', and

(b) omit subsection (9).

(4) In section 24—

(a) in subsection (1), after 'local authority' insert 'in England', and

(b) in subsection (8), omit 'in England'.

The example is confined to the first paragraph of the schedule, but it can be seen from this that the text is set out similarly to sections in the main body of the Act, albeit that the principal divisions of schedules are called paragraphs rather than sections. Use is made of italic headings to indicate the earlier piece of legislation being amended. From the text, the consequential nature of the amendments is clear: the earlier Act is being disapplied in relation to Wales (sub-paragraph (2)) and its provisions limited to England (sub-paragraphs (3) and (4)). The legislation being amended is usually set out chronologically, and a tabular presentation is sometimes employed. The amendments contained in the schedule are given effect by a provision in the main body of the Act stating, for example, that:

> Schedule 4 contains consequential amendments

or, as purists would prefer:

> The consequential amendments contained in the Schedule have effect.

The provision which gives effect to the schedule is sometimes, as in the example above, referred to in the Schedule by an italic sub-heading, or sometimes in a marginal note.

6-49 The need for such consequential amendments will be identified by lawyers when considering the effect the changes proposed have upon the whole body of existing law. Unlike most of the provisions contained in the main body of the Act, therefore, these consequential changes are matters for decision by lawyers and not the framers of the policy.

TRANSITIONAL AND SAVING PROVISIONS

6-50 The need for transitional, transitory and saving provisions is also something to be identified and, in part, determined by lawyers. It is frequently the case that the introduction of new legal provisions cuts across the operation of the provisions which they replace. Prosecutions under the pre-existing law may be in train, or actions may be pending before the civil courts. Provision may need to be made for the governance or administration of a body or activity while an old system is being phased out and a new one brought in.

6-51 In such circumstances, the enactment being proposed needs to include saving provisions to ensure that offences committed under the old law can continue to be prosecuted, and that civil actions for, for instance, compensation, can continue to be brought. It may be necessary to set up some mechanism to oversee the transfer of responsibilities and the passing of contractual and property rights from a body being abolished to its successor. Such provisions, because they are solely concerned with the move from one legal regime to another, are referred to as transitional, transitory or saving provisions. Like consequential amendments, they are needed only if the principal provisions being proposed are approved; they are not themselves vehicles for anything more than the shift from the old approach to the new. As the need for them is dependent upon the approval of the principal provisions, they need to be open to rejection or amendment while the bill is being scrutinized. Therefore, like consequential amendments, they need to be part of the bill but do not need to be included among the provisions that deliver the policy objectives. Accordingly, like consequential amendments, they are usually set out in a schedule, which is given effect by a provision in the main body of the Act. Once more, an example of a saving provision in such a schedule is taken from the Mobile Homes (Wales) Act 2013.

SCHEDULE 5
(introduced by section 58)

TRANSITIONAL AND TRANSITORY PROVISIONS AND SAVINGS

Prosecution of pre-commencement offences

7 Nothing in any provision of this Act affects the operation of any enactment in relation to offences committed before that provision comes into force.

The identification of the possible need for transitional, transitory and saving provisions, like the need for consequential amendments, is a matter for lawyers, but – unlike consequential amendments – how that need is to be met may involve decisions which need to be addressed by policy makers.[43] Lawyers, however, will need to ensure that what is done about existing rights, duties and liabilities conforms to the requirements of human rights law and natural justice. The importance of such provisions to citizens whose lives become affected by the area of the law in question while it is in the process of being changed cannot be overly stressed. Those whose focus is on implementing the change may regard them impatiently as technicalities. Lawyers and drafters will rightly insist that the issues relevant to them are thoroughly and competently addressed.

COMMENCEMENT OR COMING INTO FORCE[44]

The bill, when it has been passed and has received Royal Assent, becomes an Act. 6-52
An Act changes the law, and the law which it changes affects the lives of those bound by its terms. It is necessary therefore for those who are affected by the Act's provisions to know of them, or to be able to find out what they are, otherwise the provisions would be of little, if any, effect. Accordingly, there is a convention – not a legal rule – that an Act does not come into force until two months have passed since it received Royal Assent. If it is wished to bring an Act into force sooner than that, the convention is that the permission of the relevant law officer is obtained for doing so before the commencement provision is presented in the bill. The Attorney General is the relevant officer in the case of legislation before the UK Parliament and the Counsel General in the case of bills before the Welsh Assembly. Most commonly, such permission would be sought where the provisions

[43] See above, §§5-41–5-42.

[44] Until very recently, the term **Commencement** was in general use, but the arguably more understandable phrase **Coming into force** is also now to be found as the heading for these kinds of provision.

in question do not affect the lives of citizens generally, or where those affected by the provisions are bound to know of their effect as soon as the bill has been passed. In such circumstances, there is no reason why the provisions should not come into force and effect immediately.

The following illustrate the ways in which these commencement procedures appear on the face of a bill – where the two-month convention is being followed:

> This Act comes into force at the end of the period of 2 months beginning with the day on which it receives Royal Assent

and where permission has been obtained to waive it:

> This Act comes into force on the day on which it receives Royal Assent

or:

> This Act comes into force on the day after the day on which it receives Royal Assent

the second formula avoiding any doubt as to exactly when on the day upon which it received Royal Assent it came into force.

6-53 Frequently, particularly with lengthy or complex enactments which have a number of discrete parts, it is necessary for provisions to be brought into effect at different times. Where that is the case, it is customary to allow for their introduction by one or more commencement orders, the making of which is generally entrusted to government ministers. Such commencement orders are a form of subordinate legislation and are therefore made by statutory instrument, but because they do not themselves change the law but only introduce changes which have already been agreed by the legislature, they do not require affirmation by the legislature nor indeed that the legislature be given an opportunity to annul them. In other words, they are not subject to either affirmative or negative procedure. The section of the Act creating the power to make commencement orders has, of course, to have become effective before the orders can be made,[45] so that the relevant provisions appear in this kind of form:

> **Commencement**
> (1) This section comes into force on the day on which this Act receives Royal Assent.
> (2) The remaining provisions of this Act come into force on a day appointed by order made by the Welsh Ministers.

[45] Anticipatory exercise of such a power is permitted under s. 13 of the Interpretation Act 1978, but is rarely relied upon.

The two-month convention then applies to the provisions commenced by the order to ensure that no order can commence a provision within that time.

Where it is anticipated that the Act's provisions will require a staggered introduction, to allow for flexibility to respond to circumstances, the following kind of provision may be added: 6-54

> An order under this section may appoint different days for different purposes.

More controversially, it may be thought necessary to couple with that function an opportunity to make further transitional, transitory or saving provisions. Where the purpose of such a power is to allow consequential changes which have become necessary in the intervening period between the passing of the Act and its being brought into force, such a provision is sensible and arguably unobjectionable, although it is questionable even then whether it should be coupled with a commencement order so as not to require scrutiny by either affirmative or negative procedure given that, unlike usual commencement orders, an order containing such provisions changes the law. Where such a provision is included, it will generally read like this:

> An order made under this section may include such transitional, transitory or savings provision as the Welsh Ministers consider necessary or expedient.

It is the lack of scrutiny which makes this sort of power controversial and the exercise of such a power within a commencement order democratically objectionable. The granting of such a power is not legally challengeable, but that should not prevent its being subject to a careful application of democratic principles.[46]

EXTENT

In legislation enacted by the UK Parliament, there is frequently an extent provision. 6-55
This is often a subsection within a section at the end of the Act dealing with the short title and sometimes also with commencement. The purpose of the extent provision is to indicate within which of the United Kingdom's legal systems the enactment is to be treated as law and enforced by the courts, who are bound to take judicial notice of its provisions and apply them in cases before them. If the enactment is to be law in England and Wales, Scotland and Northern Ireland – that is, throughout the whole of the United Kingdom – no extent provision is needed as the courts in each of those jurisdictions proceed on the presumption that, in the absence of a contrary intention, Acts of the UK Parliament extend throughout the

[46] See National Assembly for Wales: Constitutional and Legislative Affairs Committee: Fourth Assembly Legacy Report, March 2016, pp. 13–14, and Recommendation 6, discussed below, §§8-01–8-02 and n. 2.

United Kingdom. A contrary intention is normally indicated by an extent provision stating, for example, that the enactment extends only to England and Wales, or, for instance, that it does not extend to Scotland.

6-56 As the Government of Wales Act 2006 expressly provides that Assembly Acts can only extend to England and Wales, there is no need for extent provisions to be included in them. Extent is not to be confused with application. Although they only apply in relation to Wales, Assembly Acts extend to England and Wales in that England and Wales is a single jurisdiction, the courts in any part of which will take judicial notice of and implement laws whether those laws apply only in relation to England, only in relation to Wales or in relation to both countries.

Chapter 7

Process and Promulgation

Policy objectives require legislation for their achievement when the means chosen for giving effect to them necessitate changing the law. Where such changes to the law affect the freedoms, duties and powers of citizens, or the granting of powers to the government or other bodies which can so affect the rules by which citizens lead their lives, in a democratic society the proposals to do that should be subjected to proper debate and scrutiny by the elected representatives of the citizens. To enable that to occur, the proposals will be presented to those representatives as a bill, the provisions of which propose the relevant changes to the law. The purpose of the legislative process is to enable that proper debate and scrutiny to take place. 7-01

It will be recalled that every legislative process involves three phases: the bringing forward of the proposal or introductory phase; consideration of the proposal in terms of its goals and how it intends to achieve them in the deliberative phase; and the final decision as to whether the change or changes proposed should be made – the decision-making phase. The manner in which a particular legislative process performs these tasks should provide for the amount of debate and scrutiny which is appropriate to decide such matters in a democratic society. Consideration must now be given to how that process is conducted in the National Assembly for Wales. The process in the National Assembly is governed by the provisions of the Government of Wales Act 2006, and the Standing Orders which the Assembly is required to have in place under that Act.[1] 7-02

THE INTRODUCTORY PHASE

The introductory phase in concerned with bringing the legislative proposal in the form of a bill before the Assembly. Those who may do so are said to have the legislative initiative and, as well as identifying who those persons are, the introductory phase is concerned with how their power to propose legislation is to be exercised. 7-03

Legislative initiative: the member in charge

The Government of Wales Act 2006 sets out who has the legislative initiative. This is done in section 110. Subject to the Standing Orders of the Assembly, a bill may be introduced by the First Minister, any one of the Welsh Ministers or Deputy Welsh Ministers, the Counsel General or any other Assembly Member (AM). The manner in which the Act presents this demarcates between members of the Welsh 7-04

[1] The provisions relating to the legislative process are to be found principally in GoWA 2006, ss. 110–111. The requirement of Standing Orders is to be found in s. 31.

Government on the one hand and other AMs who do not hold a government office.[2] The Counsel General enjoys the legislative initiative as a member of the Welsh Government even though he or she may not be an AM.

7-05 The person who is introducing the bill is described in the Act as the *person in charge*, although in the Standing Orders the person is referred to as the *member in charge*. The latter term will be used here as general usage tends to follow the Standing Orders.[3]

7-06 The member in charge must, either before the bill is introduced or at the time of its introduction, make a statement to the effect that in his or her opinion the provisions contained in the bill are within the Assembly's legislative competence. It is therefore essential that any questions concerning competence which may have arisen in the course of the bill's preparation have been resolved so as to allow the member in charge to make that statement. This includes obtaining any consent required from the Secretary of State or the Treasury for conferring, imposing, removing or modifying functions of a Minister of the Crown, a UK government department or other reserved authority.[4] Being unable to state that the provisions of the bill are within competence would mean that the bill could not be introduced.

The Explanatory Memorandum

7-07 Standing orders require that the statement by the member in charge should be made in the Explanatory Memorandum which has to accompany the bill on its introduction.[5] This Explanatory Memorandum, or EM as it is commonly known, must also set out the policy objectives of the bill. This will enable those who will later deliberate upon the proposals to form a view both as to whether they agree with the objectives of the bill and as to whether they agree with the means by which it is proposed to carry those objectives into effect. It will also be recalled that the Supreme Court has indicated that when questions arise as to the competence of the Assembly to enact provisions, the purpose of provisions can perhaps most clearly be ascertained from such documents. Clarity with regard to the policy objectives is therefore of considerable importance to ensuring its effective scrutiny and its subsequent freedom from challenge in the courts.

[2] The government members are listed in s. 110(1)(a), while the AMs are to be found in s. 110(1)(b).

[3] It may be thought that the phrase *member in charge* overlooks the power of a Counsel General who is not an AM to exercise the legislative initiative. This is not so. Standing Order 24 defines *member in charge* in terms of members of the Welsh Government, members of Assembly Committees, members of the Assembly Commission and backbench AMs. Where the Counsel General exercises the initiative, therefore, he is, like any of his government colleagues, the member of the government who is in charge, not the member of the Assembly. The same is true in the case of committee- or commission-sponsored legislation. The significance of the distinction becomes apparent if the person concerned ceases to be a member of the government, the committee or the commission, in that they cannot then continue to be the member in charge of the bill even if they continue to be AMs.

[4] See above, §§4-60–4-73.

[5] SO 26.6(i).

As well as setting out the policy objectives, the means for achieving which are the provisions of the bill, the EM is also required to reveal whether alternative methods of achieving the policy goals were considered and why the means which the bill provides were preferred. This in effect calls for the incorporation of material reflecting the evidence and analysis undertaken in determining the preferred option for achieving the policy. If due attention has been given to this in the process of policy development, it will be reflected in the quality of the EM. Likewise, the quality of the EM may expose any lack of such attention to the full glare of publicity. The EM is also required to reveal whether any consultation took place on the bill's objectives, choices of means for their achievement or indeed the detail of the bill itself. Where consultation has taken place, a summary of its results is also required. It needs to be borne in mind that the EM is admissible background material to assist the courts in interpreting the legislation, and, where protected human rights are involved, can also be used in determining how much weight to attach to the Assembly's evaluation of the competing interests. 7-08

As its title suggests, one of the key functions of the EM is to explain what each of the provisions contained in the bill is intended to achieve. This function should present the provisions in terms of their being means to give effect to the bill's policy objectives. It recognizes that the bill is not a statement of policy but, in Lord Diplock's words, the means for giving effect to that policy. While it might be thought that the clarity required should be achieved by the bill, that would confuse the means with the effect to be achieved. The provisions in the bill deliver the necessary changes to the law required to give effect to the policy; the EM is expected to explain how the legal changes are meant to achieve that. If the provisions are self-explanatory in that regard, the Standing Orders recognize that there is no need for the EM to explain them, but if information further to an explanation of the provisions is needed to explain the effect of the bill, the EM should provide it. The terminology of the Standing Orders is redolent of the 'purpose and effect' provision of the Government of Wales Act. This underlines the importance of the EM once more, not just in the context of the bill's introduction and passage through the Assembly, but also to its possible interpretation by the courts after enactment. 7-09

The EM must also address the conferral of any powers to make subordinate legislation. For each and every such power which it is intended to confer under the proposed enactment, the EM must state to whom the power is being given, why it is thought appropriate to delegate the subordinate law-making power, how it is intended that the power is to be exercised and what kind of procedure – affirmative or negative – is to be employed before the Assembly to oversee its exercise. With regard to the choice of Assembly procedure, reasons must be given as to why that procedure is thought to be appropriate and why other procedures were rejected. The level of justification demanded reflects the seriousness of giving what is a legislative function to someone other than the democratically elected legislature. 7-10

As well as setting out the policy objectives of the bill and describing the means by which it is intended to achieve them, including the means of delegating subordinate law-making functions, the EM must deal with the likely costs of pursuing 7-11 the policy objectives by these means. This should account for the administrative and compliance costs, and any other kind of cost, to which it is anticipated that the bill's provisions will give rise, and identify on whom those costs are likely to fall and when they are likely to be incurred. Once more, it will be seen that these questions are among those which should have been addressed at an early stage in the development of the policy proposals, as they relate to the questions of who is going to be affected, when and how. If it is intended that it will be necessary to incur charges against the Welsh Consolidated Fund, that is the public funds available to the Welsh Government to carry out its functions, the EM has to incorporate a report from the Auditor General for Wales setting out his or her views regarding the appropriateness of that expenditure. The Standing Orders are now also required to provide that the person in charge makes a written statement setting out the potential impact of any of the bill's provisions on the justice system in England and Wales, and Standing Orders require that this justice impact assessment has to be included in the EM.[6]

7-12 Assessments of impact are a fundamental part of policy making, and impact assessments are a record and statement of such assessments. Where proposed legislation could affect the public or private sectors, in particular small businesses, or charities or the voluntary sector, and changes to the law are being considered from which costs or benefits could accrue, a Regulatory Impact Assessment (or RIA for short) is required as part of the Explanatory Memorandum.[7] Its purpose is to provide the Assembly and other interested parties with sound estimates of the likely impact of the proposed changes.

7-13 The member in charge is required to provide the Explanatory Memorandum to the bill at the same time as the bill is introduced. The bill is introduced by being laid, and the EM must be laid at the same time as the bill.

'Laying' the bill

7-14 The notion of introducing the bill by 'laying' it reflects the terminology, and the procedure on which it is based, in the UK Parliament. There, bills have to be introduced in one of the chambers. Taking the Commons as the example, a bill is introduced at its first reading, which involves a ceremony in which the member proposing the bill proceeds from the bar marking the entrance to the Commons chamber towards the table in front of the Speaker's Chair, bowing on three occasions as he or she makes their way forward. The third bow is as the member reaches the table and places – lays – what appears to be a copy of the bill in the hands of one of the clerks who sit at the table. The clerk then reads out the title, which constitutes the first reading of the bill. It is usually the case that what appears to be a copy of the bill is in reality nothing more than a blank document with the title of the bill only on its cover. This, however, satisfies the requirements of a first reading

[6] GoWA 2006, s. 110A, inserted by Wales Act 2017, s. 11; SO 26.6(xii).

[7] SO 26.6.

at Westminster. A date is then agreed for the second reading of the bill, by which time a full version of the bill should be available to members.

There is no such ceremony – nor subterfuge – involved in 'laying' a bill before the National Assembly. The full text of the bill, in both English and Welsh unless there is a sound reason for permitting submission in one language only,[8] is forwarded to the Table Office, another term borrowed from Westminster. This is generally done electronically by sending the bill as an e-mail attachment from, in the case of government bills, the Office of Legislative Counsel. The Explanatory Memorandum will be forwarded at the same time. 7-15

Even though there in no ceremony involved in laying within the Assembly Chamber, a bill can only be introduced by being laid during a week in which the Assembly sits in plenary session. It may be introduced, however, on any working day during such a sitting week. Mondays to Fridays count as working days for bills to be laid. The only days which do not count as working days, if they happen to fall during sitting weeks, are Christmas Eve, Christmas Day, Maundy Thursday, Good Friday, bank holidays and any days which have been designated for public thanksgiving or mourning.[9] To be laid, the bill must be in proper form. What constitutes proper form is determined by the Presiding Officer.[10] 7-16

Presiding Officer's decision on competence

As well as determining the proper form for bills and ensuring that each bill presented for laying is in conformity with that determination, the Presiding Officer is required by the 2006 Act to decide whether or not, in his or her opinion, it is within the Assembly's competence to enact the provisions of the bill. Having made that decision, the Presiding Officer is required by the statute to state it in writing in both official languages. The Standing Orders require this statement to accompany the bill on its introduction and to indicate whether the provisions of the bill are within competence and to indicate if any provisions are thought not to be so, together with reasons for that opinion. 7-17

The Standing Orders interestingly, perhaps confusingly, do not refer to the Presiding Officer's duty to decide but only the duty to make the statement. The Presiding Officer's duty is, however, not to state, as is the duty of the member in charge, whether he or she believes the provisions of the bill to be within 7-18

[8] The Standing Orders provide that government bills may be in one language only if the member in charge gives specific reasons in writing as to why it would be inappropriate in the circumstances or reasonably impracticable to submit a bill in both official languages. Otherwise, a bill in one language only may be laid only in accordance with the determination of the Presiding Officer in relation to such laying: SO 26.5.

[9] Maundy Thursday is the Thursday before Easter. The bank holidays are those so designated for Wales under the Banking and Financial Dealings Act 1971.

[10] Presiding Officer's determination of proper form can be found on the Assembly website at *http://www.assembly.wales/NAfW%20Documents/Assembly%20Business%20section%20documents/PO_Determination_Public_Bills/PO_Determination_Public_Bills.pdf.*

competence, but to decide whether in his or her opinion they are. The statute is silent as to the consequences of the Presiding Officer's coming to the conclusion that they are not. The question of how the two duties differ has not been judicially considered; that they differ is apparent from the use of different words in the same statutory section. Bills have been introduced where there has been a difference of opinion.[11] Provisions which are believed to be outside competence can of course always be amended during the bill's passage or, even if they are passed by the Assembly and then found by the Supreme Court to be outside competence, amended during the Reconsideration Stage. However, one might have thought that the purpose of requiring the Presiding Officer to *decide* the matter would be to prevent wastage of time and resources in debating, scrutinizing and passing possibly invalid provisions.

7-19 The problem need not arise, however, if due care is taken in assessing before introduction whether the provisions are within competence, thus avoiding any conflict between the views of the member in charge and those of the Presiding Officer. Practice allows for the Presiding Officer's staff working for the Assembly Commission to see the bill well in advance of the date of its formal introduction so as to assess both whether it is in proper form and whether its provisions are within competence. Therefore, any clash of opinion is likely to have become apparent and, it is to be hoped, resolved before laying. The problem can still, of course, arise if the difference of views proves intractable. Some believe that there should be a formal mechanism to resolve such a question before the bill proceeds.

THE DELIBERATIVE PHASE

7-20 The deliberative phase is concerned with debating and scrutinizing the legislative proposal, the question being by whom and how that process of debate and scrutiny will be conducted. The Government of Wales Act 2006 requires that the Standing Orders of the Assembly provide for a general debate on a bill with an opportunity for Assembly members to vote on its general principles, and also provide for the Assembly members to consider the details of the bill together with an opportunity to vote on the details. Thus the answer to the question of who is to debate and scrutinize is clear: only Assembly Members, the elected representatives of the Welsh people.

7-21 Apart from insisting that there should be debate and vote on the general principles and a separate consideration and vote on the details, the 2006 Act leaves the means by which this is to be done for the Assembly itself to decide in its Standing Orders. The procedure adopted by the Assembly is to divide the process into four stages: Stage One deals with the debate and vote on the general principles, while Stages Two and Three allow for the consideration and voting on

[11] Examples include the Environment (Wales) Bill and the Public Health (Wales) Bill during the Fourth Assembly.

details in committee and in plenary session respectively. Stage Four relates to the decision-making phase and will be considered later, but a Report Stage is permitted between Stages Three and Four if some tidying up of the proposal is thought necessary at that point.

Once a bill has been introduced, the Assembly's Business Committee is required to draw up a timetable for the progress of the bill, although, if it is a government bill, it is for the government to determine how time in plenary is to be allocated for its progression.[12] The Business Committee can thereafter vary the timetable, but must give reasons for doing so.[13] 7-22

Stage One

Once the bill has been introduced, the Business Committee must also decide whether to refer the bill to the Assembly committee or committees responsible for the policy areas with which the bill deals. The Assembly is required to establish committees to examine the policy of the Welsh Government and other associated public bodies together with legislation in relation to those areas so as to ensure that all areas of devolved responsibility are subjected to scrutiny. Thus, if the bill is concerned with education, it can be forwarded to the Assembly committee that is responsible for the scrutiny of the government's education policies; if it concerns public health, it will go to the committee with that responsibility, and so on. 7-23

The purpose of referring the bill to the appropriate committee at Stage One is for the committee to consider and report on the general principles of the bill. Its report is meant to facilitate and inform the subsequent debate in plenary session at the end of Stage One as to whether the general principles of the bill should be approved. By forwarding the bill to the Assembly committee with responsibility for the scrutiny of the relevant policy area, the aim is to have it scrutinized by members who are likely to be familiar with the issues raised by reason of their wider, general responsibilities as members of that committee.[14] 7-24

[12] SO 26.7; SO 11.12.

[13] SO 26.8.

[14] During the Third Assembly (2007–11), when the Assembly had competence to legislate by means of Measures, two different approaches for such committee scrutiny were tried. During the Assembly's first year, committees were established *ad hoc* to consider proposed Measures as they were introduced. During the last three years of that Assembly, five Standing Committees for the scrutiny of legislative proposals were established, four to deal with government proposals and one to deal with those from backbench members. While the current system is thought by many to be an improvement in that the members of the responsible committee are more likely to be familiar with and better-informed regarding the issues raised, some are less convinced, believing that, as some policy areas are more productive of legislative proposals, AMs on other committees obtain less experience of legislative scrutiny, which is detrimental to the Assembly's development as a legislature. Nevertheless, many hold that this use of subject committees by the Assembly constitutes one of the most distinctive and beneficial differences between procedure there and at Westminster.

7-25 The Business Committee does not have to refer a bill to such a subject committee for consideration at Stage One, and cannot do so if the bill is a government emergency bill.[15]

Stage One – subject committee

7-26 Where a bill is passed to a subject committee for Stage One consideration, the committee will generally issue a call for evidence. It may invite interested parties, those with a particular stake in the bill's success, or otherwise, and those with expertise in the areas in question to contribute. It may invite contributions from the public generally. It may also invite persons who have submitted evidence, or whose evidence the committee feels would be useful, to attend the committee and provide oral evidence by means of presentation or by responding to questions from committee members. The committee, assisted by clerks from the staff of the Assembly Commission, will be examining the case for pursuing the plan of action which the promoters of the bill have adopted. In other words, they are gathering evidence so as to reach their own view as to whether the policy goal is desirable and whether the promoters' preferred option of achieving it meets with their approval. Although, at this stage, they are not able to propose any changes to what is proposed, the evidence being gathered and their response to and analysis of it may well lead them to propose changes at a later stage even if they are not minded to oppose the proposal as a whole. If the initial work of policy development undertaken by the bill's promoters has been thorough, the committee's deliberations should not throw up any nasty surprises. A lack of thoroughness in that initial work is likely to be exposed.

7-27 The member in charge of the bill, in the case of a government bill the relevant Welsh Minister or Deputy Welsh Minister, will certainly be called to give evidence regarding the bill's general principles. When attending a Stage One committee, a Minister is generally accompanied by two officials, either of whom he or she may call upon to answer questions on his or her behalf. At these sessions, the Minister is almost certain to be challenged regarding the preferred option to which the bill gives effect as explained in the EM. He or she is likely to be challenged regarding the evidential base for the proposal and the acceptability of the analysis which has led to the policy's adoption. It is here that the thoroughness of the initial policy development will be tested in public, and where the comprehensiveness and rigour of that initial work will pay dividends in showing mastery of the proposal. The committee is likely to utilize the evidence and analysis of the others who have contributed to its deliberations to frame its questions and challenges to the Minister. Careful attention to the evidence and the committee's discussion of it in preparation for the Minister's appearance is likely to be extremely useful. While officials may find it difficult to allocate time to attend committee sessions in the public gallery in order to monitor that process, and the temptation to rely on the

[15] The special procedure for Government emergency bills is considered below, as is the regime regarding backbench members' bills, §§7-82–7-85.

written record of committee meetings or the recorded coverage on Senedd TV may be great, nothing can rival seeing and hearing for oneself not merely the evidence given but the committee members' response to it, in terms of body language and facial expression as much if not more than verbal response. Neither the written record nor Senedd TV can provide that insight.[16]

When the subject committee has completed its hearings and the analysis of the evidence it has received, it will report to the Assembly on the general principles of the bill. It will be recalled that the Supreme Court included the reports of Assembly committees among its potential sources from which the purpose of a bill and its provisions could be ascertained. This should be borne in mind by the promoters of the bill when giving written and oral evidence, which in turn are likely to be reflected in the report. Again, it is important to remember that these reports constitute admissible background material to assist the courts in interpreting an enactment, and can also be used, where human rights are involved, to determine how much weight to attach to the Assembly's evaluation of the competing interests as it is manifested in the reports. 7-28

The Business Committee will have set a deadline in its timetable for the bill by which the subject committee is expected to publish its report. When it has done so, or has failed to do so by the due date, the member in charge may within five working days move that the Assembly agree to the general principles of the bill. If the Business Committee has decided not to forward the bill to a subject committee for consideration, the member in charge can move the approval of the bill's general principles immediately, in that there is no time needed to consider the report. 7-29

The Constitutional and Legislative Affairs Committee

As well as being considered by the appropriate subject committee at Stage One, where the policy of the bill is examined, the bill will also be sent to the Assembly's Constitutional and Legislative Affairs Committee. This is the committee charged with examining those provisions of the bill that give the Welsh Ministers, the First Minister or the Counsel General powers to make subordinate legislation. The Committee is concerned with the appropriateness of giving the government such law-making powers, and will also examine the appropriateness of the procedures – affirmative or negative – which it is proposed to use in making that subordinate legislation.[17] It will be recalled that the Standing Orders require the Explanatory Memorandum to specifically address these issues. 7-30

Like the subject committee, the Constitutional and Legislative Affairs Committee, which is frequently referred to by the acronym CLAC, can invite and take both written and oral evidence, and will also call upon the member in charge, accompanied by officials in the case of Ministers, to speak to such provisions and 7-31

[16] Senedd TV is an on-line coverage of all Assembly business which is open to the public in plenary and committee, together with an archive of such material recorded and available on-line. The cameras, however, quite properly focus primarily on the person speaking, not the reaction of the listeners.

[17] SO 21.

thereby assist in its deliberations. It is here that government ministers will find themselves politically accountable for the choices they have made between the changes to the law that are to be made on the face of the bill, and therefore undergo full debate and scrutiny, and those it wishes to be made without such scrutiny by means of subordinate legislation. This committee in effect considers the extent to which the bill respects the democratic principle that changes to the law affecting the freedoms, duties and powers of citizens should be fully debated and scrutinized by their representatives.

7-32 Like the subject committee, CLAC will produce a report for the Assembly to consider prior to the Stage One debate. The committee has acquired a reputation for unsparing criticism of failures to observe democratic principles. Once more, a government without a majority does well to monitor the progress of a bill before CLAC to gain an idea of what compromises may be required at later stages of the bill's progress with regard to subordinate law-making powers and the use of affirmative and negative procedure. Indeed, the general thrust of CLAC comments and proposals regarding these matters over the course of an Assembly or even over a longer period are worth monitoring so as to provide guidance when considering, during the preparation of later bills, what is appropriate with regard to the granting and exercise of subordinate law-making powers.

The Finance Committee

7-33 The Assembly is required to establish a Finance Committee which is charged with considering and reporting on any document that the Welsh Ministers or the Assembly Commission lay before the Assembly containing proposals for financing or the use of resources. The Committee is also allowed to consider and report on any other matter which relates to or affects expenditure out of the Welsh Consolidated Fund. Resources are used, for the purposes of the committee's remit, if they are expended, consumed or reduced in value, and this includes expenditure out of the Welsh Consolidated Fund or otherwise paid for out of taxes, charges or any other kind of revenue.[18] It will be recalled once again that the Standing Orders require the Explanatory Memorandum to specifically address issues of cost.

7-34 When called upon or when it has decided to consider a bill, the Finance Committee will, in order to facilitate and inform the Stage One debate, either report to the Assembly or to the relevant subject committee, having taken evidence in much the same manner as the other Stage One committees.

Stage One debate

7-35 The Stage One debate is on the bill's general principles. It takes place in a plenary session of the Assembly in the Senedd chamber. If the motion is not passed, the bill falls immediately. If it is passed, the bill continues to Stage Two, subject to what is said below concerning a financial motion. A government with a working majority can guarantee the success of the Stage One motion, but a minority government

[18] SO 19.

cannot. A minority government may therefore have to undertake to amend the bill in the coming stages in order to secure a sufficient number of votes to get the bill through Stage One. The extent to which such compromises may be necessary should have become apparent during the deliberations of the Stage One committees, which again makes it important that those proceedings are monitored closely so that the likely suggestions for amendment can be scoped and the promoters can consider in advance what amendments they are prepared to concede. They may well be called upon to promise such changes during the course of the Stage One debate in order to secure the votes needed from other political groups to guarantee a successful Stage One passage.[19] Such concessions may include 'upgrading' the procedures needed to make subordinate legislation from negative to affirmative in order to increase the Assembly's control over the exercise of such powers.

The opportunity to have a vote on the bill's general principles must be available at the end of the Stage One debate, but it is not necessary for a vote to actually take place. Many bills will complete this stage unopposed. That does not mean that there will not be differences of opinion as to how the detail of the bill is to carry the principles into effect. 7-36

Financial resolution[20]

Standing orders require the Presiding Officer to decide, in relation to every bill which comes before the Assembly, whether it requires a financial resolution. A bill that requires a financial resolution cannot progress beyond Stage One unless a financial resolution regarding it has been passed. Such a resolution cannot be passed until after Stage One has been completed, and, if one is needed, Stage Two proceedings cannot begin until it has been passed. It is common for a motion to pass such a resolution to be moved immediately following the completion of Stage One. 7-37

A bill requires a financial resolution if it contains a provision charging expenditure on the Welsh Consolidated Fund, or its likely effect would be a significant increase in expenditure from the Fund, or to give rise to significant extra expenditure either for new services or purposes or for existing services or purposes. Where that is the case, the bill cannot progress through Stage Two unless the Assembly has passed a financial resolution agreeing to the expenditure or the increase. The same is true if the bill imposes or increases a charge upon any person or body or requires them to make a payment which would go into the fund, and likewise if it confers a power to impose or increase such a charge or payment. However, the charge or increase must be significant, and the requirement does not apply if it is a reasonable charge for the provision of goods or is wholly or largely directed to recovering the cost of services. 7-38

[19] Again, if the preparatory work has been thorough, there will be less difficulty in assessing which amendments can be accepted without compromising the Bill's policy objectives. The less thorough that grasp, the greater the danger of accepting amendments which could undermine the goal.

[20] SO 26.68–74.

7-39 As a bill cannot proceed through Stage Two in the absence of such a resolution where the Presiding Officer has decided that one is needed, if no such resolution has been agreed within six months of Stage One having been completed, the bill falls. Only a member of the government can move a motion for a financial resolution, the government being responsible for the budget. As a consequence, even without a majority in the Assembly, the government has a mechanism by which it can cause a non-government bill to fail without being able to vote it down. By delaying moving a motion for a financial resolution for six months, the government can stop a bill which it does not wish to see become law from proceeding. This can, of course, only be done where the bill has been held to require a financial resolution. In deciding upon such a course, however, the government would need to bear in mind the risk of any backlash against its own legislative proposals if it has no guaranteed majority in the Assembly.

Stage Two[21]

7-40 Stage Two commences the working day after Stage One is completed. Stage Two is concerned with the detail of the bill. The general principles having been agreed, the question now is whether the choice of means to give effect to those principles is acceptable. At this stage, therefore, AMs are not limited to agreeing or disagreeing with what has been proposed in the bill, but can propose their own improvements to the bill provided that they do not stray into altering the principles which have already been agreed.[22] Such suggested changes take the form of amendments to the bill.

7-41 Any member of the Assembly may suggest an amendment. Amendments may be submitted as soon as Stage Two commences but they must be relevant to the bill and must be submitted in accordance with the Presiding Officer's determination of what is the proper form for amendments.[23] Members may suggest as many amendments as they wish. The member in charge may propose amendments to his or her own bill, and this is a common occurrence. On occasion, this may be done to correct some error or infelicity in the original draft, but it is also done in order to accommodate changes that have been suggested or even agreed to during the Stage One proceedings. The promise to make such changes may have been the price paid for support in getting the bill through Stage One.

7-42 Stage Two proceedings are taken entirely in committee. On the completion of Stage One, the Business Committee will either remit the bill for Stage Two proceedings to the subject committee which considered it at Stage One, or, if

[21] SO 26.16–28; 57–66.

[22] In other words, the agreed general principles determine what at Westminster is sometimes referred to as the *scope* of the bill.

[23] The Presiding Officer's determination of proper form may be found on the Assembly website at *http://www.assembly.wales/NAfW%20Documents/Assembly%20Business%20section%20documents/PO_Determination_Amendments_to_Bills/PO_Determination_Amendments_to_Bills.pdf*.

the bill had not been dealt with in a subject committee at Stage One, forward it to the appropriate subject committee. It is possible for a motion to be moved in plenary session that a bill be considered by a Committee of the Whole Assembly with the Presiding Officer chairing, but this is very unusual other than in the case of Government Emergency Bills where such a Committee of the Whole Assembly is mandatory.[24]

The Committee may not commence its deliberations at Stage Two until fifteen working days have elapsed since the completion of Stage One, and then only if any necessary financial resolution has been passed. Members wishing to submit amendments to the bill must do so at least five working days prior to the meeting at which they will be considered. There is no provision for late submission at Stage Two. As well as publishing them as they are received, the Presiding Officer can group the amendments for submission, and the amendments received will come to the committee in the form of a marshalled list. Unless the committee determines otherwise, the amendments will be dealt with according to the sequence in the bill of the sections and schedules which they propose to amend. The amendments to each section will be considered in turn, and, once the amendments to that section have been dealt with, the section is deemed to have been agreed, as are any sections to which amendments have not been submitted once they have been passed over in order. It is therefore important that members submit their amendments, particularly those to early sections of a bill, in good time for them to be included in discussion. 7-43

Amendments will only be decided upon by the committee if they are moved by a member of the committee. Members in charge, although allowed to be present in the committee and to speak to their amendments, may not move or vote upon them. As government ministers cannot be members of committees, it follows that they always have to rely on a committee member to move government amendments for them. The composition of the committee will reflect the composition of the party groupings in the Assembly itself. Therefore, if the government does not have a majority in the Assembly, it will not have a majority in the committee, and consequently cannot expect that its amendments will necessarily succeed nor that the amendments of other political groups will fail.[25] Government ministers attending the committee to speak to their amendments, and support or oppose those of others, are allowed to be accompanied by officials and to receive advice from them, but the officials are not permitted to address the committee themselves in the manner in which they were permitted to do at Stage One. 7-44

The fact that no single political party has yet succeeded in obtaining a comfortable working majority in the Assembly has meant that a culture of necessary 7-45

[24] SO 26.103.

[25] The composition of Assembly Committees was governed by statute: GoWA 2006, s. 29. However, this requirement has now been repealed by Wales Act 2017, s. 14, leaving the Assembly free to decide upon the composition of its committees in its own Standing Orders: GoWA 2006, s. 28.

cooperation has developed. In the context of bill procedure, this manifests itself in a virtual absence of wrecking amendments or amendments aimed at delaying a bill's progression. Amendments are routinely aimed at achieving what are genuinely believed by their proponents to be improvements to the bill. The lack of a government majority means that amendments can succeed; there is therefore no reason for them not to be serious suggestions for improvement.

7-46 This has implications for the members in charge of bills, and in particular government ministers. If the policy development behind the bill has been thoroughly undertaken, alternative ways of achieving the policy objective will have been scoped, and the reasons for not adopting them identified. This makes it likely that the driving motive for many, if not all, of the amendments which will be proposed as the bill progresses will have been anticipated and understood, albeit rejected. Likewise, efficient monitoring of the bill's consideration and examination at Stage One will both have revealed the likely source of amendments to the bill at Stage Two and have given a fair idea of their content. There is no reason therefore why the minister as member in charge should find himself or herself wrongfooted or embarrassed when dealing with the amendments of others at Stage Two. Indeed, the minister as member in charge retains a tactical advantage in that, although the Standing Orders require that the Explanatory Memorandum reveal whether alternative ways of achieving the bill's policy objectives were considered and why the approach taken in the bill was adopted, they do not require that the reasons for rejecting the alternative options be explained. It is the minister therefore who can come prepared to set out these reasons to the committee, and those who have to reply to him or her who will have think on the spot in response to those reasons.

7-47 Once an amendment has been submitted by an AM, it is open to other AMs to add their names to the amendment in support of it. Thereafter, if the original proposer wishes to withdraw the amendment, it will be withdrawn only if the other supporters no longer wish to continue with it. If any of them does, it will be listed in the name of the earliest of them to lend their support. When amendments come to be dealt with by the committee, they will be dealt with individually or in the groups identified by the marshalled list. When an amendment or group of amendments is reached, only members of the committee may move them; if no member of the committee does so, the amendment falls. Once moved, an amendment may only be withdrawn by the member of the committee who moved it, and then only if the committee members all agree to its being withdrawn. Amendments are accepted or rejected by majority vote of the committee. Sections or schedules which are not amended are deemed to have been agreed by the committee.

7-48 When the last amendment has been disposed of or the end of the bill reached, Stage Two ends. The bill is now in the form in which it has been amended. Where amendments have been made, the member in charge is required to produce a revised Explanatory Memorandum unless the committee has decided that this is not necessary.

Stage Three[26]

Stage Three commences on the first working day after Stage Two is completed. It is concerned with considering the detail of the bill as amended at Stage Two, but is conducted in a plenary session of the Assembly and not in committee. This ensures that every AM has an opportunity to consider, scrutinize and vote on the details of the bill. 7-49

The first Stage Three debate may not take place until fifteen working days have elapsed since the completion of Stage Two, although amendments may be submitted once Stage Three has commenced. Amendments can again be tabled by any Assembly Member and must be submitted at least five working days before the meeting at which they are to be discussed. At Stage Three, it is open to the Presiding Officer to allow amendments to be tabled less than five working days before the relevant meeting. Such amendments are termed late amendments, and they differ from those tabled on time in that it is not open to other members to add their names in support of them. All amendments must be submitted in proper form and must be relevant to the bill and not at odds with its general principles as agreed at Stage One. 7-50

Whereas at Stage Two all amendments tabled fall for consideration by the committee, at Stage Three the Presiding Officer has a discretion as to which amendments may be discussed. This is meant to enable him or her to prevent delaying and wrecking amendments, and to prevent those which have had a fair hearing at Stage Two from being aired a second time without need. In practice, during the Third and Fourth Assemblies, the Presiding Officer has never not selected for discussion an amendment which has been properly tabled. Amendments are again dealt with in plenary according to the order in which the sections or schedules to which they relate arise in the bill, and the Presiding Officer may again group amendments for consideration. It is, however, open to the Business Minister (that is the Welsh Minister with responsibility for government business before the Assembly), or the Assembly Business Committee, to move that the amendments be dealt with in a different order, and, if the Assembly agrees, the order is varied.[27] The Business Minister or the Business Committee may also move that time limits be imposed on the discussion of amendments or groups of amendments, and, if the Assembly agrees, these time limits will apply, although the Presiding Officer may still allow discussion beyond those limits if either a change in the order in which groups of amendments are to be considered occurs as a result of an amendment not being moved or if he or she feels that the limit would place an unreasonable curtailment on discussion. 7-51

[26] SO 26.29–44; 57–66.

[27] The Business Minister would move such a motion in the case of a government bill and the Business Committee in the case of other bills. Voting on the Business Committee is structured to ensure that the government cannot override the wishes of backbench members in relation to non-government business: see SO 11.5(iv).

7-52 Once an amendment has been tabled, it can be withdrawn but only if all the members supporting it are agreeable, otherwise it continues under the name of the member who registered his or her support earliest. Once moved, an amendment may not be withdrawn if any Assembly Member present objects, and, if the proposer does not move his or her amendment in the meeting, any other AM may do so. Any section or schedule which is not amended is deemed to have been agreed. Amendments are accepted or rejected by majority vote of the AMs present, the Presiding Officer having a casting vote in the event of a tie which must be cast against the amendment so as to preserve the *status quo ante*.[28]

7-53 The member in charge, including the responsible minister in the case of a government bill, may move amendments at Stage Three. Quite often such amendments are tabled in order to 'tidy' the bill as a consequence of amendments that the government did not support having succeeded at Stage Two. This will have required scoping of the effects of such amendments on the bill's achievement of its policy goal. Scoping of this sort may well have been done in preparation for the Stage Two consideration in committee, and in some cases amendments may have been withdrawn at Stage Two in return for a commitment by the government to introduce an amendment at Stage Three that is more consistent with the other provisions of the bill or with the law generally applicable to the area under consideration. With regard to bills that are not government bills, the government may promote amendments, as it may have done at Stage Two, to keep a bill to which it is not opposed from becoming inconsistent with the government's own policies.

7-54 The member in charge will speak to his or her own amendments at Stage Three, and that will be the responsible Minister in the case of government bills. As the debate is in plenary session in the Senedd chamber, officials will not be seated with the minister at this stage, but can maintain electronic communication by means of the computer terminals available at every AM's desk seat in the chamber. Voting is also conducted electronically, without members having to leave their seats. The proceedings continue until all of the amendments selected by the Presiding Officer for consideration – which so far invariably has meant all of the amendments – have been accepted or rejected.

7-55 At this point, the member in charge or any member of the government[29] may move that there be further consideration of the bill at Stage Three. This is to allow further amendments to be tabled in order to clarify the provisions of the bill as amended, to ensure that the English and Welsh versions of the bill as amended are consistent, or to deliver on promises made earlier during the Stage Three proceedings. This again recognizes the reality that, if the government does not have

[28] SO 6.20.

[29] A member of the government differs from a government member. The latter is an Assembly Member belonging to the party or, in the case of a coalition government, the political group which has formed the government; the former means the First Minister, the Welsh Ministers, the Deputy Welsh Ministers and the Counsel General. A Counsel General who is not a government member can, as a member of the government, do this: see SO 9.3 and 9.4.

a majority in the Assembly, it cannot confidently expect that the bill, whether a government bill or not, will emerge from detailed consideration in quite the form the government wishes. Further Stage Three consideration allows the bill to be 'tidied' to remove, for example, any inconsistencies or infelicities which may have arisen, as well as allowing for promises, made to obtain support, to be kept. Backbench members have the same problem, and therefore have the same opportunity, in relation to their bills.

Two issues deserve to be considered here, which are relevant at both Stage Two 7-56
and Stage Three. First, it is possible that an amendment may be made which takes a provision of the bill outside the Assembly's legislative competence. Somewhat surprisingly, the Standing Orders do not disallow such amendments. Seemingly, it is left to the government or other Assembly Members to bring the bill back into competence by subsequent amendment, or to the Counsel General or the Attorney General to spot the problem and refer the provision to the Supreme Court, a fairly drastic and expensive solution. Secondly, an amendment may introduce into the bill a provision which, had it been in the bill as introduced, would have been held to require a financial resolution. In this second scenario, the Standing Orders provide that such an amendment may not be proceeded with unless the Assembly has agreed a financial resolution.[30] At Stage Three, the Presiding Officer could, of course, not select for debate an amendment which it was thought posed either of these problems.

A motion that there be further Stage Three consideration must be voted upon 7-57
without any debate or amendment. If it is passed, Stage Three proceedings will be extended to allow further amendments to be considered in the same manner as previously in Stage Three, but these further amendments may only be tabled by the member in charge or a member of the government. This restriction manifests both the nature of the exercise and its limited nature.

When all of the amendments selected for consideration at Stage Three have 7-58
been accepted or rejected, and all unamended sections and schedules therefore deemed to have been agreed, Stage Three is completed. This may also mark the end of the deliberative phase of the legislative process, unless, that is, there is a Report Stage.

Report Stage[31]

Once Stage Three has been completed, the member in charge may move a motion 7-59
that the Assembly consider amendments at a Report Stage. The motion is not subject to amendment, but it may be debated. The member in charge may wish to explain why he or she considers a Report Stage to be necessary.

It may be necessary to consider amendments at a Report Stage to 'tidy' the 7-60
bill as amended at Stage Two or Stage Three by removing inconsistencies and

[30] SO 26.72.

[31] SO 26.45–46B.

infelicities. If these have arisen at Stage Three, the limitations upon what may be proposed by amendments at further Stage Three consideration may not have permitted what the member in charge wishes to see done. If the motion is passed, the opportunity will be provided.

7-61 Amendments at Report Stage may be tabled by any AM and are dealt with in the same manner as at Stage Three, the Presiding Officer having a discretion as to which amendments to select and there being a possibility of further Report Stage proceedings on the motion of either the member in charge or a member of the government. If the bill was amended at Stage Three, the member in charge is required to lay a revised Explanatory Memorandum, explaining the bill as amended at Stage Three, unless the Assembly has resolved that a revised EM is not needed. Where a revised EM is required, it must be laid at least five working days before the Report Stage proceedings begin.

7-62 When the amendments selected for consideration at the Report Stage have all been accepted or rejected and the unamended sections and schedules deemed to have been agreed, the Report Stage is completed, as is the deliberative phase of the legislative process of the bill.

THE DECISION-MAKING PHASE

7-63 The Government of Wales Act 2006, as well as requiring the Standing Orders to provide for a general debate on the bill with an opportunity for AMs to vote on its general principles and to provide for the consideration of the bill's details by AMs together with an opportunity to vote on them, also requires that the Standing Orders provide for a final stage at which the bill can be passed or rejected.[32] This final stage is Stage Four of the Assembly's legislative process. It is the stage at which the democratic representatives of the people of Wales decide whether or not to make the changes to the law which have been proposed in order to give effect to the policy objectives behind the legislation.

Stage Four[33]

7-64 Once Stage Three, or the Report Stage if there is one, has been completed, any Assembly Member may table a motion that the bill be passed. The motion must be tabled a working day before it is debated, and it is not ordinarily to be debated until five working days have passed since the completion of either Stage Three or the Report Stage. However, it is open to any member to propose immediately following the conclusion of Stage Three or the Report Stage that the motion to pass the bill be taken, and the Presiding Officer may allow this provided that the text of the bill is available in both official languages. In practice, it has been common for

[32] GoWA 2006, s. 111(1)(c).

[33] SO 26.47–51.

the motion that the bill be passed to be taken immediately upon the completion of Stage Three or Report, and this is what the Standing Orders originally anticipated. The above change to the Standing Orders was made during the fourth Assembly.

There is one further restriction upon the debate that the bill be passed. If the bill contains any provision which would, if it were a bill before the UK Parliament, require the consent of either Her Majesty the Queen or the Duke of Cornwall, the Assembly must not debate the question that the bill be passed until the relevant consents have been signified as forthcoming by a member of the government during proceedings on the bill before the Assembly. This is another issue, like that of Minister of the Crown consents considered earlier, which should have been spotted as requiring resolution while the bill was in preparation, although it is possible for these consents to become necessary only as a result of amendments made to the bill during its passage through the Assembly. Unlike Minister of the Crown consents, these consents do not go to the competence of the Assembly and their absence does not therefore prevent the bill's introduction. However, they need to have been obtained and reported to the Assembly by the government before the Stage Four debate can commence.[34] The need for these consents, both in relation to bills at Westminster and in the Assembly, arises from the fact that the monarch and the heir to the throne have, since the late seventeenth century, assigned, to an ever greater extent, their hereditary revenues to the Treasury in return for an annual grant called the Civil List, which by today basically supports the Royal Family and its household. The monarch, however, still retains hereditary revenues from the Duchy of Lancaster as does the heir to the throne from the Duchy of Cornwall. Therefore, if legislation affecting those revenues is proposed, it is thought proper that the relevant consents be sought, on the principle that those whose lives are affected by a change in the law should be given the opportunity to consent to it. 7-65

The motion that the bill be passed is debated without amendment. Although any member may propose the motion, it is usually the member in charge who does so. Other members may then speak as called by the Presiding Officer, and the proposer of the motion has an opportunity at the end to reply to the debate. A vote is then taken if that is necessary. It has not been unusual for bills to be passed without a vote, another indicator of the inclusive, mature style of politics that has developed in the Assembly. If a vote is taken, the bill will pass if a majority of members are in favour, otherwise it will fail. In the event of a tie, the Presiding Officer is required by Standing Orders to use his or her casting vote against passing the bill, thus maintaining the *status quo*.[35] If the bill is rejected, neither it nor a similar bill can be reintroduced within six months of its rejection. It is for the Presiding Officer to determine if a subsequent bill is so similar to the rejected bill as to fall foul of this provision.[36] 7-66

[34] GoWA 2006, s. 111(4); SO 26.67.

[35] SO 6.20.

[36] SO 26.76.

7-67 As has been mentioned earlier, the Assembly has acquired powers under the Wales Act 2017 to legislate regarding its name. This is one of a number of matters regarding which the Assembly may now legislate, but only with the agreement of an absolute majority of its members, described in the legislation as a 'super-majority'. By this is meant that a specific fraction of the Assembly membership must support the decision, not just a specific fraction of those present and voting. The super-majority required for provisions which deal with what the legislation calls a 'protected subject-matter' is two-thirds, so that as long as the number of Assembly Members remains at sixty, forty AMs would have to vote for such a provision for it to pass.[37] Both the Presiding Officer and the Deputy Presiding Officer may vote where such a majority is required.[38]

7-68 The Assembly also now has the power to legislate concerning its membership, another protected subject-matter. This power includes the ability to determine the number of its constituencies and electoral regions, the number of members to be returned for each constituency and region, the system by which members are elected and who may vote in Assembly elections. Each of these issues is a protected subject-matter, requiring provisions relating to them to be passed by a super-majority, with the exception of provisions that are incidental or consequential. The Assembly may also legislate in this way regarding the number of Welsh Ministers and Deputy Welsh Ministers who may hold office at any one time.[39]

7-69 The question of whether a provision in a bill relates to one of these protected subject-matters is one for the Presiding Officer to determine after the completion of Stage Three and any Report Stage proceedings, and before it moves to be passed or rejected at Stage Four. The Presiding Officer must state his or her decision. If the Presiding Officer has decided that the bill does contain one or more provisions relating to a protected subject-matter, the bill will require a super-majority to pass.[40] If the Presiding Officer has decided that the bill does not contain any such provisions, it can be passed by a simple majority of those present and voting.

Reference to the Supreme Court and Secretary of State intervention

7-70 If the bill is passed, the Presiding Officer must submit it for Royal Assent. This, however, must not be done until a period of four weeks has passed. During that time it is open to the Attorney General or the Counsel General to refer the bill or any provision in it to the Supreme Court of the United Kingdom to determine

[37] The term 'weighted majority' is often used in other legislatures when a specific fraction of those present and voting have to support a proposition for it to pass, distinguishing that situation from that in which an absolute majority, being a specific fraction of the overall membership, is required.

[38] SO 6.21.

[39] GoWA 2006, s. 111A, inserted by Wales Act 2017, s. 9. Some of these issues have already been considered by a panel of experts: see National Assembly for Wales, *A Parliament that Works for Wales: The Report of the Expert Panel on Assembly Electoral Reform* (November 2017).

[40] GoWA 2006, s. 111A(3), (4).

whether the bill or the provisions in question are within the legislative competence of the Assembly.[41]

Such a reference may also be made if either of the Law Officers wishes to question the Presiding Officer's decision as to whether the bill includes provision relating to a protected subject-matter. This would arise if the bill had passed by a simple majority where it is thought that it actually related to a protected subject-matter. However, a reference of this kind could also arise where a bill had been rejected, having failed to pass for want of a super-majority, where the Law Officer believes it was not correct to require one. Either way, either of the Law Officers can refer it to the Supreme Court during the four-week window.[42] 7-71

For the same period, it is open to the Secretary of State to intervene if he or she has reasonable grounds to believe that the bill or any of its provisions will have an adverse effect on a matter that is not devolved, or have an adverse effect on the operation of the law as it applies in England, or might be incompatible with the UK's international treaty obligations or the interests of defence or national security. If the Secretary of State has such a reasonable belief, he or she can make an order, stating the reasons for doing so, preventing the bill from being submitted for Royal Assent. The order, which must be laid before both Houses of Parliament at Westminster, takes effect if neither House annuls it.[43] 7-72

If any of these eventualities occurs, the Presiding Officer must not submit the bill for Royal Assent until either the Supreme Court reference has been resolved in favour of the Assembly or the Secretary of State's order has been annulled. The Secretary of State is allowed a full four-week period to consider intervention following a Supreme Court ruling. The Presiding Officer is, however, free to submit the bill for Royal Assent without having to wait for the expiry of the four-week period if the Law Officers and the Secretary of State have indicated that they do not intend to make a reference or intervene respectively. 7-73

While a reference to the Supreme Court questions whether the Assembly had the power to pass the bill in its final form, the intervention of the Secretary of State questions whether the Assembly's decision is an acceptable use of its legislative power. In effect, it allows the body which gave the Assembly its legislative power to disapprove of the use it has made of it and tacitly approve the Secretary of State's vetoing of it. It is pertinent, therefore, to ask whether the Secretary of State's power of intervention is indeed part of the decision-making phase of the Welsh legislative process. It certainly would be if it applied without any legal, as opposed to political, restriction. However, as statute requires that the Secretary of State have a reasonable belief regarding the matters over which he may intervene, thus opening his intervention to the possibility of judicial review, his or her part in the process is exceptional rather than routine. 7-74

[41] GoWA 2006, s. 112, as amended by Wales Act 2017, s. 12(2)(a).

[42] GoWA 2006, s. 111B, inserted by Wales Act 2017, s. 9.

[43] GoWA 2006, s. 114, as amended by Wales Act 2017, s. 12(2)(c). For the former intervention power relating to water resources, water supply or water quality in England, see above §4-94, n. 82.

7-75 In the event of the Supreme Court deciding that a bill or provisions in it are outside competence or an intervention order by the Secretary of State not being annulled by either House of Parliament, the bill cannot proceed to Royal Assent. Instead, it is open for it to be reconsidered by the Assembly in order that it may attempt to resolve the difficulties. The same will be the case where the Supreme Court rules that the Presiding Officer's decision as to the bill not needing a super-majority was incorrect, although here it will be not so much the content of the bill as its level of support that will need to be revisited, notwithstanding that some revision of its content may be required to obtain that extra support. Where, following the rejection of a bill, the Supreme Court finds that the Presiding Officer's ruling that a super-majority was needed was incorrect, the bill can also be reconsidered by the Assembly, although here it is much less likely that any adjustment to its content will be needed, other than where occasioned by the delay to its enactment.[44]

Reconsideration Stage[45]

7-76 It is open to any Member of the Assembly to move that a bill which has been passed be reconsidered. This may be done in any one of the following situations. First, where the Supreme Court has held that the bill or some provisions in it were not within competence. Secondly, where the Secretary of State has successfully made an order preventing the bill from being presented for Royal Assent. Thirdly, where the bill has been passed by a simple majority and the Supreme Court has held that it needed a super-majority; and, fourthly, where it failed to pass for want of a super-majority but the Supreme Court has held that it did not require one. The fifth situation, however, has not previously been canvassed: it is where either the Attorney General or the Counsel General has referred a bill or some provision in a bill to the Supreme Court and one of the issues which has arisen is whether the bill is in some way incompatible with European Union law. In such an eventuality, it is open to the Supreme Court to refer the point of European Union law to the Court of Justice of the European Union for a preliminary ruling on the point of EU law. If the Supreme Court has done that, it is open to an Assembly Member to move that the bill be reconsidered without waiting for either the resolution of the preliminary point by the European Court or the determination of the question of competence by the Supreme Court. If both references are outstanding, a motion to reconsider can be moved and, if the Assembly agrees, this causes both the reference to the Supreme Court, and therefore the reference to the European Court, to be withdrawn.[46]

[44] GoWA 2006, s. 111, as amended by Wales Act 2017, s. 10, in particular the new (6)(za), (6A) and (7).

[45] SO 26.52–56.

[46] GoWA 2006, s. 113, as amended by Wales Act 2017, s. 12(2)(b). The Presiding Officer informs the law officer who made the reference to the Supreme Court of the Assembly resolution and the law officer must withdraw the reference.

If the motion to reconsider is agreed, the Reconsideration Stage on the bill begins on the following working day, although the first meeting of the Assembly to consider the proceedings must not take place until a further fifteen working days have elapsed. The clear purpose of these Reconsideration proceedings is either to cure whatever defect in the bill has caused it to be held to be outside competence by the Supreme Court or caused that Court to refer a question regarding its compatibility with EU law to the European Court, or alternatively to amend the bill so as to satisfy the Secretary of State that there is no further need to fear that adverse consequences might ensue. 7-77

Proceedings at the Reconsideration Stage are in plenary and follow the same pattern as those at Stage Three and at the Report Stage. If the purpose is to bring the bill within competence or change its contents so as to assuage the Secretary of State, amendments will have to be made. These are governed by the same requirements as at Stage Three, but the Presiding Officer must also be satisfied that amendments to be moved are solely for the purpose of resolving the issues raised either by the preliminary reference to the European Court or the determination of the Supreme Court or the Order made by the Secretary of State. 7-78

Once proceedings at the Reconsideration Stage have been completed, and subject to the possibility of further Reconsideration Stage proceedings in the same manner as further Stage Three and further Report Stage proceedings were allowed, any member may move that the Assembly approve the bill as amended on Reconsideration. If the motion is passed, and if any required super-majority is achieved, the Presiding Officer is charged with submitting it for Royal Assent, but this is again subject to a four-week period during which the Attorney General or the Counsel General could refer the bill or any of its provisions to the Supreme Court or during which the Secretary of State could make an order preventing it going for Royal Assent because of his anxieties about its consequences.[47] If, however, there are no such references and no such intervention, the Presiding Officer may submit the bill for Royal Assent. 7-79

Royal Assent

On receiving Royal Assent, the bill becomes an Assembly Act and its provisions part of the law of England and Wales applying in Wales. This moment is not to be confused with the achievement of the policy objectives which underlie it. 7-80

SPECIAL PROCEDURES

The discussion above has focused on the progress of a Welsh Government bill through the Assembly, and the vast majority of bills before the Assembly are introduced by the Welsh Government. Bills can also be introduced by Assembly 7-81

[47] GoWA 2006, ss. 112–115, as amended by Wales Act 2017, s. 12.

Members who are not members of the government on behalf of an Assembly Committee or on behalf of the Assembly Commission, as well as in their own capacity as Assembly Members.

Assembly Committee and Assembly Commission bills[48]

Assembly Committee bills must concern the remit of the committee in question while Assembly Commission bills must be concerned with that body's functions. In the case of Committee bills, it is not usually necessary for the general principles to be sent to a responsible subject committee for Stage One consideration as the responsible committee will be the committee proposing the bill.[49] A member of the committee will be the member in charge of a Committee bill, while a member who sits on the Commission will be the member in charge of a Commission bill.

Member bills[50]

7-82 The Standing Orders require the Presiding Officer to conduct periodic ballots of Assembly Members who are not members of the Welsh Government to determine who may be allowed an opportunity to bring forward a bill for consideration by the Assembly. Assembly Members who wish to participate in a ballot must submit the proposed title of their bill together with its policy objectives. As it is not a government bill, it cannot be assumed that there is a mandate for the change proposed. A member who is successful in the ballot then has twenty-five working days to table a motion requesting leave to introduce the bill, together with an Explanatory Memorandum setting out the proposed bill's policy objectives and indicating what support they know exists for their proposal and an initial assessment of any costs or savings it involves. That motion must be debated within thirty-five working days of the ballot, the latter period measured exclusively by working days during weeks in which the Assembly is sitting.[51] If the Assembly agrees to permit the Member to introduce the bill, he or she then has thirteen months within which to introduce it. Upon introduction, it progresses through the stages of the legislative process described earlier. Member bills must not seek to amend existing taxes or introduce new ones.

[48] See SO 26.80–84.

[49] For this reason, until 2017, Standing Orders had precluded sending Committee Bills for Stage One subject committee consideration.

[50] SO 26.85–94A.

[51] Sitting weeks are weeks during which the Assembly sits in plenary session, while working days are weekdays – Mondays to Fridays inclusive – other than Christmas Eve, Christmas Day, Maundy Thursday, Good Friday, bank holidays and days appointed for public thanksgiving or mourning. See also above, §7-16 and n. 9.

Government emergency bills[52]

As the name suggests, these bills may only be introduced by a member of the Welsh Government and can only be introduced in an emergency, that is a situation in which primary legislation needs to be passed within a timescale which does not allow for the usual requirements of the legislative process to be observed. 7-83

It is therefore necessary for the introduction of such a bill to be justified. Reasons for requesting the exceptional procedure must be given, together with an estimate of the cost and other consequences of not proceeding swiftly. The member of the government requesting the Assembly's permission to proceed in this manner can also request that the need for an Explanatory Memorandum be excused, and even that all stages of the bill be taken on a single day. As a consequence of the compressed timetable which will apply, detailed consideration at Stage Two is undertaken by a Committee of the whole Assembly, and the Presiding Officer is entrusted with determining how amendments to such a bill shall be taken. In effect, every stage of the bill's progress is undertaken in plenary session of the Assembly. 7-84

This does not, however, prevent the provisions of a government emergency bill which has been passed by the Assembly from being challenged prior to Royal Assent. Indeed, the Agricultural Sector (Wales) Act 2014, which was passed as an emergency bill, was subjected to such a challenge, albeit unsuccessfully, by the UK Attorney General. 7-85

Private bills and hybrid bills

One of the principles of the rule of law identified by Lord Bingham was that the laws of the land should apply equally to all, save to the extent that objective differences justify differentiation.[53] The notion therefore that a private individual should expect the law to be changed in his or her favour or that the state should seek to disadvantage identifiable individuals to achieve its goals would appear to contradict that principle and contravene the rule of law. The special procedures for private and hybrid bills seek to balance the occasional need for such legislation with the requirements of the rule of law by ensuring that the voice of those directly affected can be directly heard, and not left to the offices of their elected representatives. The more targeted interference is balanced by a more direct voice in the legislative process. 7-86

A private bill is one that is introduced in order for an individual to obtain powers or benefits which they would not otherwise by law enjoy or which even conflict with what other people enjoy under the law. The individual in question – who may be a private person or a body corporate or an unincorporated association – acts as the promoter of the bill. The provisions of the bill will relate to the private interests of the promoter, which may be estate or property interests, 7-87

[52] SO 26.95–104.

[53] Tom Bingham, *The Rule of Law* (London, 2010), p. 55.

or matters relating to their status or style. In short, the promoter seeks to change the law in order to gain an advantage which they would otherwise not enjoy. This might, for example, relate to the compulsory acquisition of property.

7-88 A hybrid bill, on the other hand, is a government bill which affects the private interests of certain individuals or bodies in a way which is different from the manner in which it affects other persons of that kind. Here, it is the particular disadvantage that will be inflicted and suffered, rather than the particular advantage sought, that marks out the proposal as requiring special treatment. The disadvantage may, for instance, result from the compulsory acquisition of the property of specific persons or the consequences that they will suffer from the approval of works of construction.

Private bills[54]

7-89 The promoter of a private bill must first seek permission from the Presiding Officer to introduce it, and this may involve an agreement of what fees may need to be paid for its being processed. The promoter will also need to demonstrate that any statutory consultation requirements have been complied with. The bill will need to be accompanied by an Explanatory Memorandum, and, if the proposals would require amendments to primary legislation, a Keeling schedule illustrating the effects of those changes on that legislation will be needed. The promoter will also need to show how adequate opportunity is to be given to others to raise objections to the bill's proposals, and how publicity is being given to what is proposed so as to raise awareness regarding it and thereby facilitate either informed support or informed opposition. Objections received will be formally listed and published.

7-90 The Assembly establishes a Private Bill Committee to consider the bill's proposals. The committee is required to consider the bill impartially and to base its conclusions on the evidence which has been received. Each member of the committee is required to agree to act thus at the committee's first meeting. The committee's initial consideration is whether to recommend that the bill should be allowed to proceed. If it determines that it should, and the Assembly resolves on the motion of its Business Committee that the bill may be introduced, the Initial Consideration ends and the committee proceeds to a detailed consideration of the bill, requiring as with all bills consideration of its general principles as well as the objections that have been raised and the detailed provisions of the bill.

7-91 During this Detailed Committee Consideration, the committee may hear oral argument from the promoter, the Welsh Government and any objectors, and it is open to the committee to appoint assessors to consider the objections. Having taken such evidence, the committee reports to the Assembly on the general principles and objections, and, if no motion is at that point tabled to prevent the bill proceeding, or, if tabled, no such motion is passed, the Assembly is deemed to have agreed to the general principles of the bill. This procedure in effect takes the place of Stage One of the legislative process for public bills. As with public bills, it is at

[54] SO 26A.

this point that the Presiding Officer must determine whether a financial resolution is required. If it is, a member of the government may move it, and without it the bill will fall.

If all this is accomplished, the committee then returns to a consideration of the bill's detail. At this point, it is open to Assembly Members generally to table amendments to the bill, which fall to the committee to consider and determine. This corresponds to Stage Two of the legislative process for public bills. 7-92

Once the amendments received have all been disposed of, the Detailed Committee Consideration ends and Detailed Assembly Consideration begins. This corresponds to Stage Three of the legislative process for public bills, and, as with Stage Three proceedings, proceedings are now conducted in plenary session, any member may table an amendment, but the Presiding Officer can choose which amendments shall be debated. Only three kinds of amendment are admissible during Detailed Assembly Consideration of a private bill. These are: amendments to clarify the text, including amendments to remove inconsistencies between the two language versions; amendments which deliver on commitments made during Detailed Committee Consideration; and amendments arising from recommendations made by the Private Bill Committee when reporting on the general principles of, or objections to, the bill. When all the selected amendments have been disposed of, opportunity can be provided for Further Detailed Committee Consideration and for Further Detailed Assembly Consideration if that is necessary. 7-93

Thereafter, the Final Stage of the private bill's passage is undertaken in plenary, as with Stage Four of public bills, when any Assembly Member may move that the bill be passed. No amendments are allowed at the Final Stage. Prior to the Final Stage, as is the case with public bills, a member of the government must report as to whether any relevant consents have been forthcoming from Her Majesty the Queen or the Duke of Cornwall. If the private bill is passed, it proceeds to Royal Assent in the usual manner, with opportunity having been given for reference to the Supreme Court by the Law Officers on questions of competence or for intervention by the Secretary of State. Should there be such a reference or intervention, the private bill could return to the Assembly for reconsideration, as is the case with public bills. 7-94

Hybrid bills[55]

Hybrid bills differ from private bills in that they are proposed by the government. They are similar to private bills in their concern, in whole or in part, with the interests of particular individuals in their private capacities rather than as members of the public. Here, however, it is the disadvantage which the government seeks to inflict on private individuals that differentiates them from private bills on the one hand and public bills on the other. 7-95

The special procedure for hybrid bills is very similar to that for private bills. Publicity and opportunity for objection from those affected is required, and a Hybrid Bill Committee is established to consider impartially and on the evidence 7-96

[55] SO 26B.

whether there is a case for permitting such legislation. After Initial Consideration, however, it is a member of the government as the member in charge who tables the motion that the bill be allowed to proceed, and, at Detailed Committee Consideration, there is an additional issue for the committee to consider, namely whether there are any proposals to create subordinate law-making powers contained within the bill. In other respects, the procedure for hybrid bills is, *mutatis mutandis*, almost identical to that for private bills.

To date, the Assembly has not dealt with any private or hybrid bills.

Chapter 8

Implementation and Interpretation

COMMENCEMENT OR COMING INTO FORCE

Royal Assent signifies that the changes to the law – changes that the bill proposed should be made in order to provide the means for giving effect to the underlying policy objectives – have been agreed. The changes will be made when the Act's provisions come into force and effect by being commenced. As stated earlier,[1] by convention, the provisions of an Act are not commenced until two months have passed since Royal Assent. This is to allow those who are affected by the changes to the law and those who advise them to find out what changes are in the offing. Any departure from the convention requires the permission of the relevant government law officer – the Attorney General in the case of Acts of the UK Parliament; the Counsel General in the case of Assembly Acts. As has also been shown, it is not uncommon to provide for the moment of commencement to be determined by a government minister, or for the provisions to be introduced in stages by a series of commencement orders made by ministers where this has been agreed to be appropriate by the legislature as part of the Act's provisions. The Act will therefore provide for its own commencement, including provisions for the making of any commencement orders, which will generally be made by statutory instrument. Such instruments, however, do not usually have to be laid before the legislature for either express approval by affirmative procedure or even implied approval by negative procedure as they themselves make no changes to the law whatsoever, but merely put into effect changes to which the legislature has already agreed. This is why it is controversial to include within commencement orders transitional, transitory or saving provisions, as such provisions do make changes which have not been 8-01

[1] See above, §6-52.

previously agreed and therefore merit some degree of scrutiny by the legislature, even where the changes are of a minor nature.[2]

8-02 Commencement orders, being the exercise of a power given by a statute, are subject to review in the same manner as the exercise of any other executive function.[3] In that their content determines when changes to the law come into force and effect, it is of considerable importance that they should themselves be accessible to those who may be affected by those changes. Accordingly, they are made, registered and published as statutory instruments, and, although they do not require the express or implied approval of the legislature, are nevertheless reported to it. The National Assembly's Constitutional and Legislative Affairs Committee requires that all commencement orders made by the Welsh Ministers are to be received by it and reports on them. Thus it is that the Committee has reported unfavourably on the practice of including incidental, consequential, transitional, transitory or saving provisions in the same instrument as a commencement order.

SUBORDINATE LEGISLATION

8-03 Where an Assembly Act has delegated the power to make subordinate legislation to the Welsh Ministers in the form, for example, of regulations, rules or orders, the Act will also have specified the procedure in accordance with which the Assembly requires that the legislation made by exercise of that power is to be scrutinized by

[2] National Assembly for Wales: Constitutional and Legislative Affairs Committee: Fourth Assembly Legacy Report, March 2016, pp. 13–14, and Recommendation 6:

> It is standard practice that no procedure is prescribed for commencement orders. Such orders commence provisions within Assembly Acts (or Measures). However, in the course of our work scrutinising Bills we have become increasingly concerned that some commencement powers permit incidental, supplementary, consequential, transitory or transitional provisions. We have taken the view that such orders should be subject to the negative procedure as they do more than simply announce a date for the commencement of a particular provision. We do not consider the absence of a procedure to be satisfactory ... Although we are content that no inappropriate use has been made of commencement orders, we remain of the opinion that there is a risk of them being used inappropriately.
>
> **Recommendation 6.**
> We recommend that our successor committee scrutinises incidental, supplementary, consequential, transitory or transitional provisions contained within commencement orders ...

The Welsh Government's disagreement with this view is acknowledged by the Report.

[3] Although Ministers are not under a duty to commence such provisions, they must consider whether and when to exercise the power. They may not decide that the provisions are never to be brought into force, as that would override the provisions enacted by Parliament. See *R* v *Secretary of State for the Home Department*, ex parte *Fire Brigades Union* [1995] UKHL 3, [1995] 2 AC 513, [1995] 2 WLR 464, [1995] 2 All ER 244, a majority decision of the House of Lords (Lord Keith of Kinkel and Lord Mustill dissenting).

it.[4] These procedures are intended and designed to allow the representatives of the people to approve or disapprove of the manner in which members of the executive exercise a legislative function which properly is the preserve of the legislature not the executive. The choice of procedure will have been made when the Act providing it was passed, and the factors which should govern that choice have been considered earlier when discussing the application of democratic principles to the choice of the kinds of legislation to be employed as the means of achieving the policy goals.[5] The question is essentially one concerning the appropriate level of scrutiny that the law-making requires in a representative democracy. The choice lies between allowing the executive to make the legal changes subject only to the possibility of annulment by the legislature or requiring that the executive's law-making be expressly approved by those entrusted by the people with the function of making laws.

As has been seen, the purpose of the legislative process for the making of primary legislation is to give the democratically elected representatives of the people the opportunity to deliberate upon the general principles of a proposal and to scrutinize its detail, with the opportunity to amend that detail. It is at the end of that process of deliberation and scrutiny that a final decision is taken as to whether to approve the changes to the law proposed. The process of making subordinate legislation differs in that there is no opportunity for such thorough scrutiny and no opportunity at all for amendment by decision of the members of the legislature. That being so, the content of subordinate legislation should not alter the general principles that were agreed when the enabling Act was passed, and should not propose changes of detail that require more than simple agreement or disagreement, that is should not be such as should benefit from the opportunity of amendment. If the change to the law proposed is one to which it is proper that the consent of the people's representatives should be sought, the affirmative procedure should be used, whereas if the opportunity to object is sufficient, the negative procedure will be appropriate. At the stage of making subordinate legislation, of course, these choices will already have been made; all that is now required is that the procedure chosen be followed. The Standing Orders of the Assembly set out what the various procedures require.[6] 8-04

Although it is open to the legislature to devise a procedure of its choice regarding the exercise of any subordinate law-making power delegated to others, the vast majority of such legislation follows one of two principal patterns – the affirmative or negative procedures. Which of these procedures is to apply will depend on whether the enabling Act, that is the Act creating the subordinate law-making power, requires the statutory instrument containing the subordinate legislation to be laid before the legislature for approval or merely, and more commonly, laid before 8-05

[4] Almost all subordinate legislation, apart from commencement orders, is now made in the form of regulations.

[5] See above, §§3-61–3-74.

[6] SO 27 and 28.

the legislature so as to give the legislature the opportunity of annulling it. While there are no standard formulas for expressing these requirements, the affirmative procedure is often established by the words:

> 'must be laid before, and approved by a resolution of, the National Assembly',

while the words:

> 'is subject to annulment in pursuance of a resolution of the National Assembly'

indicate the choice of the negative procedure.

8-06 Regardless of the procedure chosen, when the statutory instrument containing the subordinate legislation is laid before the legislature, it will have to be accompanied by an Explanatory Memorandum. In the case of the National Assembly, this requirement is set out in the Standing Orders. The Explanatory Memorandum is needed so as to inform Assembly Members why the changes in the law made by the statutory instrument are needed and that the case for the actual changes being made has been properly considered by those proposing them. It should explain what the instrument proposes to do and the reasons for so doing, paying particular attention to matters that the proposers wish those who will scrutinize the proposal to bear in mind. It should set out clearly the legal basis for the exercise of the law-making power and describe the use that is being made of it in terms of the problem the exercise of the power intends to resolve or the benefit it is aimed to provide, the need for the intervention intended and clarity as to who or what is going to be affected by the proposal. In other words, the EM is meant to satisfy the Assembly of the thoroughness and quality of the policy development underlying the proposal. The proposal may also need to be accompanied by a Regulatory Impact Assessment (RIA), where one is needed to comply with the code for carrying out such assessments when making subordinate legislation which the Welsh Ministers are required to have in place under the Government of Wales Act 2006.[7] The Act defines the assessment as being of 'the likely costs and benefits of complying with the relevant Welsh subordinate legislation', and the code addresses the need to assess the impact of such law-making on, for instance, the business community, the voluntary sector, local authorities and others likely to be affected, as well as how the proposals fit in with the Welsh Ministers' commitments regarding issues such as equality of opportunity, sustainable development, the Welsh language and the rights of children as protected by the UN Convention on the Rights of the Child.[8] The EM, together with a RIA, if needed, and a report from the Auditor General

[7] GoWA 2006, s. 76.

[8] As incorporated into the domestic law applicable in Wales by the Rights of Children and Young Persons Measure 2011.

for Wales giving his views on the appropriateness of any expenditure that may be charged against the Welsh Consolidated Fund in consequence of the legislation's provisions, must accompany the statutory instrument when it is laid before the Assembly for approval or to provide the opportunity for its annulment.[9]

Affirmative procedure

Where the enabling Act requires that the Assembly expressly approve the subordinate legislation, the Standing Orders require that a member of the government – that is, the First Minister, a Welsh Minister, a Deputy Welsh Minister or the Counsel General – table a motion that the instrument be approved. The motion cannot be considered by the Assembly in a plenary session until either the committee or committees considering the instrument have reported or twenty days have elapsed since the motion was tabled. Instruments are invariably forwarded to the Constitutional and Legislative Affairs Committee of the Assembly for consideration of both the legality and the propriety of the proposal, and instruments relating to devolved taxes will also be considered by the Finance Committee.[10] Any other committee of the Assembly may also choose to report on the instrument provided that it gives notice of its intention to do so to the Welsh Government within seven days of the instrument having been laid. The member of the government who laid the instrument, or another member of the government designated for that purpose by the First Minister, may attend the committees when they are considering the statutory instrument and participate in the proceedings, but may not vote as they are not members of the committee. Whereas it is not open to the Assembly or its committees to amend the proposed legislation, if they report that there are errors in it or in regard to its making, the government may withdraw the instrument at any time before the motion is considered. 8-07

Once the committee or committees have reported or once the twenty-day period has elapsed, the Assembly may consider the motion that the instrument be approved. If it is approved, the Minister may then sign it and arrange for it to be registered by the UK's Office for the Publication of Statutory Instruments (OPSI), which ensures that it is accessible to the public. The instrument then comes into force on the date specified in it. 8-08

The consideration of the instrument by the Constitutional and Legislative Affairs Committee of the Assembly allows the lawfulness of the exercise of the law-making power to be confirmed, but may also extend to the quality, including the clarity, of the drafting and the propriety of achieving the legislative goal by 8-09

[9] The requirement of a justice impact assessment imposed by GoWA 2006, s. 110A, inserted by Wales Act 2017, s. 11, is limited to the introduction of bills. There seems no logical reason, however, why the Standing Orders should not require them for statutory instruments also.

[10] SO 27.8A.

means of subordinate rather than primary legislation (so-called 'technical reporting points'). During the Fourth Assembly, CLAC was prepared to engage with the merits of the use of subordinate law-making powers as part of its regular function of scrutiny (so-called 'merits reporting points'), and indicated in its legacy report at the end of the Assembly term that it fully intended to continue doing so.[11]

8-10 If the motion that the instrument be approved is not passed by the Assembly, then the subordinate legislation is not made and the law on the matters concerned remains unchanged. It should be noted that a government with a majority in the Assembly would be able to force through its subordinate legislation without difficulty, whereas a government without a majority would not be able to do so. In the event of a tied vote on the approval of a statutory instrument, the motion would not have been passed and the Presiding Officer would be required under Standing Order 6.20 to use his or her casting vote against the motion.

Negative procedure

8-11 The more common method of making subordinate legislation is by allowing the legislature the opportunity of annulling the statutory instrument containing it. Where this is the procedure which the enabling Act requires, the Minister responsible will make the subordinate legislation by signing the instrument containing it. At that point, it becomes law, although it will not generally come into force and effect until at least twenty-one days have elapsed since its making. This allows time for those affected by the changes made to the law to become aware of how those changes affect them and to take appropriate action. To enable them to become aware of those changes, the instrument will be registered by OPSI as soon as it has been made by the Minister.

8-12 Having made the subordinate legislation, the member of the government responsible for its making will lay the statutory instrument containing it before the Assembly so as to give the Assembly the opportunity to annul it. Members of the Assembly then have a period of up to forty days to table a motion that the instrument be annulled. If no such motion is tabled, the subordinate legislation contained in the instrument will remain law.

8-13 Given that the Assembly is allowed forty days to annul the instrument, it is customary to delay the coming into force and effect of the legislation until after the forty days have passed, even though it is permissible to bring the legislation into force after twenty-one days have elapsed since its making. By not relying on the twenty-one-day period, the difficulties that could result if the instrument had to be annulled having come into force are avoided. It is a sensible approach. Exceptionally, where the content of the legislation relates to an emergency which

[11] National Assembly for Wales: Constitutional and Legislative Affairs Committee, Fourth Assembly Legacy Report, March 2016.

has arisen, such as the outbreak of a notifiable disease in either the human or the animal population, subordinate legislation may come into force before the twenty-one-day period has elapsed. Where circumstances require this, the Presiding Officer needs to be notified and informed of the reasons for the departure from normal practice.[12]

The legislation contained in the instrument will be considered by the Constitutional and Legislative Affairs Committee, which will report on it. If any Assembly Member tables a motion for the instrument's annulment, it will be for the Assembly's Business Committee to decide whether the motion requires debate in plenary or simply that it be put and voted upon. If there is a motion and the motion fails, the legislation contained in the instrument remains law, but, if the motion is passed, the government will have to revoke the instrument and thereby repeal the subordinate legislation in question by making an order under section 5 of the Statutory Instruments Act 1946. Alternatively, further subordinate legislation may be made revoking the instrument that needs to be annulled and making fresh legislation, which it will be hoped will not be disapproved by the legislature. 8-14

Similar to what was noted above in discussing the affirmative procedure, a government with a majority in the Assembly can use that majority to prevent its subordinate legislation being annulled, but a government without a majority does not enjoy that advantage. Arguably, the latter situation could make for better subordinate legislation and more responsible exercise of delegated law-making powers. It is worth noting, however, the implications for subordinate law-making of a tied vote on a motion to annul a statutory instrument containing subordinate legislation. As the instrument is made by being signed and remains valid unless a motion is passed annulling it, a tied vote means that the motion has not been passed. In such circumstances, the Presiding Officer is required under Standing Order 6.20 to exercise his or her casting vote against the motion, thereby allowing the instrument to remain valid. It is a worrying feature therefore of a 'tied Assembly' that a government unable to guarantee the success of its own proposals for primary legislation may return to the strategies of the first two Assembly terms in the years 1999–2007 when, in the absence of primary law-making powers, ways were sought to implement policy by the exercise of powers to make subordinate legislation. If the powers have been given to allow this to occur, then, by use of the negative procedure, the government would be able to get such legislation through even without a majority. This possibility underlines the need 8-15

[12] See Statutory Instruments Act 1946, s. 11A(4), inserted by GoWA 2006, Sch. 10, para. 3.

for vigilance in the granting of subordinate law-making powers by use of the negative procedure.[13]

Super-affirmative procedure

8-16 A major difference between the scrutiny of primary and secondary legislation by the legislature is the absence, in the case of the latter, of the opportunity to propose amendments. It has already been noted that, when the Assembly ceased to be responsible for making subordinate legislation in 2007 and the function passed to the Welsh Ministers, there was some resistance to the change, primarily because of the loss of the ability – albeit little used – to amend such enactments. As the Assembly gradually became accustomed to its primary law-making rôle and more demands were made on its time to scrutinize Assembly bills, so the new situation became more acceptable. Nevertheless, there remains a feeling, which manifests itself from time to time, that the Assembly should be able to have some input into the content of subordinate legislation and not be confined to simply approving or annulling the content presented to it by the Welsh Ministers.

8-17 One method, which is occasionally employed to allow something like amendment of subordinate law-making proposals, is the so-called super-affirmative procedure. Unlike the affirmative and negative resolution procedures considered above, the concept of super-affirmative procedure is not a term of art; rather it describes a variation of the affirmative resolution procedure that requires more than is usually asked for by the affirmative procedure. What is asked for by a super-affirmative procedure can vary from case to case, in that, as always, the relevant procedure is that laid down by the Act which conferred the subordinate law-making function.

[13] The situation, which actually obtains in the Fifth Assembly following the result of the May 2016 Assembly General Election, could also militate against officials moving on from the 'comfort zone' of thinking of primary legislation as a vehicle for obtaining subordinate law-making powers, and consequently returning to regarding subordinate legislation as the preferred method, or even the default method, for policy implementation. In the Fifth Assembly, discounting the seats of the Presiding Officer and the Deputy Presiding Officer, the governing party group and the combined opposition party groups have twenty-nine seats each. In the event of a tied vote, the Standing Orders require the Presiding Officer to cast a negative casting vote if no further discussion is possible (SO 6.20). This means that in the event of a tied vote at Stage Four, the bill fails. Given the choice between risking a bill being rejected and proceeding by subordinate legislation, the temptation to do the latter is as clear as it is understandable. Moreover, given that the same fate might await a statutory instrument containing subordinate legislation where an affirmative vote is needed, there would also be a temptation to prefer negative procedure, for, in that case, it would be the motion to annul the instrument that would fail on a tied vote, leaving the subordinate legislative provisions in force.

While that strategy might appeal more to the Government than the Assembly, both would probably be relieved to find that broad powers to make subordinate legislation given by Assembly Acts or Measures under the conferred-powers settlement might enable devolved competence to survive losses of legislative competence for the future arising as a consequence of the move to the reserved-powers model.

In both instances, however, the loss is to the development of a mature democracy in Wales.

The extra element that is required is usually that a draft of the proposed instrument be provided well in advance of its formally being laid for approval so as to allow opportunity for amendments to it to be proposed. In effect, it is a form of statutory consultation. The enabling Act, for instance, may require that a draft of the instrument be laid before the Assembly for sixty days, during which time Assembly Members may suggest amendments to it. The procedure, however, goes no further than allowing for amendments to be suggested. It does not allow the Assembly itself to deliberate upon those suggestions nor to decide as to their fate. When the sixty days are ended, it is for the Minister to consider whether to act upon any of the suggestions and to decide whether to amend the proposed content of the instrument. The Minister may, however, be required to report as to how he or she has responded to the suggestions made when formally laying the instrument in its final form before the Assembly for its approval. Clearly, a majority government has little to fear from super-affirmative procedures, while a government without a majority will be obliged to be more inclusive in its response if it wishes its proposals to bear fruit. In essence, super-affirmative procedure works by adding an extra dimension to the affirmative resolution procedure. The extra dimension may require consultation on draft subordinate legislation with interested parties outside the Assembly rather than expecting them to raise concerns through their AMs.[14]

Enhanced negative procedure

Nor is there anything to prevent such an extra dimension being added to the 8-18
negative resolution procedure. Having wisely eschewed describing this as 'super-negative', the term 'enhanced negative procedure' has been coined. Basically, it requires a draft of an instrument to be published before it is formally laid to allow an opportunity for amendments to be suggested. Again, this may be an opportunity confined to Assembly Members or could involve the consultation of outside parties. The government may be required to report on any changes made when laying the instrument once made to allow the Assembly the opportunity to annul it. Once again, although amendments can be suggested, it is ultimately the Minister who deliberates upon the suggestions and decides whether to make the suggested amendments. As with super-affirmative procedures, it is only the opportunity to propose changes that is afforded, unlike bill procedures where not only is that initiative shared, but also the function of deliberating and deciding upon changes.

Joint statutory instruments

Although Assembly Acts are unlikely ever to create such subordinate law-making 8-19
powers, some subordinate law-making powers created by Acts of the UK Parliament require that the relevant statutory instrument be made by both the Welsh Ministers

[14] See, for instance, the provisions of the Social Services and Well-Being (Wales) Act 2014, ss. 32, 33, 140 and 141.

and the Secretary of State acting together. Where this is the case, it is essential that the two governments reach the earliest possible agreement upon the substance of the legislative proposals. Without this, the legislation will not be able to be made. Once that agreement has been reached, and responsibilities allocated for the production of the legislation, the process for making it will involve it being laid before both the two Houses of Parliament at Westminster and the National Assembly in Cardiff for approval, if the enabling legislation required the affirmative procedure, or for the opportunity of annulment, if it was the negative procedure that had been chosen.

8-20 Such joint law-making should not be confused with the situation where the Secretary of State and the Welsh Ministers have concurrent powers to make subordinate legislation. In that instance, each may act alone according to the relevant procedure in the respective legislature to which they are accountable.[15]

Special procedures

8-21 In the same manner as the House of Lords at Westminster has a procedure by which private individuals who are affected by some proposed subordinate legislation may petition regarding it, Standing Order 28 of the National Assembly makes provision with regard to the opportunity for such petitioning with regard to Welsh subordinate legislation. In effect, the procedure prevents the making or confirming of subordinate legislation by the Welsh Government unless the provisions of the Standing Order have been observed. The Standing Order applies wherever a special Assembly Procedure is required for the making of subordinate legislation by the virtue of an enactment.

Opportunities for challenge

8-22 Express or implied approval of subordinate legislation by the legislature does not mean that the delegated legislation is free from the risk of challenge before the courts. Political endorsement does not oust the possibility of legal challenge. In that the power to make subordinate legislation has been conferred by the legislature, its exercise must conform to the requirements which the legislature has set. Therefore, it is open to anyone with a legitimate interest in the matter, including in particular those who may have been prejudiced by its terms, to challenge its legality, as opposed to its merits, before the courts. This would normally be done by means of judicial review. If the matter raised concerns as to whether or not the Welsh Ministers had the power to make such subordinate legislation or in making it have exceeded their powers, the matter will constitute a devolution issue to be

[15] Where the Secretary of State acts alone, this has the unfortunate consequence that the legislation produced is expressed in English only.

tried in accordance with the provisions of Schedule 9 to the Government of Wales Act 2006.[16]

The Welsh Ministers can make subordinate legislation only where they have been given the power to do so by Parliament or the Assembly. In the absence of such a power, any purported exercise by them of that function can be challenged in the courts and set aside as being invalid. Likewise, if they have exceeded a subordinate law-making power which they have been given, or exercised it for a purpose for which it was not intended, or in bad faith, or in a manner which is wholly unreasonable or lacking in proportionality, the legislation so made can be set aside as invalid on review. Nor can any legislation made by them be incompatible with European Union law or the Convention rights protected by the Human Rights Act 1998, again on pain of invalidity. Subordinate legislation made by them may also be challenged and adjudged invalid if they have failed to consult properly where required to do so either by the enabling Act or as a consequence of their having raised a legitimate expectation that they would do so in the process of obtaining the law-making powers being exercised or in statements made regarding the exercise of those powers. All of this ensures that in the exercise of its subordinate law-making functions, the Welsh Government – like the Welsh Assembly when enacting primary legislation – is subject to the rule of law and answerable for its activities before the courts. 8-23

Codes of conduct, guidance and directions

Acts of the UK Parliament and of the Assembly can also give powers to ministers to influence or determine conduct without resorting to formal law-making. As has been shown earlier, items of so-called 'soft' law such as the issuing of codes of conduct, guidance or directions can be effective methods of achieving policy goals, and can be made to have a significant effect on conduct by requiring, for instance, that 'regard' or 'due regard' be had to their content on pain of it being presumed that the conduct fell short of the required standard by failing to do so or had reached the required standard by dint of compliance.[17] Whether or not specific procedures need to be followed in the making of such norms depends, as always, upon the terms of the enactment that conferred the power to make them. Where a procedure is required, it has to be followed for the rules or guidance made to be valid. On occasion, their making may require the same form of affirmative or negative procedure as subordinate legislation made by statutory instrument. However, unlike subordinate legislation made by statutory instrument, these less formal sources of law – if indeed they constitute law – do not need to be registered with OPSI and are not automatically published by the Stationery Office. The result is that they are not as readily accessible as subordinate legislation made 8-24

[16] See above, §§3-60; 4-86–4-91. For a full discussion of judicial review in the Welsh context, see David Gardner, *Administrative Law and the Administrative Court in Wales* (Cardiff, 2016).

[17] See §§3-29; 6-27.

formally, which is a cause of criticism and controversy.[18] Moreover, it is open for such informal items of subordinate legislation to be made – that is, made effective by being signed – by properly authorized officials rather than by the Minister in person. This is permitted in accordance with the general principle regarding the delegation of ministerial functions known as the *Carltona* principle.[19] It would be highly unlikely that such a delegation would be permissible with regard to the making of subordinate legislation by statutory instrument unless it was specifically contemplated and provided for in the enabling enactment. The default position is that where a legislature has entrusted a function, including a legislative function, to another, that other should be accountable to the legislature for its exercise, and only ministers, as opposed to officials, are so accountable. Therefore, for the *Carltona* principle to be operable, the circumstances must be such that the legislature would not in delegating the function have expected the minister to perform it in person even though no express power to delegate had been given.

JUDICIAL INTERPRETATION

8-25 Whether a power to delegate a function can be implied even though none has been expressed on the face of the legislation is a question of how to interpret the legislation in question. The rôle of the courts in implementing legislation is not confined to determining whether the exercise of a law-making power is lawful by, for instance, judicial review, but also extends to providing authoritative determinations on the meaning of legislative provisions by resolving questions of interpretation. Lord Bingham in his survey of the modern meaning of the rule of law regarded the provision of means to resolve disputes as a key feature of that constitutional requirement. 'Means must be provided', he wrote, 'for resolving … disputes which the parties themselves are unable to resolve'.[20] Sometimes such disputes turn upon the meaning of a legislative provision.

8-26 It has been said that in ideal legislation 'the intended meaning of every legislative proposition would be clear beyond doubt from the natural meaning of the words used'.[21] On the other hand, it is doubted that legislation would be ideal if it were thought that 'those words would put beyond doubt the legislature's intention

[18] A report was commissioned into the problem at the conclusion of the Second Assembly in 2007: see A. Jones-Evans, *Publication of Pre-2006 Non-Statutory Instrument Legislation: A Scoping Study*, *http://webarchive.nationalarchives.gov.uk/20080912102143tf_/http://new.wales.gov.uk/publications/publicationscheme/?lang=en*, and follow the related link for 'Publication of Pre-2006 Non-Statutory Instrument Legislation: A Scoping Study – Executive summary'.

[19] After the leading case in which the principle was settled, *Carltona Ltd* v *Commissioners of Works* [1943] 2 All ER 560.

[20] Bingham, *The Rule of Law*, pp. 85–9.

[21] Daniel Greenberg (ed.), *Craies on Legislation* (11th edn, London, 2017), 16.1.1.

in respect of the application of the proposition to every possible practical case'.[22] The fact that to attempt the second would render the legislation so lengthy and cumbersome as to be virtually unusable implicitly accepts that legislative provisions need to be framed at a level of generality which allows them to be applied as intended in circumstances that are not particularized in the legislation itself.

It is therefore necessary to apply laws which have been expressed at a level of generality higher than the facts of particular situations to those particular situations. Where disputes arise with regard to whether a law is meant to apply to a particular situation and, if so, how, that question is not returned to the legislator or legislature for determination.[23] Instead, that function of answering such questions is entrusted to courts and tribunals. It is their function to apply the law to the facts of particular cases and determine the outcome which the law demands. This is what is meant by administering justice in accordance with the law. Stating the result of applying the law to the facts of a particular case – stating what the law is on those facts in that case – is one meaning of jurisdiction. 8-27

The English word *jurisdiction* is derived from two Latin words – *dicere* meaning 'to state' and *ius* which is a Latin word for 'law'. The word *ius*, however, does not mean 'a law which has been made as the result of a process of enactment'. The Latin word for that, as has been seen,[24] is *lex*. *Ius* means law in the sense of 'what is just or right in a particular situation', always remembering that what is just or right in a particular situation must be determined according to the law. This difference between two meanings of the word *law* is to be found in many European languages, particularly those derived from Latin or used in countries which have been influenced by the legal tradition of Rome. Thus, in French, *loi* is distinguished from *droit*; in Spanish, *ley* from *derecho*; in Italian, *legge* from *diritto*, and in German, *Gesetz* from *Recht*. There is no such clear verbal distinction in English, nor for that matter in Welsh, but the existence of the two meanings, though less obvious, needs to be borne in mind. 8-28

The jurisdiction of the courts involves their authority to state the result which a law (*lex*) requires in a particular case – to state what the law (*ius*) is in that case. The exercise of that authority requires them to apply the law to the facts. In so far as the application of the law will depend upon the nature of the facts, if the facts are in dispute, the courts need the authority to determine what the facts actually are. Such determinations are frequently the principal questions to be resolved in, for instance, criminal trials – 'did the accused do it or didn't he?' and, on the basis of the answer to that question, 'is the accused guilty or not guilty?' Much the same can be true of the importance of determining the facts in civil trials where the issue is one of liability for harm, injury or damage suffered, rather than guilt. 8-29

[22] Ibid.

[23] It is unlikely that the legislature would be composed of the same members as when the legislation was passed. Hence, the significance of the words 'in this present Parliament assembled' in the enactment clause.

[24] See above, §1-01.

8-30 Disputes, however, are not always concerned with the facts to which the law needs to be applied. They can relate to the law itself, in terms of the meaning to be given to the legal provisions which are to be applied. In order to perform the function of applying the law to the facts, the courts therefore need to be able to determine such questions of law as well. In other words, they need to have the authority to state what the law actually is when such questions arise.

8-31 When the courts exercise the authority to determine questions of law, it is important not only that their determination should be accepted as correct in the case before them but also that their determination should thereafter be accepted on that point of law in subsequent cases. If that were not so, the same issue could arise whenever the law in question needed to be applied and, as well as cost in time and effort, the risk would arise of inconsistent decisions being made in relation to the same matter. It is to avoid such problems that the law of England and Wales has developed the doctrine of binding precedent, whereby the decisions of points of law by courts at a certain level of seniority in the judicial hierarchy are treated as binding when the rule falls to be applied in later cases. Basically, decisions of the Supreme Court are binding upon all other courts, and the Supreme Court itself will only depart from its own previous decisions in the most exceptional of circumstances. Beneath the Supreme Court, the Court of Appeal's decisions are also binding upon all lower courts and upon itself when considering and applying the law in later cases. Beneath the Court of Appeal, decisions of lower courts are not strictly binding, but those of the High Court are regarded as being of persuasive authority although not technically binding. The doctrine of binding precedent means that judicial decisions on points of law are in themselves authoritative in settling what the law is in disputed cases. Given, therefore, the authoritative nature of judicial interpretation of the law, it is of the greatest importance that those interpretations should be objective and not expressions of the subjective views of the judges entrusted with the rulings. For those involved in the process of legislative enactment, it also emphasizes the premium to be placed upon clarity of meaning when making the law, so as to ensure that it is definitely the will of the law-makers that the courts enforce, not the courts' interpretation of it. As will be seen, it also increases the importance of clarity with regard to the legislative intention in sources to which the courts may refer when seeking to establish the legislative intention, some of which will either be produced or influenced by officials engaged in the preparation and passing of the legislation in question.

Literal interpretation

8-32 The purpose of the judicial interpretation of legislation is to discover objectively and authoritatively what the legislature intended when a provision was passed.[25]

[25] Professor Andrew Burrows discussed and challenged this approach to interpretation in his Hamlyn Lectures during 2017: see A. Burrows, *Thinking about Statutes: Interpretation, Interaction, Improvement*, The 2017 Hamlyn Lectures (Cambridge, 2018).

This is not the same as asking what individual members of the legislature may have intended. The process assumes that an objective legislative intention existed, and it is the duty of the courts to discover and declare it in a disinterested manner. The principal approach taken to discovering the intention of the UK legislature for the greater part of the nineteenth and twentieth centuries, and an approach which remains important today, is by examining the express words used by the legislature in making the law. This literal approach to legislative interpretation was neatly described by Willes J almost a century and a half ago, when he said:

> the general rule is that the language of an Act is to be read according to its ordinary grammatical construction … [26]

In essence, that, without more, would sum up a strict literal approach. However, Willes J was aware that such a strict approach might defeat rather than achieve the object of the exercise, and he therefore added:

> unless so reading it would entail some absurdity, repugnancy or injustice.[27]

These words make it clear that the courts will assume that the legislature never intends to enact provisions which are absurd, repugnant or unjust, even if such a result might be required according to the 'ordinary grammatical construction' of the words used. Instead, the courts proceed on the assumption that such consequences are not to be taken as intended simply because of the ordinary grammatical construction of words. It could be argued that it is not for the courts but for the legislature to cure such linguistic faults, but to insist upon such a pure view of the separation of powers would be manifestly inconvenient to all concerned, Parliament as much as the parties to the case. If the question of what the legislature intended can be properly resolved even if it involves departing from a strict, literal interpretation, it is submitted that the courts are correct in considering the departure justified. For this reason, some would prefer to describe 'the general rule' of interpretation as expressed by Willes J as the 'Cardinal rule' or the 'Golden rule' rather than the literal rule. Nevertheless, it remains the traditional approach of the UK courts to statutory interpretation, and, where departure from the ordinary grammatical construction of the language used by the legislature is required, leaves unanswered the problem of how else the courts can discover the objective intention of the legislature.

[26] *Abel* v *Lee* (1871) LR 6 CP 365, at 370.

[27] Ibid. Contrast with the unmitigated literal rule as adumbrated by Jervis CJ in *Abley* v *Dale* 11 CB 391: 'if the precise words used are plain and unambiguous … we are bound to construe them in their ordinary sense, even though it leads … to an absurdity or a manifest injustice'.

Logical or purposive interpretation

8-33 If the literal approach, tempered by its expression in the form of the cardinal or golden rule, is the traditional approach of the UK courts to statutory interpretation, it is certainly not the traditional approach of legal systems in many other countries, particularly those of our nearest neighbours in mainland Europe who belong to the civil law tradition based on ancient Roman law rather than the common law tradition of England. There, a logical approach to legislative interpretation has been followed, according to which interpretation of legislation aims to promote the underlying purpose of an enactment rather than simply determine the meaning of the enactment's provisions. Traditionally, the courts in this country have shied away from seeking to promote an enactment's purpose, regarding this as a dangerous encroachment upon an activity which is the preserve of executive and legislative government rather than the fulfilment of a judicial function.

8-34 Doctrinal legal writing in the civil law jurisdictions of mainland Europe[28] distinguishes three criteria which are employed in the task of logical interpretation. These they refer to as the teleological, historical and systematic criteria. The teleological criterion asks what is the aim of the legislative provision, what is it that it intends to achieve, and then seeks to interpret the provision so as best to fulfil that aim.[29] This is contrasted with the historical criterion, which asks what was the problem that the legislation aimed to solve, thereby looking at the issue from a different perspective. The provisions would then be interpreted according to that criterion so as to assist in solving the underlying problem. Both of those criteria, particularly the second, bear a close resemblance to the approach to statutory interpretation called in England the 'mischief rule' or sometimes the 'rule in *Heydon's case*'.[30] This approach has more recently been described by Lord Nicholls in *Wilson* v *First County Trust Ltd (No. 2)*[31] by saying:

> It has long been established that the courts may look outside a statute in order to identify the 'mischief' Parliament was seeking to remedy.

The systematic criterion, on the other hand, has not been as influential in England as it has been on the continent, at least not until arguably the last quarter of the twentieth century. According to it, the courts seek to interpret legal provisions in one enactment so as to ensure that they fit rather than conflict with other laws on the same topic or within the same legal system. In England and Wales, the criterion could certainly be identified in the manner in which courts would set about

[28] That is the writing of academic commentators on the law, which writing has a more significant part to play in interpretation in civil law as opposed to common law systems. See further, n. 32 below.

[29] The word *teleological* is derived from the Greek word, τελος (*telos*) meaning 'end', in the sense here of a goal or a target.

[30] From the case in which it was famously described: (1584) 3 Co. Rep. 7a.

[31] [2003] UKHL 40; [2004] 1 AC 816.

interpreting a provision within a body of legislation dealing with a particular policy area, such as a provision to be found in one of a number of Acts concerning education. This would be described in the United Kingdom as contextual interpretation. However, within jurisdictions in mainland Europe, the approach is taken much further, attention being paid to a whole area of law, such as the civil law or criminal law, or even the entire law of the country concerned. It has become common for systematic interpretation to extend to ensuring that the domestic law of the country concerned blends in well with the laws of the European Union – not merely being compatible with them, and in Germany has gone so far as to attempt to achieve a good fit with not only the law of the European Union but also the legal regimes of other member states.[32] In the United Kingdom, neither the Supreme Court nor its predecessor, the Appellate Committee of the House of Lords, has traditionally regarded seeking to achieve harmony amongst the laws of Scotland, Northern Ireland and England and Wales, as part of its remit, although that could of course change with the advent of legislative devolution within the United Kingdom and perhaps a wish to avoid unnecessary and unhelpful divergence as between the laws of the several nations, and of the laws applicable in Wales and those applicable in England in particular, given that England and Wales remains a single jurisdiction. The Supreme Court has indeed noted the significance that interpretation of the terms of the legislation relating to the several devolution settlements might have one upon the other.[33]

One area, however, in which the systematic criterion may be discerned to 8-35
have played a rôle in judicial interpretation of legislation in the United Kingdom concerns the interpretation of European Union law. Following the entry of the UK into the European Economic Communities, as they then were, in 1973, the courts faced the question of whether they should interpret EEC law in the same manner as they traditionally interpreted native, domestic law. Realizing that, if they did so, their literal interpretation might prove to be at variance with the interpretation arrived at in other member states and thereby pose difficulties which could result in increased and unnecessary levels of litigation, the courts decided that in interpreting EU law they would adopt a purposive approach, that is seeking to establish the purpose of a provision and then to interpret it so as to assist in achieving that purpose. This was not entirely new to courts in the UK, as they had adopted a similar approach to the interpretation of international treaties where the same problem could have arisen.

[32] At this point, an important difference between interpretation in civil law and common law jurisdictions needs to be noted. Whereas in countries of the common law tradition, the interpretation of legislation is a function which the courts perform in the process of deciding the cases which come before them, in civil law jurisdictions it is academic writers rather than judges who deal with questions of interpretation in their commentaries on the law. In civil law countries, judicial decisions do not generally have the force of authoritative determinations on questions of interpretation and therefore there is no doctrine of binding precedent.

[33] See, for instance, *AXA Insurance* v *Lord Advocate* [2011] UKSC 46, at ¶42 *per* Lord Hope and at ¶99 *per* Lord Reed.

8-36 As with the gradual adoption of the principle of proportionality considered earlier,[34] so with the adoption of purposive interpretation, what began in the particular context of the interpretation of EU legislation has gradually spread to encompass the interpretation of UK legislation as well. This can be seen – as can its connection with the native 'mischief rule' – from two further statements made by Lord Nicholls in *Wilson* v *First County Trust Ltd (No. 2)*. With regard to the mischief rule, he said:

> When interpreting a statute … the court may need enlightenment on the nature and extent of the social problem (the 'mischief') at which the legislation is aimed.[35]

However, he went further and contemplated not merely asking what problem the legislation was meant to solve but also what policy objective it was meant to achieve, that is what continental jurists would describe as the teleological approach. He said:

> as when interpreting a statute, so when identifying the policy objective … or assessing the 'proportionality' of a statutory provision, the court may need enlightenment.[36]

He even linked the development with the use of the principle of proportionality.[37]

8-37 This raises the question of how the courts are to achieve 'enlightenment' as to 'the social problem (the "mischief") at which the legislation is aimed' or the underlying 'policy objective'. In both instances, Lord Nicholls had no doubt as to where to look for such enlightenment. This, he thought, could be found in what he termed 'additional background material', which could be found in 'published documents, such as a government white paper', 'ministerial statements in the course of debate', and in explanatory notes.[38] Each of these suggested sources of additional background material would have been prepared as part of the process of proposing the bill containing the legislation to the legislature. The published documents, whether a government Green Paper or a White Paper, would have been the fruit of the policy development work undertaken by officials prior to the introduction of the bill. Likewise, the ministerial statements would have been the result of official briefings and may even have been written for the minister by officials. Likewise, the Explanatory Notes. In each case, the importance which these documents now have for the success of the policy is greatly increased by

[34] See above, §§3-11–3-20.

[35] *Wilson* v *First County Trust Ltd. (No. 2)* [2003] UKHL 40, at ¶¶63–4 *per* Lord Nicholls, [2004] 1 AC 816, at 842.

[36] Ibid.

[37] As with the principle of proportionality, it is questionable whether the UK courts would wish to revert to their earlier attitude in the event of the UK withdrawing from the EU.

[38] Above, n. 35.

the willingness of the courts to use them as background material in the task of interpreting the legislative provisions that are means for giving effect to the policy. Properly thought through and competently executed, they can be key to the policy's success. Poorly thought through or incompetently executed, they may reduce the chances of success or even cause the policy to fail. As has been noted, this could be the difference between the legislation being 'a powerful force for good' or a cause of 'untold unfairness and misery'.[39]

Admissible background materials

Whereas the civilian jurisdictions of the European mainland have for long been 8-38
prepared to use such extraneous materials to assist in the interpretation of legislation, traditionally the courts of England and Wales had set their face very much against employing them. Once more, a change of heart occurred and that within a generation of the UK's accession to the European Union. Given that interpretation in other countries would take account of such additional background material, or *travaux préparatoires* as they are termed abroad, it would have been risky when interpreting EU law for the UK courts to ignore them. Having been prepared to access such materials when seeking to interpret EU law, it became difficult to justify continuing to refuse to employ equivalent native materials when it came to the interpretation of the domestic legislation of the United Kingdom. One of the sources of such additional background material which the courts had steadfastly refused to access was reports of proceedings in Parliament, the debates recorded in Hansard. A major objection to the citing of Hansard before the courts was long believed to be the terms of article 9 of the Bill of Rights of 1688, which reads:

> **Freedom of Speech.**
> That the Freedome of Speech and Debates or Proceedings in Parlyament ought not to be impeached or questioned in any Court or Place out of Parlyament.

The constitutional significance of this enactment and its connection with the Glorious Revolution which introduced a constitutionally limited monarchy at the end of a century that had seen protracted disputes and even civil war between king and Parliament made the courts very wary of trespassing upon the privileges guaranteed to parliamentary debates. Nevertheless, the experience of the usefulness which background material had been found to provide in the interpretation of EU legislation and perhaps the confidence which that use had given that it was not an interference with Parliamentary privilege, led to the courts revising their position on the matter in the ground-breaking decision of *Pepper* v *Hart* in 1993.[40]

[39] Based on Daniel Greenberg, see above, §§2-29–2-30.

[40] *Pepper (Inspector of Taxes)* v *Hart* [1993] AC 593. As with the principle of proportionality and the adoption of a purposive approach in legislative interpretation, it is submitted that it is unlikely that the UK courts will revert to their earlier approaches in the event of the UK withdrawing from the EU.

8-39 In that case, the House of Lords decided that a limited use of the parliamentary record was permissible. As envisaged in *Pepper* v *Hart*, however, that use was to be limited. The record of debates in Parliament was to be used only where the legislation falling for interpretation was ambiguous or obscure, or the literal meaning led to absurdity – a condition echoing one of the occasions on which the cardinal or golden rule allowed for departure from the ordinary grammatical construction of the legislative text. In such circumstances, use could be made of the parliamentary record, where understanding could be achieved by relying on statements made in introducing the bill by the responsible Minister, in the case of a government bill, or the bill's promoter, if it were a backbench proposal, or of other parliamentary material, such as reports or White Papers. However, reliance on such background material was permissible only if the statements to be relied upon in them were in themselves clear. There was no point in shifting the argument from an ambiguous provision in a statute to an ambiguous statement in a speech or document.

8-40 With hindsight, the decision in *Pepper* v *Hart* may well be seen as a Trojan horse, which succeeded in getting extraneous material into the arsenal of interpretation under cover of a limited use which was bound to be expanded. Somewhat unsurprisingly, statements made by Ministers in Parliament when introducing bills regarding their intentions as to how powers within them would be used have been held sufficient to raise legitimate expectations which must not be disappointed. Thus, a statement in debate that a power would not be exercised without prior consultation, for example, could lead to the legality of exercising that power without such consultation being challenged before the courts by judicial review by those with a legitimate interest in being consulted. The fact that the legislation itself was silent on the matter, and therefore betrayed no ambiguity on its face, would not be an obstacle.

8-41 One of the more controversial uses of such additional background material has arisen in the context of assessing whether legislative provisions are compatible with the Convention rights incorporated into the domestic law of the United Kingdom by the Human Rights Act 1998. As has already been shown, Welsh Assembly legislation that is incompatible with these rights can be struck down as invalid by the courts. In assessing whether legislative provisions are incompatible with Convention rights, the question arises of the use to be made by the courts of extraneous materials relating to the passing of the legislative provisions being challenged. In the *Asbestos Diseases* case,[41] the issue arose as to whether the provisions in the bill which permitted the Welsh Ministers to recover the costs to the Welsh NHS of treating those diseases not only from liable employers but also from their insurers, who would not have been aware of this potential liability when entering into the contracts of insurance concerned, amounted to an undue interference with the insurers' right to peaceful enjoyment of their possessions under Article 1

[41] *Recovery of Medical Costs for Asbestos Diseases (Wales) Bill: Reference by the Counsel General for Wales* [2015] UKSC 3.

of the First Protocol to the European Convention on Human Rights. This article, A1P1 as it is commonly referred to, states that:

> (1) Every natural or legal person is entitled to the peaceful enjoyment of his possessions. No one shall be deprived of his possessions except in the public interest and subject to the conditions provided for by law and by the general principles of international law.
>
> (2) The preceding provisions shall not, however, in any way impair the right of a State to enforce such laws as it deems necessary to control the use of property in accordance with the general interest or to secure the payment of taxes or other contributions or penalties.

The majority of the Supreme Court, in the judgment delivered by Lord Mance, described the approach to be taken when assessing compatibility in such cases as follows:

> The general principles according to which a court will review legislation for compliance with the Convention rights … are
>
> (i) whether there is a legitimate aim which could justify a restriction of the relevant protected right,
> (ii) whether the measure adopted is rationally connected to that aim,
> (iii) whether the aim could have been achieved by a less intrusive measure, and
> (iv) whether, on a fair balance, the benefits of achieving the aim by the measure outweigh the disbenefits resulting from the restriction of the relevant protected right.[42]

In relation to the fourth stage, it was held that the court would accept the legislature's judgment regarding what was in the public interest unless that judgment was totally unreasonable, but the court refused to accept that that precluded it from assessing for itself whether the public interest being pursued justified interference with an individual's protected right. The court would examine the legislature's decision to determine whether it had struck a fair balance between the competing interests involved.[43]

This raises the question as to how the courts are to determine whether the 8-42
legislature's decision that the interference is in the public interest is not totally unreasonable, and, if not, whether a fair balance was struck between the competing

[42] Ibid., ¶45.

[43] 'The court will accept the legislature's judgment as to what is "in the public interest" unless that judgment is "manifestly without reasonable foundation". But "an interference with peaceful enjoyment of possession" must nevertheless strike a "fair balance" between the demands of the public or general interest of the community and the requirements of the protection of the individual's fundamental rights': ibid., ¶48 *per* Lord Mance.

interests when deciding that the public interest outweighed the claims of the individual's protected right. Lord Mance, speaking for the majority, held that this required an examination of the quality of the decision-making in the legislature. He said:

> There is in this connection a potential tension. If, at the fourth stage when the court is considering whether a measure strikes a fair balance, weight attaches to the legislative choice, then the extent to which the legislature has as the primary decision maker been in or put in a position to evaluate the various interests may affect the weight attaching to its assessment: …

In doing this, the majority was of the view that 'admissible background material' could form the basis of the court's judgment to see whether:

> the background to the Bill had consisted of a full presentation and appreciation of its implications by those responsible for promoting and passing the legislation.[44]

Drawing on Lord Nicholls's words in *Wilson* v *First County Trust Ltd (No. 2)*, Lord Mance plainly believed that the record of proceedings in the Assembly and its committees together with published documents such as government White Papers and explanatory memoranda could all be used to determine whether the legislature's determination that a fair balance had been struck between the competing interests was sustainable.

8-43 In saying this, Lord Mance was fully aware that he was questioning the quality of the decision-making of an elected legislature in a court outside that legislature in a manner forbidden with regard to the Westminster Parliament by the Bill of Rights. Regarding this, he said:

> Perhaps in the light of article 9 [of the Bill of Rights] there is a relevant distinction between cases concerning primary legislation by the United Kingdom Parliament and other legislative and executive decisions.[45]

Although his views on this matter were shared by the majority of the court, the minority dissented from them. The Lord Chief Justice, Lord Thomas of Cwmgiedd, delivering the minority judgment, expressly disagreed, saying:

> Although the Welsh Assembly is a body, like the Scottish Parliament and Northern Ireland Assembly, to which section 9 of the Bill of Rights does not apply, I would find it difficult to make any logical distinction in the context of the United Kingdom's devolved constitutional structure between these legislatures and the United Kingdom Parliament in according weight to the evaluation

[44] Ibid., ¶67.

[45] Ibid., ¶56.

> of the different choices and interests in respect of matters which are within the primary competence of the legislatures.[46]

Nevertheless, as the law currently stands, the judgment of the Assembly as to what is a fair balance between the public interest and an individual's protected rights is open to question before the courts, and published government documents, ministerial statements in the course of debates and explanatory materials are all admissible to provide evidence of the quality or otherwise of the Assembly's decision-making. This again emphasizes the importance that needs to be attached to the thoroughness with which the underlying policy is developed and the clarity with which the findings of that process are presented to the legislature. Poorly thought through policy leading to incompetently executed legislative decision-making can lead to the legislation being declared invalid.

It should, however, be noted that there are limits to what is admissible as additional background material. In the *Agricultural Sector (Wales) Bill* case, as has been seen,[47] the Supreme Court indicated that it was prepared to look at reports that gave rise to the legislation or reports of an Assembly committee where it might find 'the clearest indication' of the purpose of legislative provisions[48] so as to determine whether they were within competence. However, it was not prepared to admit correspondence between government departments or between the UK and Welsh governments where that correspondence had not been made public and had not been referred to in the legislature. It was said that it 8-44

> would be wholly inconsistent with the transparent and open democratic process under which Parliament enacts legislation to take into account matters that have passed in private between two departments of the Executive or between the Executive of the UK and a devolved Executive.[49]

Bilingual legislation

A distinctive feature of Welsh legislation, whether Acts of the Assembly or subordinate legislation made by the Welsh Ministers, is that almost invariably it is enacted or made in both English and Welsh. In being bilingual, it is markedly different from the legislation of the UK Parliament and government. It is important to stress that Welsh legislation is bilingual at all points of the legislative process, unlike the legislation of countries such as the Republic of Ireland which generally completes its passage through the legislature before being translated into the second language. In Wales, Assembly bills are required to be introduced into 8-45

[46] Ibid., ¶119.

[47] See above, §4-14.

[48] *Agricultural Sector (Wales) Bill: Reference by the Attorney General for England and Wales* [2014] UKSC 43, ¶50.

[49] Ibid., ¶¶36–9.

the Assembly in both languages, and all the accompanying documentation such as explanatory memoranda have also to be bilingual. Consideration by the Assembly in both plenary and committee is of the text in both languages, and amendments at Stage Two, Stage Three and on Report are dealt with in both of the official languages. Assembly Members and others who participate in committee proceedings by, for instance, giving written or oral evidence do so in the language of their choice. The final text of a successful bill passes into law as a bilingual text, and virtually all of the subordinate legislation made by the Welsh Ministers, like that made by the Assembly between 1999 and 2007, is made in both languages.

8-46 One consequence of this is that, having been enacted or made in both English and Welsh, the English and Welsh legislative texts are required by the Government of Wales Acts 'to be treated for all purposes as being of equal standing'.[50] One such purpose is the interpretation of the text by the courts. As has been accepted by the Law Commission of England and Wales in its report on the *Form and Accessibility of the Law Applicable in Wales*,[51] it would be wrong and unacceptable to ignore the existence of the other language version in seeking to interpret the text. This places at the disposal of the courts an interpretative tool which is absent from the interpretation of legislation framed in one language only, namely the opportunity of referring to and comparing the terms of both texts to discover the intention of the legislature. In this, Welsh legislation is similar to the texts of international treaties made in more than one language, United Nations conventions, European Union law and the laws of many other states which adopt a bilingual or multilingual approach in law-making. It is to be hoped that, as the Law Commission has recommended, the courts will develop techniques for interpreting bilingual Welsh legislation which will further enrich the learning of statutory interpretation in this country.[52]

8-47 It is worth noting that the preparation of legislation in more than one language, and in particular its drafting, in itself decreases the risk of ambiguity in the language used. An extra pair of eyes, seeking the meaning of the draft in one language when seeking to express that meaning in another, is likely to detect latent ambiguities which may have escaped the notice of earlier drafters. The iterative process involved in creating bilingual bills and draft subordinate legislation is likely to decrease the incidence of ambiguity, and goes far to eliminate the risk of absurdity or outright error. It is therefore of great importance that due respect is paid to those responsible for producing a second text and those who check the two texts to ensure legal and

[50] GoWA 2006, s. 156(1). A similar provision was to be found in GoWA 1998, s. 122(1).

[51] Law Commission, *Form and Accessibility of the Law Applicable in Wales / Ffurf a Hygyrchedd y Gyfraith sy'n Gymwys yng Nghymru* (Law Com. No. 366), ¶¶12.1–12.56.

[52] Ibid., ¶¶12.39–12.40.

linguistic equivalence, and sufficient time given them in the process of preparing draft legislation to achieve optimum performance of their tasks.[53]

Correcting obvious errors – *casus omissus*

It is occasionally the case that, despite the best endeavours of those who draft and amend legislative proposals, errors occur. The question then arises as to what the courts should do, if anything, when confronted by obvious error. A strict application of the literal rule would suggest that the court should do nothing other than apply the ordinary grammatical construction of the language used. However, as noted, the cardinal or golden rule rejects such a strict approach if the result would be absurdity, repugnance or injustice. 8-48

While the courts have traditionally eschewed correcting the text of legislation when confronted with mistakes, there has been in the last half century a slight relaxation of their attitude. Arguably, this can again be traced to the willingness to adopt a purposive approach to statutory interpretation and, even more recently, the admissibility of additional background material capable of confirming not merely the existence of error but even the true intention of the legislature or even the correct wording required. 8-49

The contemporary stance of the courts on this issue is admirably summed up in the words of Lord Nicholls of Birkenhead in *Inco Europe Ltd* v *First Choice Distribution (A Firm)*, when he said: 8-50

> It has long been established that the role of the courts in construing legislation is not confined to resolving ambiguities in statutory language. The court must be able to correct obvious drafting errors. In suitable cases, in discharging its interpretative function the court will add words, or omit words or substitute words …
>
> This power is confined to plain cases of drafting mistakes. The courts are ever mindful that their constitutional role in this field is interpretative. They must abstain from any course which might have the appearance of judicial legislation. A statute is expressed in language approved and enacted by the legislature. So the courts exercise considerable caution before adding or omitting or substituting words. Before interpreting a statute in this way the court must be abundantly sure of three matters: (1) the intended purpose of the statute or provision in

[53] For a full discussion of law-making in more than one language, see Colin D. Robertson, *Multilingual Law: A Framework for Analysis and Understanding* (London and New York, 2016). For bilingual legislation in Wales in particular, see Dylan Hughes and Huw G. Davies, 'Accessible Bilingual Legislation for Wales' (2012) 33(2) *Statute Law Review* 103; Dylan Hughes and Huw G. Davies, 'Deddfwriaeth Hygyrch a Dwyieithog i Gymru' (2012) 33(2) *Statute Law Review* 122; C. F. Huws, 'The Day the Supreme Court was unable to interpret Statutes' (2013) 34 *Statute Law Review* 221; T. G.Watkin, 'Bilingual Legislation and the Law of England and Wales' (2014) 2(2) *The Theory and Practice of Legislation* 229; C. F. Huws, 'The Law of England and Wales: Translation in Transition' (2015) 22(1) *International Journal of Speech, Language and the Law* 1; T. G. Watkin, 'Bilingual Legislation: Awareness, Ambiguity and Attitudes' (2016) 37 *Statute Law Review* 116.

> question; (2) that by inadvertence the draftsman and Parliament failed to give effect to that purpose in the provision in question; and (3) the substance of the provision Parliament would have made, although not necessarily the precise words Parliament would have used, had the error in the bill been noticed. The third of these conditions is of crucial importance. Otherwise any attempt to determine the meaning of the enactment would cross the boundary between construction and legislation.[54]

It is evidence with regard to this crucial third matter which has now become more readily available in consequence of the admissibility of additional background material.

8-51 It goes without saying that the process of producing bilingual legislation reduces the risk of the kind of error contemplated here, and the existence of two language versions is an invaluable source for correcting any error that might occur in the process of amendment during the passage of a bill.

[54] [2000] 1 WLR 586.

Chapter 9

Other Legislatures and Their Legislative Processes

LEGISLATIVE PROCESS IN THE WESTMINSTER PARLIAMENT

Introduction

The Westminster Parliament continues to enact primary legislation that directly affects Wales. Although this is primarily in relation to matters that are not devolved, the proposition that the Westminster Parliament remains competent to legislate on all matters, including those which are within the legislative competence of the devolved legislatures, applies in relation to Wales as in relation to the other territories.[1] The Parliament of the United Kingdom, at Westminster, therefore, is still responsible for legislating for Wales in a number of ways. 9-01

Because there is as yet no separate legal jurisdiction of Wales, primary legislation of the Westminster Parliament extends to Wales, even where it is not desired for it to affect Wales in practice. This is less likely in relation to Scotland or Northern Ireland. The confusing result of this is that there is Westminster legislation which 'extends to England and Wales' but has no effect in relation to Wales, as well as legislation of the National Assembly for Wales which 'extends to England and Wales' but has no effect in relation to England. This causes difficulty and confusion for the vast majority of people who are not immediately aware of the technical, legal distinction between extent and application.[2] 9-02

Even after a series of expansions to the legislative competence of the National Assembly, there is a range of matters on which the Westminster Parliament remains the usual legislature in relation to Wales, and on those matters primary legislation will be required to emanate from Westminster. 9-03

There is also a range of secondary legislation that relates wholly or partly to Wales and that involves the Westminster Parliamentary scrutiny process in one way or another. This includes instruments which are made jointly by a United 9-04

[1] GoWA 2006, s. 107(5) explicitly states that the devolution of legislative competence to the Assembly 'does not affect the power of the Parliament of the United Kingdom to make laws for Wales'. The Wales Act 2017, s. 2 has added to this a new subsection (6), which reads: 'But it is recognised that the Parliament of the United Kingdom will not normally legislate with regard to devolved matters without the consent of the Assembly.' This provision enshrines in statute the previously existing convention to that effect, but it has been confirmed by the Supreme Court that its incorporation into statute does not made it legally enforceable: *R (on the application of Miller and another)* v *Secretary of State for Exiting the European Union* [2017] UKSC 5, at ¶¶136–51.

[2] See above, §§6-55–6-56.

Kingdom Minister of the Crown in relation to England and by the Welsh Ministers in relation to Wales, and which engage scrutiny processes at both Westminster and the National Assembly.

9-05 For all these reasons, it is desirable for the student of Welsh legislation to have a basic understanding of some of the legislative procedures in Westminster. This is one of the purposes of this chapter.

Initiation of legislation

9-06 In some respects the power to initiate legislation in the Westminster Parliament is highly diffuse, and it is more open than in the National Assembly for Wales to individual members and groupings of members to propose legislation and to obtain time for its consideration.

9-07 But this diffusion of power is largely illusory. In an average Session it is not uncommon for more than 100 Bills to be introduced, of which perhaps 70 or 80 per cent may be introduced by non-Government Members of Parliament or peers. But the reality is that government bills are almost certain to pass unless withdrawn for some reason; and genuine private members' bills are very unlikely to pass, and will not pass without at least benevolent neutrality on the part of the Government.

9-08 Even the well-known Ballot for Private Members' Bills in the Commons is a largely illusory process in terms of the right to initiate legislation, for two reasons. First, because of the way the Standing Orders of the House of Commons allocate time to private members' business, only the top seven ballot places each year out of the twenty names drawn have a chance of poll-position on a private members' Friday for Second Reading, which is a strategically crucial point when a bill is faced with more than the very mildest of backbench opposition. A bill faced with serious Government frontbench opposition is most unlikely to pass, even if it comes in the top seven in the ballot.

9-09 The second reason why the private members' ballot is an illusion of backbench power to initiate legislation, is that it is nowadays entirely normal for a number of the bills proposed, often including some in the top seven, to be 'handout' bills, that is to say Government bills masquerading as private members' bills, and being taken through the Commons by a private member in order to obtain favour with the Government.

9-10 In the House of Lords, any peer may introduce a bill at any time; but the prospect of time being found to discuss it is remote, and the prospect of its becoming law is even more remote.

9-11 So the reality is that while members in either House have unlimited power notionally to introduce as many bills as they like, in terms of obtaining time to discuss them, and even more so in terms of securing enactment, the Government has a virtual monopoly on the initiation of primary legislation.

9-12 The one real exception to this relates to private bills (as opposed to private members' bills): these are initiated by local authorities, corporations or other entities that need to promote a change in the law to facilitate the performance of their functions or for some other reason, and who cannot achieve that change otherwise than by primary legislation. These are genuinely initiated by non-Government organizations; although, again, the Government has, in effect, a veto when it comes to the question of whether the legislation once initiated will ever be enacted.

Explanatory material

In relation to bills introduced in the Westminster Parliament there is a document which serves part of the same purpose as the Explanatory Memorandum required by the Standing Orders of the National Assembly for Wales. But it only performs part of that purpose, and unlike the National Assembly its production is not a requirement of Standing Orders, but a facility made available to the Government by the House Authorities, for the assistance of members. 9-13

These Explanatory Notes are a relatively recent creation, originating in an experiment begun in around 1995. Because the Explanatory Notes are a document printed by the House Authorities, although the Government is responsible for preparing them, there are limitations imposed by the Houses on what may be included. Much of the useful background information and policy justification that is required by the Standing Orders in the National Assembly for Wales, is actually prohibited in relation to the Westminster Explanatory Notes. Put simply, they are required to confine themselves to explanation of what the Bill does as a matter of law, as distinct from justification of why the policy achieved by the bill is desirable. 9-14

Before the bill is introduced, the explanatory notes are cleared in draft with the Public Bill Office in each House; and if the Clerk of Legislation detects matter of an argumentative nature in the notes, he or she will require it to be removed before the notes are printed. The explanatory notes are printed first around the time of introduction of the bill, although there may sometimes be a short delay. They are then reprinted, broadly speaking, at the time when the bill passes between the two Houses, and they are reprised and reissued once the bill is enacted. At that point they cease to be Parliamentary documents and become Government publications; so it is theoretically open to the Government to reinsert into the explanatory notes as published after Royal Assent, matter of a background or argumentative nature that would not have been permitted in the notes as published by the House. But this is rarely done to any significant extent. 9-15

Although the explanatory notes begin with a disclaimer as to forming part of the bill and as to their having been approved in any sense by Parliament, the courts have established a practice of being prepared to have regard to the notes under conditions similar to the use of Hansard under the rule in *Pepper* v *Hart*, to resolve ambiguities or uncertainties. 9-16

The explanatory notes routinely include publication of the statement which a Minister introducing a bill in either House is required to make by section 19 of the Human Rights Act 1998. The requirement is either to state that the Government is satisfied that the bill is compatible with the Convention rights under that Act, or that it is not but the Government wants to proceed anyway. It is very rare for the statement to deny compatibility, but there have been a small number of instances. 9-17

The explanatory notes routinely include discussion of the analysis of any fundamental rights engaged by the bill, showing why the Government has concluded that the bill is Convention-compliant.

Laying the bill

9-18 The Westminster procedures for physically introducing a bill into either House have been adumbrated in chapter seven, in drawing the contrast with the National Assembly.[3]

Speaker's role

9-19 There is of course no equivalent, in Westminster, of the Presiding Officer's decision on competence, that not being a relevant concept for the Westminster Parliament. Nor does the Speaker in either House have any control or discretion in relation to the introduction of bills. There are matters, such as the use of short titles which are thought to be more about propaganda than information, as to which the Speaker may express a view: but in neither House does the Speaker have the power to refuse the presentation of a bill whether by the Government or any other member. As to whether the bill will receive time to be discussed or will proceed, again that is generally not a question for the Speaker's discretion, and some of the factors controlling it have been referred to above.

The deliberative phase

9-20 Broadly speaking, the system required to be achieved by Standing Orders for the National Assembly for Wales, as required by the Government of Wales Act 2006 and its predecessor, is intended to mirror the essence of the arrangements for Westminster. There are, however, some significant differences of substance, and a number of differences of nomenclature which make the similarities more difficult to spot.

9-21 Apart from the fact that, at Westminster, stages of consideration of the Bill are referred to as Readings and not as Stages, there is the fundamental and confusing difference that in both Houses of Parliament the First Reading is a mere formality which does not actually take place in any meaningful sense, in contrast to Stage One in the National Assembly which is an important substantive stage. The Westminster equivalent of Stage One is therefore the Second Reading, which in the same way is intended to be a debate on the general principles of the bill.

9-22 Amendments of the text of the bill are not tabled at Second Reading. In the House of Commons it is normal for the Second Reading of a Government bill to occupy either a whole or half day of Government time (allowing for Questions, Statements and other minor matters). In the House of Lords, the Second Reading of a Government bill routinely lasts for the whole of a day's business (again allowing for Questions and other minor matters); and in the case of a bill of particular complexity or importance, the Second Reading might be taken over more than one day.

[3] See above, §§7-14–7-16.

As in the National Assembly, at the end of the Second Reading of a bill in either House of Parliament it is committed for what is commonly known as line-by-line scrutiny, although the modern reality is that few if any bills actually receive scrutiny at that thorough a level of detail. 9-23

In the House of Commons the most usual form of committal is to a Public Bill Committee. Unlike the National Assembly for Wales, this is not a standing committee dealing with the subject-matter to which the bill relates, but is an *ad hoc* committee constituted for the purpose of examining the bill and then dissolved. That can make a real difference to the quality of the scrutiny, as members may not have much in the way of experience in relation to the relevant subject-matter; nor are they likely to expect to be involved in post-legislative scrutiny of the bill or even in informal consideration of how it is implemented and whether or not it achieves its objectives. 9-24

Like the National Assembly Committees, however, a Public Bill Committee routinely takes evidence from interested stakeholders in relation to a bill, generally for around two to four sessions before beginning its formal clause-by-clause scrutiny of the bill. 9-25

In the House of Lords, the norm is for a bill to be considered in Committee of the Whole House in the Chamber; and whether that is the case or a bill is committed to Grand Committee in the Moses Room, in neither case is evidence taken before considering the bill. 9-26

A Public Bill Committee in the House of Commons considering a Government bill of around 100 pages might be expected to hold anything between ten and twenty sessions to consider it. In the House of Lords, a Committee stage of a Government bill of that size would be likely to be spread over two or three days. 9-27

There are a number of committees which consider a bill outside the context of formal proceedings on it, but with a view to influencing or informing those proceedings, in a manner similar to the Constitutional and Legislative Affairs Committee of the National Assembly. The House of Lords has for some time maintained a delegated powers committee which scrutinizes, in relation to bills and amendments, proposals by the Executive to take powers in relation to the making of subordinate legislation or other matters. That committee routinely reports its findings about the powers proposed to be taken, and it is common to have those findings referred to in the course of later debates, particularly in the House of Lords. The Committee is relatively influential, and it is not uncommon for the Government to make concessions on, in particular, the appropriate level of Parliamentary scrutiny proposed in relation to a delegated power, and to table amendments to give effect to that compromise at a later stage of the bill. 9-28

There is no Westminster equivalent of the Constitutional and Legislative Affairs Committee in the National Assembly in relation to bills. A similar function is performed in relation to statutory instruments by the Joint Committee on Statutory Instruments and in the Select Committee on statutory instruments in the House of Lords. The delegated powers functions are scrutinized by the delegated powers committee in the Lords, but apart from that there is no formal consideration of the 9-29 technical matters in relation to bills that the Constitutional and Legislative Affairs Committee routinely considers.

9-30 Bills and amendments are, however, routinely considered by the Joint Committee on Human Rights and by the House of Lords Constitution Committee, both of which may report aspects of Bills or amendments to the Houses; and those reports may be referred to in debate and may inspire opposition or backbench amendments or Government concessions.

Financial motions

9-31 Financial motions are required in relation to bills in the House of Commons, and, indeed, the financial motion procedure in the National Assembly is broadly reflective of the House of Commons supply procedures.

9-32 In essence, a bill that imposes a charge on public funds cannot proceed to the Committee stage in the House of Commons unless a money resolution has been moved: since money resolutions can be moved only on the recommendation of the Crown, this effectively gives – and is intended to give – the Government a veto over legislative proposals that would entail the expenditure of public money. Ways and means resolutions play a similar role in relation to the imposition of charges on the people: broadly speaking, new taxes or increased taxes, but the concept is a technical one and there are anomalies on either side of the line.

Amendments

9-33 In the course of Westminster legislation, significant numbers of amendments are expected to be tabled in both Houses of Parliament and are tabled freely by the Government, by the opposition and by backbenchers on all sides. On a Government bill of significant size it is not uncommon to have tens or even hundreds of amendments, which are likely to pass into law. Opposition amendments are much less likely to succeed, but some will be accepted by Ministers in principle and then followed by Government amendments giving technically accurate effect to the original policy.

9-34 The process of amendments is basically the same at the Westminster Parliament Committee Stages and Report Stages as it is in the National Assembly at Stages Two and Three. In particular, the amendments 'toolkit' is exactly the same: amendments may remove text, add text or substitute text.

9-35 The main difference in practice between Westminster and Cardiff is the common lack of a working majority for the Government in the House of Lords, as a result of which amendments are sometimes moved against the Government's wishes and passed. Although a Government with an effective majority in the House of Commons can always reverse Lords amendments, it is often considered not politically adroit to do so. Because of the lack of a necessarily entrenched Government majority, and the ability to provide significant amount of time in the Chamber for the scrutiny of a bill at Committee and Report, it is thought by some that the House of Lords is able to provide effective legislative scrutiny of a kind not found in a unicameral chamber such as the National Assembly, where the single chamber is necessarily dominated by the Government. That opinion is held, in particular, by many members of the House of Lords. The reality is rather more nuanced, but it is certainly true that on some occasions the nature of the second chamber allows it to give significantly more effective legislative scrutiny than is true of the first chamber.

In the Commons, Third Reading is not in any meaningful sense a separate stage from the Report Stage (which is an opportunity for the whole House to move amendments to the bill). While technically it is the decision-making phase at the end of the proceedings of the bill in the House of Commons, in reality it is rarely anything more than a formality. Amendments are not taken in the House of Commons at Third Reading, while in the Lords it is a separate amendable stage, albeit with rules designed to deprecate the tabling of significant new matters by way of amendment. 9-36

Recommitment is a technical possibility for bills in both Houses of Parliament but very rarely happens. 9-37

Relationship between the House of Commons and the House of Lords

The two Chambers of the Westminster Parliament mean that the to-and-fro process, commonly called 'ping-pong', is a key difference between the Westminster procedure and the procedure in the National Assembly. 9-38

Amendments made by the second House return to the first for approval, and a series of messages can pass between the two Houses proposing a series of compromise positions until agreement is reached. Failure to reach agreement results in the bill falling, but this happens very rarely, as the unelected House of Lords accepts that failure to give way to the elected House would be likely to hasten the Lords' demise. 9-39

The same is true of the general balance between the two Houses in relation to the passage of bills: the Parliament Acts allow the Commons to dispense with the Lords' agreement on a bill introduced in the Session after a bill in the same terms has been rejected or delayed by the Lords.[4] This does happen occasionally, but is rarely necessary as the Lords tend to back down and pass a Bill sent to them from the Commons. 9-40

Bills that are certified by the Speaker of the House of Commons as Money Bills (broadly speaking, dealing only with public expenditure or taxation) have additional protection under the Parliament Acts, and in effect the Lords have only one month to consider them: if not passed within that period they proceed to Royal Assent despite the Lords. 9-41

Timetable

The predicted timetable for the progress of a bill varies greatly between bills, and even Government bills do not progress through the two Houses at anything like a uniform rate. 9-42

[4] The Parliament Act 1911 required two rejections by the Lords before the Commons could proceed to Royal Assent on the third occasion without troubling the peers further. This timescale was reduced to one rejection by the Parliament Act 1949. See also above, §§1-38–1-41.

9-43 For the most part, bills are Sessional: a bill that is introduced early or reasonably early in the Parliamentary Session is likely to be completed before the summer recess; and, as a rule, bills that are not completed before the end of the session fall. The process of carrying over bills from one session to the next used to be reserved for private bills; however, in recent years this has been extended, to a limited extent, to Government bills.

9-44 As a general rule, a Government bill of medium size is likely to pass through the two Houses at something like the following rate: an interval of a couple of weeks between introduction and Second Reading; a couple of weeks between Second Reading and the beginning of the Committee Stage; four to six weeks or so in Public Bill Committee in the Commons; an interval of a week or so between Committee and the Report Stage on the floor of the Chamber; a couple of weeks between passing from the first House to the second House and having Second Reading in the second House; a couple of weeks' interval between Second Reading in the Lords and the first day allocated to Committee; the Committee Stage in the Lords held over a week or two; a short interval between the last Committee Stage day and Report; a short interval of a few days between Report and Third Reading.

Interval for reference

9-45 There is no equivalent in the Westminster Parliament to the interval allowed for reference to the Supreme Court in relation to bills in the National Assembly. This is for the obvious reason that, as there are no legal limits to the competence of the Westminster Parliament, its enactments are not open to challenge. Likewise, there is no equivalent to the opportunity for Secretary of State intervention, as there is no body to which to turn for political approval of such a move. Although the validity of Parliamentary legislation may be challenged by reference to incompatibility with European Union law, and although a declaration of incompatibility with the European Convention on Human Rights could be sought under the Human Rights Act 1998, no special arrangements are made to allow time for such a contingency between the passage of a bill and the giving of Royal Assent.

9-46 For pragmatic reasons, if the Government feared a successful challenge on grounds of contravention of European Union law, they might choose to delay Royal Assent or implementation; but this would be a matter of political strategy, not law.

Royal Assent

9-47 The arrangements for Royal Assent are broadly the same for Westminster Bills as for the National Assembly.

9-48 The timing of presentation of Bills for Royal Assent is entirely in the hands of the Government; and a short delay is not uncommon, although for Westminster this is rarely as long as is commonly the case for the National Assembly.

Although the Government chooses the time of presentation for Royal Assent, there is a convention, which one would not expect the Government to breach, that once it has decided to present any of the bills currently awaiting Royal Assent for that purpose, it cannot pick and choose which to present but must seek Royal Assent to all or none. 9-49

'English Votes for English Laws' – EVEL

One feature of the consideration of bills and statutory instruments in the Westminster Parliament, which is necessarily absent from the National Assembly, is the 'English Votes for English Laws' procedure created by Standing Orders of the House of Commons to address (to a limited extent) the complaint that it is inequitable for Scottish, Welsh and Northern Irish Members of Parliament to have a vote on legislation in relation to England in circumstances where English MPs would not have a vote in relation to the same topics in relation to Scotland, Wales or Northern Ireland. 9-50

The process applies to almost all Government bills and to statutory instruments. The Speaker has a duty to determine whether in his opinion bills or elements of bills, and amendments, attract the special rules. Where the process applies, the members of a public bill committee will be chosen only from MPs representing constituencies in England (or England and Wales, in the case of a bill applying to both countries). The process also creates three stages that a bill can go through between Report Stage and Third Reading: Legislative Grand Committee; Reconsideration; and Consequential Consideration. The Legislative Grand Committee considers a consent motion for the application of a bill or provision to England, or England and Wales. The Reconsideration and Consequential Consideration stages exist to resolve disagreements at the first stage. There is no equivalent of the process for the House of Lords. 9-51

Addressing the *EVEL* issue by amending the House of Commons procedures regarding bills which apply only to England solves one anomaly at the expense of creating others. Whereas the question of whether the provisions of an Assembly bill fall within devolved competence is one ultimately for courts to determine, the same question asked regarding a Westminster bill is determined by the Speaker and that determination is not justiciable. Likewise, if the provisions of an Assembly bill or Act are incompatible with the Convention rights protected by the Human Rights Act 1998, in the case of Wales-only legislation the provisions can be struck down by the courts, while England-only legislation, being enshrined in a UK Act of Parliament, is only subject to a declaration of incompatibility, leaving the decision whether to repeal or amend to political judgment. 9-52

Statutory instruments

The arrangements for Parliamentary scrutiny of statutory instruments in the Westminster Parliament match those in the National Assembly. In particular, there is 9-53 the same choice of scrutiny procedures, and the most common are draft affirmative procedure, negative resolution and no express scrutiny. The Joint Committee on Statutory Instruments performs a similar function to the technical scrutiny which can be performed by the Constitutional and Legislative Affairs Committee or the subject-focused Committees in the National Assembly.

EUROPEAN UNION LEGISLATION

Introduction

9-54 The legislative process in the European Union is fundamentally different from the process in either the Westminster Parliament or the National Assembly for Wales. Overall, it more closely resembles a process of political negotiation through a series of increasingly focused draft policy proposals than it does the production of legislation in a legislature.[5]

9-55 That is primarily attributable to the fact that much European Union legislation, and almost all the European Union legislation that is intended to have the most significant effect, takes the form of skeleton instruments which are required to be transposed into law in each of the member states and are therefore not intended to be fully formed legislation at the point when they leave the EU institutions.

9-56 Even those legislative instruments which are intended to have immediate legal effect in the member states without further transposition tend to have the attributes of political documents as well as, and sometimes instead of, the attributes expected to be found in legislative instruments in accordance with the United Kingdom's legal traditions.

9-57 Despite this, much of the legislation that emanates from the European Union either affects people and businesses in Wales directly, or can be expected to affect

[5] *Craies on Legislation* (11th edn, by D. Greenberg, London, 2017), para. 31.1.21; cited with approval in *Assange* v *Sweden* [2012] UKSC 22:

> European union legislation is framed in a very different way to United Kingdom legislation. Whether out of principle or political necessity, the text of legislation is arrived at through a process of political compromise, and individual words may be chosen less for their legal certainty than for their political acceptability. Once negotiated and passed, however, legislation from the EU has to be applied and implemented within each Member State, and despite the additional freedom imparted by a purposive approach to construction, it must have sufficient legal certainty to enable consistent application and implementation. The difficulties in drafting style resulting from the political process by which EU legislation is constructed were acknowledged for many years, and resulted in the establishment on December 22, 1998 of an interinstitutional agreement on common guidelines for the quality of drafting of Community legislation. While those guidelines are to be regarded as instruments for internal use by the institutions and are not legally binding, they are noteworthy and likely to be helpful for all engaged in legislative (or indeed other) drafting, whether international or national.

them indirectly once transposing legislation has been made, under section 2(2) of the European Communities Act 1972 or otherwise.[6]

An account of legislative processes in relation to Wales would therefore be incomplete without a brief description of the relevant features of the European Union legislative process. That, therefore, is the second purpose of this chapter. 9-58

Overview

Only the European Commission can initiate legislation within the European Union. 9-59

The European Commission consists of the Commissioners, one appointed by each of the member states and then entrusted with responsibility for a particular policy area, much in the manner of cabinet ministers. The Commissioners are served by a large staff, who are often also referred to as being the European Commission, although strictly, in legal terms, the Commission is the body composed of the Commissioners. 9-60

The ordinary legislative procedure (formerly co-decision) gives the European Parliament and the European Council equal power in relation to the progress of legislation; and there are certain special procedures for specific cases in which the Parliament has only a consultative rôle, and certain other issues, notably taxation, in relation to which the European Parliament gives only an advisory opinion through the consultation procedure. 9-61

Although the European Parliament does not have power to initiate legislative proposals, it can ask the Commission to do so and in practice this is a significant source of new legislation. 9-62

The European Parliament is a unicameral body of over 700 members, elected by constituencies within the member states, although the Members of the European Parliament, or MEPs, tend, when elected, to form party groupings based on their political rather than their national allegiance. 9-63

The European Council is a body composed of government ministers from each of the member states, each state being represented as occasion requires by a minister with responsibility for the policy area under discussion or requiring a determination. At its highest level, it is the quarterly meeting of the European Council of Heads of State or Government. The European Council needed at one time to be unanimous for a law to be made, but in many – but not all – instances this has now ceased to be required and is replaced by a system of qualified majority voting or QMV. This requires that a legislative proposal be supported in the Council by at least 55 per cent of the members of the Council representing the participating member states, which states must comprise more than 65 per cent of the participating member states' combined populations. To block such a decision, opponents must comprise a minority consisting of Council members representing more than 35 per cent of the population of the participating member states. Where 9-64

[6] This will continue to be the case, at least until such time as the United Kingdom may cease to be a member of the European Union and thereby ceases to be affected by its legislation.

unanimity is required, abstention by a member state does not prevent adoption of the proposal.[7]

Ordinary legislative procedure

9-65 The European Union Treaties as amended provide for different legislative procedures in relation to different matters.

9-66 The ordinary legislative procedure deals with a wide range of issues, including economic governance, immigration, energy, transport, environment and consumer protection. It involves, in effect, the joint adoption of law by the European Parliament and the Council. The ordinary legislative procedure is the successor to what used to be called the co-decision procedure which was introduced by the Maastricht Treaty on European Union in 1992 and extended by the Amsterdam Treaty in 1999. It was renamed as a result of the Lisbon Treaty in 2009.

9-67 Under the ordinary legislative procedure, the power of initiation of legislative proposals rests in the European Commission, which submits a legislative proposal to the European Parliament. The College of Commissioners adopts a proposal by the Commission through a written procedure, without public discussion, or through an oral procedure that involves public discussion. If the proposal is controversial, a decision on initiation is taken by simple majority vote of the Commission. Something in the region of one hundred legislative proposals are made each year by the Commission under the ordinary procedure, which accounts for very roughly 90 per cent of the legislative proposals emanating from the Commission altogether.

9-68 Once initiated by the Commission through a proposal, the legislation needs to be given a first reading in the European Parliament. There is no specific deadline by which this needs to be achieved, and whether taken in Committee or in a plenary session the decision will be taken by a simple majority vote. At the point at which a proposal is sent by the Commission to the European Parliament a process of citizen consultation begins through the appointment of *rapporteurs*, who are appointed on a party political basis. At the first reading in the European Parliament the Commission's proposal may be rejected, adopted or amended.

9-69 On arrival at the European Parliament a legislative proposal from the European Commission is referred to a relevant Committee by the President of the Parliament in consultation with civil servants. As with the National Assembly, there are subject-based standing Committees to which proposals are referred, rather than the *ad hoc* approach of the Westminster Public Bill Committee. Also as with the National Assembly, more than one Committee may be invited to give an opinion on a cross-subject legislative proposal.

9-70 The next stage of the consideration of a proposal for legislation is the first reading in the European Council (although preparatory work is undertaken by the Council at the same time as the first reading in the European Parliament). Once the Parliament has adopted a position in relation to a legislative proposal, it

[7] Treaty on European Union, Article 238.

is open to the Council to consider the Parliament's position and either to adopt the legislative proposal or to change it, in which case a first reading position from the Council is sent to the Parliament for a second reading. There is no fixed timing for the process of the first reading in Council. The decision-making in Council focuses on working parties which are made up of political representatives of the member states and chaired by the holder of the rotating Presidency, assisted by the Council Secretariat. Intermediate stages open to the Council to adopt are to reach agreement in principle – a general approach – which may take place before the European Parliament has delivered a position, although this rarely happens. More usually, the Council may reach a political agreement on the broad outline of a proposal before the Parliament adopts a position.

Once the European Council has reached a position on a legislative proposal, the 9-71
proposal returns to the European Parliament for a second reading. There is a fixed time period within which the European Parliament must examine the Council's position: three months, with a potential extension to four months. Second reading begins with examination by the relevant subject committee of the Parliament, which prepares a recommendation for second reading which takes place in plenary. There is some scope for the making of amendments in the plenary session. Overall, there are four standard outcomes to the second reading process: approval of the Council's position and adoption of the legislative proposal; failure to take a decision within the relevant time, in which case the act is adopted as amended by the Council at its first reading; rejection of the Council's first reading position, in which case the Act falls; and the proposal of amendments to the Council's first reading position, which results in a second reading in the Council.

Most legislative proposals are adopted at the second reading stage in the 9-72
European Parliament. If, however, a legislative proposal is not adopted at that stage then it returns to the European Council for a second reading. The Council has another three-month period (which can be extended to four months) to examine the second reading position taken by the European Parliament, in the light of the European Commission's communicated position on amendments suggested by the Parliament. The European Council has the option of approving the amendments proposed by the European Parliament, and if it does so then the legislative act is adopted at that point. If the Council does not approve all the amendments proposed by the Parliament, then a meeting of the Conciliation Committee has to be called by the President of the Council together with the President of the Parliament.

Underlying the essentially political rather than legislative nature of this process, 9-73
official-level bilateral meetings between representatives of the Parliament and the Council, and sometimes the Commission, are expected to take place in parallel to the whole of this process and are often likely to be determinative. These are much more significant and quasi-formal than the corridor conversations that inevitably take place around the stages of legislation in the National Assembly for Wales or in the Westminster Parliament.

The Conciliation Committee is convened in cases where the European 9-74

Council does not approve all amendments proposed by the European Parliament at its second reading. The purpose of the Conciliation Committee is to allow the Parliament and the Council to negotiate directly with the aim of reaching an agreement in the form of a joint text: again, this underlines the essentially political nature of the legislative process and the legislative text in the European Union institutions. (The only slightly similar procedure approaching it in the United Kingdom context would be the Reasons Room consideration of messages between the two Houses of Parliament, but even that is purely unilateral and does not take the form of substantive bilateral negotiations.)

9-75 The time limit for the convening of the Conciliation Committee is six weeks, with a possible extension by agreement to eight weeks, following the end of the Council second reading and its notification to Parliament of non-acceptance of its second reading amendments.

9-76 The purpose of the Conciliation Committee is to deal with the Council's refusal to adopt the European Parliament's position at second reading. Within the allotted period the aim is to decide on a joint text based on the combination of the second reading position of the Parliament and the Council. If a joint text does not emerge from the Conciliation Committee, that is fatal to the proposed legislation and ends the procedure.

9-77 If a joint text does emerge from the Conciliation Committee, it is forwarded to the European Parliament and to the Council for a further reading in each institution. As with all the proceedings in the European institutions, the formal process happens in parallel with negotiations at official level, amounting to technical and policy three-way discussions between the Parliament, the Council and the Commission; and each of those bodies reports to its appropriate delegation within the Conciliation Committee.

9-78 As its name implies, the Conciliation Committee is designed to produce a compromise on amendments to resolve outstanding differences. A range of negotiation techniques is used, including four-column working documents with translations into all the official languages: so this is a very unwieldy process, different from anything that takes place in the Westminster Parliament or the National Assembly. The parallel political negotiations are in practice of enormous importance to the resolution of the differences between the institutions and party groupings within them, dwarfing in importance the casual informal political negotiations that take place in the corridors of Westminster and Cardiff.

9-79 Once a joint text has been agreed it is sent to the European Parliament and European Council for approval. There is another six-week period, again with a potential extension to eight weeks, during which each institution must make a decision on the text, and neither can amend it. If the two institutions approve the joint text then the legislative proposal is adopted in that form; if approval by both institutions is not achieved within the time limit, the legislative proposal falls. (The Council can be expected to approve the joint text because of the composition of the Council's delegation on the Conciliation Committee, and that has been the invariable practice to date.)

The equivalent of Royal Assent is that, once the final text of a legislative proposal has been approved by the European Parliament and the European Council, it is signed by the Presidents and Secretaries-General of each institution and promulgated by publication in the Official Journal. If the proposal never gets to the stage of joint approval of a joint text, it falls and cannot be formally revised, although in practice it could be replaced by a new proposal from the Commission. 9-80

For Regulations which have direct effect throughout the European Union, publication in the Official Journal is enough to give them force of law. Directives come into force on publication or otherwise as specified in their own terms; but they require transposing domestic legislation to give them effect. Decisions will also have full effect on promulgation, subject to their own terms, in the cases to which they apply. 9-81

Other legislative procedures

As well as the ordinary legislative procedure, a number of special legislative procedures are used for a variety of purposes. The consent procedure (formerly the assent procedure) was introduced by the Single European Act in 1986 to deal with association agreements and access agreements. It now applies to a slightly wider area including ratification of agreements negotiated by the European Union, cases of fundamental rights under Article 7 of the Treaty on European Union and in relation to taxation arrangements or withdrawal arrangements from the EU. 9-82

Other specific procedures carried out for particular purposes include special procedures for the consideration of voluntary agreements that are proposed instead of legislation. 9-83

There is also a procedure for codification of a number of Acts and their replacement with a single Act, which amounts to an expedited procedure similar to that used for Consolidation Bills in the Westminster Parliament. 9-84

Additionally, a range of procedures for implementing provisions and delegated provisions broadly follow the policy approach of delegated legislation in the Westminster Parliament and the National Assembly. 9-85

For as long as the UK remains in the EU, legislation made in Wales by the National Assembly and the Welsh Ministers will continue to have to be compatible with EU law. The proposed withdrawal of the UK from the EU will end the current competence of EU institutions to legislate for the UK and therefore for Wales, and the requirement that Welsh legislation comply with EU law will also cease. It is not yet clear what will replace those arrangements in the future. 9-86

Afterword

Writing about the law is like taking a still photograph of a moving object; the result immediately belongs to the past. That is certainly true of writing about Welsh devolution, where changes have been frequent. At the time of this book's completion, further changes are in the offing, but one cannot be certain about their outcomes. A-01

Three such potential changes deserve mention – the consequences of the UK's proposed withdrawal from the European Union; the issue of the single legal jurisdiction of England and Wales; and the powers given to the Assembly by the Wales Act 2017 to alter its name and its electoral arrangements.

WITHDRAWAL FROM THE EUROPEAN UNION – SO-CALLED *BREXIT*

The case for this momentous change is essentially political. A majority of the UK electorate who voted in the June 2016 referendum were in favour of leaving the EU. The European Union (Withdrawal) Act 2018, which effects the changes to UK law necessitated by withdrawal, received Royal Assent on 26 June 2018. A-02

The Act provides for the repeal of the European Communities Act 1972 and the incorporation into UK domestic law of the rules of EU law as they exist on the date of withdrawal – exit day. The rules of EU law so incorporated will form a distinct body of law within the UK, termed 'retained EU law'. Thereafter, the institutions of the EU will no longer be able to change rules in that retained body of law; only legislatures within the UK will be able to do so.

The Act empowers UK Government ministers to make changes to retained EU law to overcome 'deficiencies' resulting from references within it to EU institutions. This includes the power to make changes to other laws which present similar problems. Where laws made by the devolved institutions contain such 'deficiencies', their respective governments are empowered to effect such changes provided they do not conflict with the changes made by the UK ministers. In Wales, such changes to Assembly legislation and Welsh Government subordinate legislation will be made by the Welsh Ministers. In every instance, the changes will be made by regulations, subordinate legislation contained in statutory instruments.[1]

The retained EU law will contain what remains in force of the law with which devolved legislation currently has to be compatible to be within competence. Much of that law relates to matters that are not reserved under the devolution settlements. It was originally proposed that, after exit day, only the UK Parliament would be able to make changes to that body of law, the rules contained in it being placed outside the competence of the devolved legislatures. The rationale for this approach

[1] EU (Withdrawal) Act 2018, ss. 1–7; ss. 8–9, and s. 11 and Schedule 2.

was that common rules were necessary to ensure a single market for goods and services across the UK, a commonality achieved prior to exit day through compliance with EU law. This approach was opposed by the devolved institutions in both Wales and Scotland, who succeeded in having the proposal amended.

The Act as passed removes the requirement that devolved legislation must be compatible with EU law, so that, with regard to Wales, the National Assembly will be able to amend retained EU law provided it is otherwise within its competence to do so. However, the Act also introduces a new restriction. This restriction prevents the Assembly from making changes to retained EU if the change is of a description specified in regulations made by a UK government minister. To be made, such regulations need to be approved by resolution of both Houses of Parliament, and prior to being laid before Parliament, the regulations must undergo a statutory consent procedure before the Assembly. This procedure allows the Assembly a period of 40 days to either agree to the regulations, decide not to agree to them, or to refuse to agree. The Minister may not lay the regulations before Parliament for approval until either a consent decision has been made or the 40-day period has expired. If the Minister lays regulations without the agreement of the Assembly, he or she must present a statement explaining why it has been decided to do so together with any statement provided by the Welsh Ministers giving their opinion as to why the Assembly has not agreed. Thereafter, it is up to Parliament to decide whether the regulations should be made. The power to make such regulations expires two-years after exit day, and regulations made in pursuance of it become subject to the Assembly's legislative competence five years after they are made.[2]

As a consequence of this change of approach, the National Assembly resolved to consent to the passing of the EU (Withdrawal) Bill. The Scottish Parliament did not. It is worth noting that if, during the relevant two-year period, the UK government were to attain a majority in the House of Commons, its ability to proceed in defiance of the Assembly's not having agreed would mean that it would be up to the House of Lords whether to approve the regulations. By convention, the unelected second chamber does not overrule the will of the democratically-elected representatives in the other chamber. However, on devolved matters, one can legitimately ask which is the relevant democratically-elected chamber – the House of Commons or the National Assembly. On these issues, the UK is entering uncharted constitutional territory

After withdrawal, the UK will (subject to the terms of any agreement with the EU) be free to enter into trading agreements with other states, whereas currently such agreements are made by the EU and are binding on its member states as part of EU law. If in future, the UK's trading agreements will be part of its international

2. EU (Withdrawal) Act 2018, s. 12, amending section 108A(2)(e) of the Government of Wales Act 2006 (as amended by the Wales Act 2017, s. 3), and inserting a new section 109A into the 2006 Act, together with Schedule 3, para. 43, inserting a new section 157ZA into the 2006 Act. Similar restrictions are placed upon the powers of Welsh Ministers with regard to their subordinate law-making powers: EU (Withdrawal) Act 2018, Schedule 3, para. 2, amending Government of Wales Act 2006, s. 80(8).

obligations, then instead of having to be compatible with EU law to be valid, devolved legislation may be tested for compatibility with those international obligations. Whereas, at present, compatibility with EU law is a question of law for the courts to determine, compatibility with international obligations is a matter for Secretary of State intervention. Such a development would be damaging to the legislative competence of the devolved administrations in Wales and Scotland, although in Northern Ireland there is already a provision in the devolution settlement allowing the Secretary of State to refuse to present a bill for Royal Assent if he or she considers its provisions 'would have an adverse effect on the operation of the single market in goods and services within the United Kingdom' – a phrase for which perhaps a future beckons in the devolution settlements generally.[3]

The Assembly's legislative competence may also be adversely affected by the manner in which functions currently exercised by EU institutions are re-allocated within the UK upon withdrawal.[4] Wherever a function which does not relate to a reserved matter is given to a public authority which is not a devolved Welsh authority, the competence of the Assembly to legislate in relation to that function and therefore in relation to that devolved matter will be restricted. The need for Minister of the Crown consent in such situations would be a useful way to protect the UK government's view of what 'would have an adverse effect on the operation of the single market in goods and services within the United Kingdom'. Doubtless the allocation of functions by the UK government will not be done in ignorance of that opportunity.

It is simply not possible to predict with any certainty what the future holds on these issues, and one is consequently left wondering what the long term effects of Brexit will be upon Welsh devolution.

The UK is scheduled to leave the EU on 29 March 2019, but it is expected that transitional arrangements will continue to operate until at least the end of 2020.

A WELSH JURISDICTION

Mention has been made on several occasions in this work that England and Wales is a single legal jurisdiction, whereas both Scotland and Northern Ireland have separate legal systems.[5] This means that in Scotland and Northern Ireland, it is the courts of those countries which enforce the laws made for them by their legislatures. The extent and application of their laws correspond. A-03

That is not the case in England and Wales. Because England and Wales is a single jurisdiction, the laws which apply only in relation to Wales and the laws which apply only in relation to England, all extend to both countries, as do the laws which apply to both. A court anywhere in England can, subject to rules of

[3] Northern Ireland Act 1998, s. 14.

[4] See EU (Withdrawal) Act 2018, s. 8(6); Schedule 2, paras. 4–7.

[5] See above, §§6-55–6-56; 9-02.

court about forum and allocation of proceedings, deal with litigation concerning laws which apply only in Wales and *vice versa*.

Not surprisingly, the existence of legislative and executive devolution within Wales has led to questions being asked as to whether the judicial function should also be devolved. This became a matter of considerable controversy during the passage of what became the Wales Act 2017, because it became apparent that several of the restrictions being placed upon the Assembly's legislative competence resulted from the perceived need to maintain the integrity of the single legal jurisdiction of England and Wales.[6]

Arguably, there are three issues which suggest that some distinct jurisdictional arrangements are required.

First, there is now developing a distinct body of law which applies only to Wales, as there is also a distinct body of law which applies only to England. Both of those bodies of law will increase in size as divergent legislation is enacted in one or other country.

Secondly, within the body of Welsh law are laws which have been enacted or made in both English and Welsh, with the result that, by law, the two language versions must be treated as of equal standing for all purposes.[7] It is difficult to see how courts across England are meant to respond to this, or indeed why they should continue in theory to have to do so.

Thirdly, and unconnected with legislative and executive devolution, under the Welsh Language Acts, parties before the courts in Wales – but not in neighbouring England – have the right to be heard in either Welsh or English. When trials are listed to be heard or moved outside Wales for administrative convenience, this right is forfeit. The distinct right simply does not fit appropriately into the pre-existing single jurisdiction.

For these reasons, it is submitted, there is arguably a case for change – but there is more than one option available. During the passage of what became the Wales Act 2017, the Welsh Government produced its own draft Wales Bill, which proposed a complete separation of England and Wales as law districts.[8] Others hold that, while a considerable body of law continues to apply in both countries, the inconveniences which such complete separation would cause militates against that solution, preferring instead the idea of developing distinct but formal jurisdictional arrangements which could keep pace with the expansion of the divergent bodies of law.

The First Minister of Wales, the Right Hon. Carwyn Jones AM, has established a Commission on Justice in Wales under the chairmanship of the former Lord Chief Justice of England and Wales, Lord Thomas of Cwmgiedd. Its terms of reference

[6] These included the restrictions placed on the making of ancillary enforcement provisions and the restrictions upon modifying private law and criminal law; see above, §§4-47–4-51; 4-57–4-58.

[7] GoWA 2006, s. 156(1).

[8] See *http://gov.wales/docs/caecd/publications/160526-wales-bill-draft-en.pdf*.

include examining the jurisdictional arrangements of Wales and the distinct issues which arise here.[9] It is expected to report in 2019.

THE FUTURE OF THE ASSEMBLY

Mention has also already been made of the various powers given to the National Assembly in the Wales Act 2017 to enable it to change its name, the method by which members are elected, the constituencies for which they serve and their number, and the voting age.[10] Consideration of these issues has already commenced as noted earlier.[11] It is very likely that the Assembly will decide to change its name. While the choice of name may be a matter of keen popular debate, it is not likely to be seriously controversial. The same cannot be said for any proposed increase in its membership. At a time when discontent with the political establishment has arguably resulted in the vote in favour of the major constitutional upheaval of leaving the EU, there is need to be wary of the possibility of a popular backlash when proposing further growth of political institutions. A-04

CONCLUSION

The process of devolution in Wales has certainly therefore not come to a close. It is virtually inevitable that further changes, some major, will occur within the next few years. While one cannot predict the outcome of those changes, one thing is certain. If they are to be of benefit to the people of Wales, they must be properly thought through and competently delivered. To proceed otherwise risks unfairness and misery. It has been the purpose of this book to raise awareness of what such sound policy and effective legislation requires. A-05

[9] *Update on the Commission on Justice in Wales* (Written Statement by the Welsh Government: 20 November 2017).

[10] See above, §§7-67–7-68.

[11] Ibid.

Select Bibliography

Better Governance for Wales / Trefn Llywodraeth Well i Gymru (2005)

Bingham, Tom, *The Rule of Law* (London, 2010)

Burrows, A., *Thinking about Statutes: Interpretation, Interaction, Improvement*, The Hamlyn Lectures 2017 (Cambridge, 2018)

Bush, Keith, 'Approaches to UK Legislative Drafting: the Welsh Perspective' (2004) 25 *Statute Law Review* 144–50

Cabinet Office, *Guide to Making Legislation* (July 2017), *https://www.gov.uk/government/publications/guide-to-making-legislation*

Commission on the Powers and Electoral Arrangements of the National Assembly for Wales, Report 2004 (The Richard Commission)

Davies, R., *Devolution: A Process Not an Event*, The Gregynog Papers, vol. 2, no. 2 (Cardiff: Institute of Welsh Affairs, 1999)

Dicey, A. V., *An Introduction to the Study of the Law and the Constitution* (London, 1885)

Empowerment and Responsibility: Financial Powers to Strengthen Wales / Grymuso a Chyfrifoldeb: Pwerau Ariannol i Gryfhau Cymru (Commission on Devolution in Wales, 2012) (The Silk Commission – Silk I)

Empowerment and Responsibility: Legislative Powers to Strengthen Wales / Grymuso a Chyfrifoldeb: Pwerau deddfwriaethol i gryfhau Cymru (Commission on Devolution in Wales, 2014) (The Silk Commission – Silk II)

Gardner, David, *Administrative Law and the Administrative Court in Wales* (Cardiff, 2016)

Greenberg, Daniel, *Laying Down the Law* (London, 2011)

Greenberg, Daniel (ed.), *Craies on Legislation* (11th edn, London, 2017)

Hailsham, Lord, 'Elective Dictatorship', The Richard Dimbleby Lecture, *The Listener*, 21 October 1976

Hailsham, Lord, *The Dilemma of Democracy* (London and Glasgow, 1978)

Hohfeld, W. N., 'Some Fundamental Legal Conceptions as applied in Judicial Reasoning' (1913) 23 *Yale Law Journal* 16

Hughes, Dylan and Huw G. Davies, 'Accessible Bilingual Legislation for Wales' (2012) 33(2) *Statute Law Review* 103

Hughes, Dylan and Huw G. Davies, 'Deddfwriaeth Hygyrch a Dwyieithog i Gymru' (2012) 33(2) *Statute Law Review* 122

Huws, C. F., 'The Day the Supreme Court was unable to interpret Statutes' (2013) 34 *Statute Law Review* 221

Huws, C. F., 'The Law of England and Wales: Translation in Transition' (2015) 22 *International Journal of Speech, Language and the Law* 1

Jones-Evans, A., *Publication of Pre-2006 Non-Statutory Instrument Legislation: A Scoping Study*, *http://webarchive.nationalarchives.gov.uk/20080912102143tf_/http://new.wales.gov.uk/publications/publicationscheme/?lang=en*, and follow

the related link for 'Publication of Pre-2006 Non-Statutory Instrument Legislation: A Scoping Study – Executive summary'
Law Commission, *Form and Accessibility of the Law Applicable in Wales / Ffurf a Hygyrchedd y Gyfraith sy'n Gymwys yng Nghymru* (Law Com. No. 366)
Law Commission, *Thirteenth Programme of Law Reform* (Law Com. No. 377)
Miers, D. R. and A. C. Page, *Legislation* (2nd edn, London, 1990)
Morgan, Rhodri, *Rhodri: A Political Life in Wales and Westminster* (Cardiff, 2017)
National Assembly for Wales, *A Parliament that Works for Wales: The Report of the Expert Panel on Assembly Electoral Reform* (November 2017)
National Assembly for Wales: Constitutional and Legislative Affairs Committee, *Fourth Assembly Legacy Report* (March 2016)
Oliver of Aylmerton, Lord, 'A Judicial View of Modern Legislation' [1993] *Statute Law Review* 1
Palmer, G., 'Law Making in New Zealand: Is There a Better Way?' (the Harkness Henry Lecture) (2014) 22 *Waikato Law Review*, 1–40 (Victoria University of Wellington Legal Research Paper Series Palmer Paper No. 82/2015).
Powers for a Purpose: Towards a Lasting Devolution Settlement for Wales / Pwerau at Bwrpas: Tuag at Setliad Datganoli sy'n para i Gymru (Cm. 9020, 2015)
Robertson, Colin D., *Multilingual Law: A Framework for Analysis and Understanding* (London and New York, 2016)
Rose, R., *Do Parties make a Difference?* (2nd edn, London, 1984)
Salmond on Jurisprudence (12th edn, by P. J. Fitzgerald, London, 1966)
Steiner and Woods EU Law (13th edn, by L. Woods, P. Watson and M. Costa, Oxford, 2017)
Thring's Practical Legislation: The Composition and Language of Acts of Parliament and Business Documents (3rd edn, by M. MacKenzie and D. Purdie, Edinburgh, 2015)
Thornton, G. C., *Legislative Drafting* (4th edn, Haywards Heath, 1996)
Watkin, T. G., 'Bilingual Legislation and the Law of England and Wales' (2014) 2(2) *The Theory and Practice of Legislation* 229
Watkin, T. G., 'Bilingual Legislation: Awareness, Ambiguity and Attitudes' (2016) 37 *Statute Law Review* 116
Watkin, T. G., 'Dadleuon Dichellgar a Datganoli' / 'Devious Debates and Devolution', in T. G. Watkin (ed.), *The Welsh Legal Triads and Other Essays* (Bangor, Welsh Legal History Society, vol. 11, 2015), pp. 96–132
Welsh Government, *Interpreting Welsh law: an interpretation act for Wales* (WG33701: December 2017, version 2).
Welsh Government, *Legislation Handbook on Assembly Bills* (August 2017): *http://gov.wales/docs/legislation/170830-legislation-handbook-cy.pdf* *http://gov.wales/docs/legislation/170830-legislation-handbook-en.pdf*
Xanthaki, Helen, *Legislation Drafting – Art and Technology of Rules for Regulation* (Oxford, 2014).
Zander, Michael, *The Law-Making Process* (6th edn, Cambridge, 2004)

Index

M

N

Q

R

S